A Millennium of Archdeacons

The Archdeacons of Winchester from the 11th to the 20th Centuries

Editor: John Guille

Consulting Editor: Richard Buxton

George Mann Publications

Published by
George Mann Publications
Easton, Winchester,
Hampshire SO21 1ES
01962 779944

A CIP catalogue record for this book
is available from the British Library

ISBN 0-95-416346-X

George Mann Publications

Contents

Foreword

Fifteen years as a bishop, in two very different Dioceses, have educated me about the critical significance and value of Archdeacons! But if this is so in our own time, how much more must it have been the case in days when the Bishop was rarely in the Diocese, the Crown was habitually on the look-out for opportunities for pillage, and the Law a good deal less predictable and transparent than at its best it is today!

So I am grateful for the opportunity, on behalf of a millennium of those who have the privilege of signing themselves "Winton:", to offer appreciative thanks for, and to, the long and honourable succession of our Archdeacon colleagues; and especially to thank John Guille and all whom he has persuaded (a necessary talent in an Archdeacon!) to collaborate in producing this intriguing and illuminating book.

+Michael Winton

The Right Reverend Michael Scott-Joynt
Bishop of Winchester

Acknowledgements

This book owes the large amount of research that lies behind it, its writing, compilation and publication to the encouragement and support of many people. I shared the original idea with Michael Till, Dean of Winchester, explaining that I hoped to bring together a group of people associated with Winchester Cathedral who would explore with me the lives of the Archdeacons of Winchester from the 11th to the 20th-century. With his support this is what a group of us have done. A list of the contributors and a brief curriculum vitae of each contributor is listed overleaf. I am deeply grateful to each member of the group for their dedication to the task and the fun we have shared together. My dear friend Richard Buxton as consulting editor has guided us wisely at every step of the way and enthusiastically encouraged us.

I extend my thanks also to members of the Dean and Chapter of Winchester Cathedral for permission to use material held in the Cathedral Library and Archives and to John Hardacre for his eye to detail. To the Friends of Winchester Cathedral and Paul Bray as their chairman for agreeing to be associated with this project. To my wife Sue who has encouraged me, to Michael Scott-Joynt, Bishop of Winchester, to Christine Williams, my secretary, and to Vicky Rutherford and Brenda Kipling for their help. Finally to our anonymous benefactor who has lent us the money to cover our costs prior to publication, and to George Mann for his professional advice and work in the publication process itself.

Any financial surplus generated by the sales of this book, after all expenses and the loan have been repaid, will be donated to the Friends of Winchester Cathedral.

John Guille
Archdeacon of Winchester
January 2003

Notes on Contributors

Major General Paul Bray C.B., B.A. (Hons), M.A., was a career soldier finishing as Paymaster-in-Chief, the last officer to be so appointed with the creation of the Adjutant General's Corps. On leaving the Army in 1992, he read History, Politics and Philosophy at Southampton University followed by a Masters in Historical Studies.

The Revd Richard Buxton, BSc.(Eng), M.A., PhD, is retired from stipendary ministry and lives in Porthmadog, Gwynedd. Originally a chemical engineer, he has been previously and successively Tutor and Lecturer on the staff of Salisbury and Wells Theological College, and lecturer in Liturgy in the University of Manchester.

Elizabeth Crawley B.A., was educated in the U.S.A. and at St. Mary's School, Calne, and graduated with a B.A. (Hons) in History from Westfield College, London University; Social Science Certificate, LSE; worked in London in the voluntary help field and as a charity administrator until 1985, when she was appointed Diocesan Adviser to Community Care Groups, based in Winchester. Now retired: helps as a Cathedral Guide and Library volunteer.

Naomi Davidson B.A., trained at the Royal College of Music in London and has the L.R.A.M., A.R.C.M., and G.R.S.M. Diplomas. During her teaching career she held Head of Department posts in Cornwall and Shropshire. She was Senior Housemistress at Wycombe Abbey. Since retiring in Winchester she completed a B.A. (O.U.) and now undertakes some voluntary work at the Cathedral.

Sheila Gray, Dip.Eng. Loc.Hist, is a researcher in English local history, with a particular interest in genealogy. She has taught research methods and contributed to a variety of books and journals. For almost twenty years she has been a voluntary Guide at Winchester Cathedral.

The Ven. John A. Guille, BTh. is Archdeacon of Winchester.

John Hardacre, B.A., A.M.A. read his first degree at Durham and after a career in museums is now Curator of Winchester Cathedral.

Pat H. Mather, M.A., after graduating in history from Southampton University and two years' research, worked as an archivist in Northamptonshire. This was followed by a spell at Portsmouth Museum running a loan service for schools. Marriage brought a return to Southampton with work in the city Record Office and involvement in her husband's historical studies.

Professor A. J. Harding Rains, CBE, FRCS is a retired surgeon who was Professor of Surgery at Charing Cross Hospital, 1959–1981, and a member of Council, Vice-President and Hunterian Orator of the Royal College of Surgeons. Also a post-graduate dean, editor of the Journal of the Royal Society of Medicine and author and editor of Surgical texts.

Abbreviations in the Main Text

B.A.	Bachelor of Arts
B.Cn.L.	Bachelor of Canon Law (until 1535)
B.D.	Bachelor of Divinity
B.Th.	Bachelor of Theology
C.M.G.	Companion of (the order of) St Michael & St George)
D.C.L.	Doctor of Civil Law (Oxon)
D.Cn.L.	Doctor of Canon Law
D.D.	Doctor of Divinity
Lic.C.L.	Licentiate of Civil Law (Oxon)
LL.D.	Doctor of Civil Law (Cantab.)
M.	*Magister* (indicating a university graduate)
M.A.	Master of Arts
M.D.	Doctor of Medicine
SCH.C.L.	Scholar of Civil Law
S.T.B.	*sanctae theologiae baccalaureus*, Bachelor of Sacred Theology
T.C.F.	Temporary Chaplain to the Forces

Archdeacons Then and Now

In reflecting upon the lives of the Archdeacons of Winchester during the period of the second Christian Millennium there is an invitation to examine the roots of this office and to discover how the role of archdeacon has developed over the centuries. Through the lives of these individuals and their involvement with the church in the Diocese of Winchester and beyond, a greater awareness of the social and religious history of England during this period is obtained.

Canon Law of the Church of England (Canon C 22) states that no one may be appointed archdeacon until he has served a minimum of six years in holy orders and must be in priest's orders at the time of the appointment. '*Every archdeacon shall within his archdeaconry carry out his duties under the Bishop and shall assist the bishop in his pastoral care and office, and particularly he shall see that all such as hold any ecclesiastical office within the same perform their duties with diligence, and shall bring to the bishop's attention what calls for correction or merits praise.*' He shall within his archdeaconry hold annual visitations and '*shall also survey in person or by deputy all the churches, chancels, and churchyards and give direction for the amendment of all defects in the walls, fabric, ornaments, and furniture of the same, and in particular shall exercise the powers confirmed on him by the Inspection of Churches Measure 1955; he shall also, on receiving the directions of the bishop, induct any priest who has been instituted to a benefice into possession of the temporalities of the same.*' Since 1994,

Sources

1 *A History of the Church of England* J.R.H.Moorman p 48
2 *The Fifteenth Century,* E F Jacob p 277
3 *The Reformation of Cathedrals,* S E Lehmberg, p 258
4 ibid p260
5 ibid p 260
6 Quotation used by R L Ravenscroft in his *The Role of an Archdeacon Today.*
7 *The Diocesan Revival in the Church of England c.1800-1870,* A Burns, p 74.

- *A History of the Church in England,* J.R.H. Moorman (1973)
- *Church Life in England in the XIII Century,* J.R.H. Moorman(1946)
- *The Canons of the Church of England*
- *The Revival in the Church of England c.1800-1870.* A Burns
- *The Reformation of Cathedrals S E Lehmberg.* (1988)
- *Ecclesiastical Law,* Mark Hill (1995)
- *The Oxford History of England:*
  - Anglo Saxon England, F Stenton (1971)
  - The Thirteenth Century, M Powicke (1962)
  - The Fourteenth Century, M McKisack (1959)
  - The Fifteenth Century, E.F.Jacob (1961)
- *"Oculus Episcopi",* compiled by Hugh Buckingham
- *The Role of the Archdeacon Today,* R.L. Ravenscroft
- *Winchester Cathedral 1079-1979,* F. Bussby, 1979
- *Aspects of Cathedral Life,* Alec Knight.

women who meet the above qualifications, are eligible for appointment as Archdeacon.

St. Jerome makes reference to archdeacons as early as the fourth century. The archdeacon was the principal deacon of the local church and he assisted the bishop at the altar, in preaching and in the distribution and management of ecclesiastical revenues. By the seventh century his duties had been extended in that, he was often given the chief care and inspection of a diocese, in subordination to the bishop.

In our own country however, very little is known about the existence or office of archdeacons in English dioceses before the Norman Conquest in 1066. Wulfred had been archdeacon to Archbishop Aethelheard before being appointed himself as Archbishop of Canterbury in 805. Two archdeacons are named in the Canterbury Charters of 830 and *c*.850 by the names of Cyneheard and Dunning and it would seem that Archbishop Ceolnoth was assisted by four archdeacons between 833-878. In 889 an archdeacon occurs in a group of clergy belonging to the see of Rochester. Apart from Canterbury, the only diocese in which an archdeacon can be traced between 900 and 1066 is that of York. The Pre-Conquest diocese of Winchester covered an enormous area and documents of the ninth century mention the names of several bishops who seem to have assisted each diocesan of this great West Saxon see. It is quite possible therefore, that archdeacons of Winchester functioned at this time as well, though there is no direct evidence for this, and it is not capable of proof. J. R. H. Moorman is confident that by the tenth century the office of archdeacon had acquired a recognised status in ecclesiastical jurisdiction.(1)

After the appointment of Archbishop Lanfranc in 1070 many reforms were introduced as an important part of Norman policy. Norman churches were to replace previous Saxon buildings and Winchester Cathedral was no exception. Lanfranc achieved his reforms by summoning a number of Church Councils and one was called to meet in Winchester in 1072; another followed in London in 1075 and in Winchester again on April 1st 1076. The Councils concluded that each diocese should hold synods twice a year, archdeacons were to be appointed, simony to be prohibited and vagrant clerks and monks were to be rounded up. By the time of Lanfranc's death in 1089, separate Eccesiastical Courts were in place for the operation of Canon Law and territorial archdeaconries had been established as the first step in remodelling diocesan administration on continental lines. It is possible that the principal factor in raising the status of the office of archdeacon under William the Conqueror was the intention to end the Anglo-Saxon practice of referring ecclesiastical business to the local courts. R.S. Mylne in Canon Law (1912) writes,

> *'the prevalent idea in the Middle Ages was that the Church and State were two co-ordinate institutions, each with its own separate jurisdictions, independent of each other, and yet more closely connected. Thus each kingdom possessed its Archbishop as well as its King. In like manner the Bishop possessed similar territorial jurisdiction to the feudal noble, and together these formed the upper House of Parliament. And in England, as each county had its Earl and Sheriff, so each county also had its Archdeacon.'*

The number of archdeacons increased at this time and often included more than one archdeacon for each bishop.

Thomas à Becket was appointed archdeacon on his being ordained deacon in 1154 and therefore, it was as an archdeacon he came to Winchester Cathedral in 1162 for his ordination to the priesthood and his consecration as Archbishop of Canterbury by the then bishop of the diocese Henry of Blois. It is sometimes suggested that archdeacons were in priest's orders to enable them to discharge their responsibilities more effectively. However, it is not clear when this change occurred. Anselm's Canons issued at Westminster in 1102 record 'that archdeacons be deacons'. In 1126 the canons are still showing that an archdeacon is in deacon's orders: 'that none be promoted... to an archdeaconry but a deacon.' As archdeacon, Becket was the holder of an office which was rather more secular than ecclesiastical in character, in that he was in charge of the legal work of the diocese of Canterbury.

The office of archdeacon was commonly bestowed at this time by the bishops on their own sons or members of their extended families because it was regarded as an easy and lucrative form of livelihood and a stepping stone to preferment. The reputation of archdeacons in the twelfth century was not good in that they were often given to extortion and injustice. The king on one occasion, when informed about such malpractices in York diocese declared that the archdeacons annually extorted more money from the inhabitants of his kingdom than he himself received in revenue! Archdeacons were also accused of keeping parishes vacant in order to benefit from the fees generated during an interregnum. An archdeacon was entitled to a third of the profit from the sequestration when the vacancy came to an end. By the end of the thirteenth century England (including Wales) was divided into 17 dioceses and 40 archdeaconaries. There were approximately 9500 parishes. The Register of Bishop Pontissara lists 345 churches in the Winchester Diocese at this time.

During the medieval period the archdeacon's court was very powerful. It passed judgement upon the moral behaviour of the inferior clergy and laity. During this period, the reputation of the archdeacon suffered because of the court's concern with adultery and fornication. Consequently the archdeacon's court became known as the '*bawdy court*'. In 1222 Archbishop Langton's *Constitution* records the involvement of the archdeacon in minute detail;

> *'we ordain that every Church have a silver chalice with other decent vessels, and a clean white linen cloth for the altar: let the old corporals which were not fit for the altar be put in the place appointed for the relics, or be burnt in the presence of the archdeacon (if they are consecrated). And let the archdeacon take care that the cloths and other ornaments of the altar be decent; that books be fit for singing and reading; and that there be two suits of vestments for the priests: and that the attendants at the altar wear surplices, that due esteem be paid to divine office.'*

By the fifteenth century when a vacancy occurred in a diocese the king selected for appointment as bishop one whom he thought appropriate and submitted his name to the Pope for ratification. The Archbishop of Canterbury and the Cathedral Chapter where the bishop was to be 'elected' had little influence in the appointment. Once appointed the new bishop would undertake a 'primary visitation' and then often retire from the diocese to devote himself to affairs of state. The diocese was mainly administered from the episcopal manors where the clergy were summoned when asked to meet with their bishop. Being absent so frequently however, the bishop delegated much of the routine work to the vicar-general (usually a member of the Cathedral Chapter) and an assistant bishop. In matters of discipline the bishop depended upon his 'oculus', the archdeacon, but the archdeacon, 'came into contact with his own subjects, clerical and lay, through his official, through whom the visitation of the archdeaconry was often concluded: it was the official who normally increased the procurations (taxes) and which the archdeacon was entitled to collect, and who acted as the moral supervisor of the laity.' (2)

During the period of the Reformation the lives of the Archdeacons of Winchester are probably representative of archdeacons generally and how they fared. For example, an archdeacon was in post in the person of William Boleyn during the key periods of King Henry VIII's reign and John Philpot was burned at the stake in May 1554 for heresy. Stanford E Lehmberg has uncovered some interesting facts concerning the archdeacons of the sixteenth and seventeenth centuries who were associated with Cathedrals. Of 53 archdeacons, where their social background is known, 7 were the sons of commoners or tenant farmers, 12 of merchants, artisans or tradesmen, 24 from the gentry and 2 of noble birth. He writes, 'the files contain information about 256 deans (including 43 men who were priors of monastic cathedrals before the Reformation) and 352 archdeacons who held Cathedral positions (this includes 65 men who were both deans and archdeacons, and are counted in both categories).' (3) About half of the deans and archdeacons held doctoral degrees with many of the archdeacons holding doctorates in canon and civil law. It was also relatively unusual for men to be appointed as deans or archdeacons without having previously held some Cathedral office. Approximately two-thirds of the archdeacons had had experience as prebendaries or canons. Archdeacons more than deans were frequently drawn from the Cathedral Chapter itself rather than from outside; this was the case in nearly a third of the appointments of archdeacons. Similarly, nearly all deans and archdeacons were pluralists holding offices in several cathedrals and quite frequently in several parishes as well. '43 archdeacons held 2 archdeaconries concurrently or successively, while 9 held 3 each and 4 men held 4 archdeaconries apiece.' (4) At this time 62 archdeacons were appointed to the bench of bishops. 'At least 129 of the 195 men consecrated as bishops between 1485 and 1603 had previously been prebendaries, canons, archdeacons, or deans.' (5)

By the beginning of the eighteenth century bishops often spent more than half of the year in London and the administration of their dioceses was largely left to the archdeacons except during the four or five summer months when the bishops left London. For those bishops who were conscientious they then engaged in a busy round of visitations, confirmations, ordinations and entertainments.

The Victorian archdeacon is epitomised for all time by Anthony Trollope:

> *'To define – or rather to make intelligible by any definition – an archdeacon's powers and duties, would be difficult... The archdeacon holds a court, and makes visitations. These visitations may be made pretty much at pleasure. He inquires as to the administration of the services, seeing that the canons are maintained, but has no power to alter aught; and as*

there seems to be much difficulty in knowing when and by what the canons are maintained, and by when and what they are not maintained, we may imagine that the enquiries of a discreet archdeacon into the practices of a respectable and efficient parson will not be too close or searching in this matter of the canons. He must be an earnest working parish clergyman, or he would hardly have been selected as an archdeacon... And he walks just a head taller than other clergyman around him, receiving the pleasant attitude from the modest authority which he carries... but an archdeacon is not raised by his dignity above a capability for jovial intimacy...' [(6)]

In our own day the archdeacon remains an officer of the bishop and the description 'Oculus Episcopi' still holds true. However, as the Bishop of St. Albans writes in the foreword to the latest handbook for new archdeacons:

'the mythology surrounding archdeacons is very considerable, ranging from those medieval discussions about whether or not archdeacons were worthy of eternity to Trollope's magnificent Archdeacon Grantley. That mythology continues in our own day so you will hear countless boring references to gutters and graveyards. The reality, of course, is very different. Rooted as the ministry of an archdeacon is, in the priesthood of Christ's Church, it necessarily encompasses all that makes up the earthly institution of the Church whilst also, through prayer and sacrament, through administration and teaching, it reflects something of the grace and the glory of God.'

Today there are just over 100 archdeacons serving in the Church of England and the average number of clergy per archdeaconry is approximately 100 and the number of parishes is 115. The role varies from diocese to diocese but the core duties and responsibilities are largely the same. An archdeacon works closely with his or her bishop, Rural and Area Deans and lay chairs of synod. They have a particular association with Churchwardens and their Annual Visitations and, as has been demonstrated, these visitations are of ancient origin. The modern visitation focuses upon the Admission of the Churchwardens to office for the ensuing year and their responsibilities under the Care of Churches and Ecclesiastical Jurisdiction Measure 1991. The archdeacon delivers a charge at the visitation sharing with those present the matters he wishes to draw to their attention. The role continues to be administrative and pastoral and ecclesiastical legislation directs much of his work.

The modern archdeacon works very closely with the Diocesan Advisory Committee under the provisions of the Care of Churches and Ecclesiastical Jurisdiction Measure 1991. He manages the process with regard to any pastoral reorganisation under the Pastoral Measure in co-operation with the Diocesan Pastoral Committee. Similarly he is involved to a greater or lesser extent (depending on the practice followed in a particular diocese) with the appointment of the clergy to parochial posts under the Patronage Benefices Measure 1986. In both of these areas of work he is in close contact with the Rural/Area Deans and Churchwardens. He regularly undertakes Parochial Visitations and is drawn into the pastoral care of the clergy and their families. He is an ex officio member of the Diocesan Synod and currently one archdeacon from each diocese serves on the General Synod.

Thus the archdeacon has been at the heart of ecclesiastical affairs throughout most of the second millennium, and therefore through the portraits of their lives a series of pictures in microcosm of the church and society in which they lived, ministered and administered, is obtained. These portraits also reflect the vast changes that went on occurring throughout the millennium.

In medieval society, the bishops occupied some of the great offices of state, and ecclesiastics of middling rank were frequently involved in administrative tasks for the state as well as the church; they were effectively the civil servants of their day. Benefice and other ecclesiastical income was used to maintain them, to provide them with their salaries, as it were. Given the premises on which medieval society was based, few would have argued that this was an unreasonable arrangement. A relic of this remains to this day in that an Anglican clergyman/clergywoman is still legally described as a 'clerk in holy orders'.

In the sixteenth and seventeenth centuries the Archdeacons of Winchester were inevitably caught up in the religious, and consequent civil turmoil of their times; that John Philpot perished at the stake has already been mentioned. What is perhaps more surprisingly is that for much of the time they seemed to have been able to carry on with their normal duties more or less unhindered.

In the politically calmer conditions of the eighteenth and early nineteenth centuries, many of the clergy settled down to live the lives of country gentlemen, reasonably diligent at the same time in leading worship and in the pastoral care of their parishioners, but very much part of the squirarchy all the same. (It should be noted however, that much of this work would be done for the more influential clergy by unbeneficed curates). This pattern is evident in the lives of some of the eighteenth century archdeacons. What is also noticeable is the extent to which many of the archdeacons of this time were related to the upper echelons of society and indeed the aristocracy, who used their power of patronage to advance their interests. This latter is something that was regarded as entirely ethical at the time; benefices and their incomes were a form of property that they were entitled to enjoy.

Towards the end of the first half of the nineteenth century a change occurs, for most of the things we associate with modern Anglican church life had their origins in this period, and the clergy, in overseeing all of this, became conscientious and hard-working in the running of all the multifarious activities in their parishes as never before, and in a way that we would now recognise.

> *'The archdeaconries saw centre and locality combine to achieve diocesan reform... At the fulcrum was the contribution of the episcopate, risking bold appointments and encouraging energy and enthusiasm. Together they transformed a decayed institution into an effective one which nevertheless was consistent with, and drew legitimation from, the charismatic and hierarchical diocesan structure.'* [(7)]

In this respect, Charles Hoare may be judged the first modern Archdeacon of Winchester.

And this continues to the present day. Never previously has there been such a sustained period of time when the clergy have been better trained, or more conscientious in the performance of their duties, then the last 160 years or so. And yet it has sadly to be acknowledged that this has coincided, during the last two-thirds of this time, over the last 125 years or so, with an era of almost continuous decline in church going, and regular frequent involvement in church life on the part of many people. This seems a very poor reward for the dedicated labours of the clergy over the last century and a half, labours exemplified by the Archdeacons of Winchester during this time, as the later biographies in this volume illustrate.

All this 1000 years of general history is reflected in detail in the lives of the Archdeacons of Winchester over the last millennium. Thus this study of their lives is set forth, confident that it will make a contribution to the history of this part of England, and of our understanding of the English church and society as a whole. And perhaps we can be confident too that this study of the past may provide us with some pointers and directions for the present time, at the start of the third millennium.

12th-Century Archdeacons

The twelfth century is generally accepted as being a period of cultural renaissance[(1)] in England and in the wider world. The development of institutionalised higher education in the form of Universities is a phenomenon of the twelfth century as is the widespread enrichment of English cathedrals, monastic and parish churches with wall-paintings, and elaborate decorative and architectural carving in stone. It was the period when book production and illumination began again, at Winchester after a break of over a century, and when 'the riotous imagination of the Romanesque' is seen at work in all the visual arts. It was also a century of Crusades and hitherto unparalleled contact with the Byzantine and Arab world. The Winchester Bible[(2)], a product of the monastic scriptorium of St Swithun's Priory is the supreme example of this artistic renaissance at Winchester.

In Rome, Adrian IV (Nicholas Breakspear) was the only Englishman (so far) to have been elected Pope, between 1154 and 1159, and in Winchester the century was dominated by Henry of Blois, Bishop 1129 - 1171. He was preceded by William Giffard, Bishop 1100 (although he was not consecrated until 1107) - 1129 and succeeded by Richard of Ilchester, 1173 - 1188 and Godfrey de Lucy, 1189 - 1204.

The first recorded Archdeacon[(3)] in the Winchester Diocese may be William of Chichester in a charter which implies

Sources

1 For a general introduction to Romanesque Art see Zarnecki et al., *English Romanesque Art 1066 – 1200*, London 1984

2 The Winchester Bible, c.1160 – c.1180. Winchester Cathedral Library MS. XVIII

3 For a detailed discussion of the Episcopal household see M.J.Franklin, *English Episcopal Acta VIII, Winchester 1070-1204*, OUP for The British Academy, 1993.

4 For a detailed discussion of Archdeacons' households and staff see B.R. Kemp *Twelfth-Century English Archidiaconal and Vice-Archidiaconal Acta*. The Canterbury and York Society, 2001.

5 He appears as 'Richer monk' among the witnesses of a charter of Henry of Blois c.1150. See A.W. Goodman, *Chartulary of Winchester Cathedral*. Winchester, 1927

6 See W. de Gray Birch *The New Minster Liber Vitae*, Hampshire Record Society, Winchester, 1892. p.30. 'Frater noster Richerius archidiaconus, Monachus et sacerdos.'

Also Joan Greatrex, *Biographical Register of the English Cathedral Priories of Canterbury c. 1066-1540*, Oxford 1997.

Franklin p. 39, Hyde-Jumièges 1139 – 1141.

the existence of an archdeacon of the Bishop of Winchester, but the attestation *Willelmo Cicestrie archidiacono* could equally mean William, Archdeacon of Chichester. After the consecration of William Giffard on 11 August 1107, two archdeacons, Henry and Stephen undeniably existed; the latter is called Archdeacon 'of Surrey' in later texts. Franklin detects 'a faint hint of internal promotion' in the fact that Richard (*capellanus episcopi* or Bishop's Chaplain) succeeds Henry sometime after Henry became Bishop of Verdun in 1116. In Giffard's last years he is found attesting the first Episcopal grant to the initial Cistercian abbey of Waverley as well as the settlement with St Swithun's. He became a monk(4) of Hyde Abbey before his death(5).

The archdeacons appointed by Henry of Blois are rarely found attesting charters; this, taken with the 'relatively late' use of territorial titles for archdeaconries in this diocese has led to doubts about the succession. The later titles 'of Winchester' and 'of Surrey' are used particularly by Robert de Inglesham Archdeacon of Surrey between 1155 and 1186 and Ralph, Archdeacon of Winchester perhaps from 1142 until 1179/80. On two occasions Ralph, when attesting with Robert, is styled 'of Hampshire'. One of these references almost certainly dates from the 1160s suggesting that there was still doubt about the territorial title of an archdeaconry at that time.

Franklin also doubts the validity of calling Hugh de Puiset (later Bishop of Durham 1153 – 1195) Archdeacon 'of Winchester' and argues that the line becomes clearer if he is considered as Archdeacon 'of Surrey' and if the reference to him as *archidiaconus Wintonie* in 1153 is best understood in the non-territorial sense as an archdeacon of the Winchester Diocese. Jocelin de Bohun who attests an act(6) and appears as *Iocelino Wintoniensi archidiacono* is probably the first true archdeacon of the Winchester line. He vacated his archdeaconry on his consecration as Bishop of Salisbury (Old Sarum) in 1142: his episcopate at Old Sarum lasted for over 40 years. He resigned in 1189 shortly before his death in November of that year.

Bishop Richard of Ilchester's sole appointment of Roger I was made after his return from Normandy in 1180. The last dated occurrence of his predecessor, Ralph as Archdeacon of Winchester is 1178 and he had died before September 1180.

13th-Century Archdeacons

Following the martyrdom of Thomas à Becket in 1170 tension continued between King and Pope over fiscal and legal matters throughout the reigns of John, Henry III and Edward I. The clergy had to endure both papal taxation in order to fund the Crusades and the demands of the Kings for money to mount their campaigns in Scotland, Ireland, Wales and France. King John incurred papal wrath and the imposition of the Great Interdict (1208 - 1213) when he refused to accept Innocent III's nominee, Stephen Langton, as Archbishop of Canterbury. While all the churches were closed for services, John took the opportunity of plundering them. He was excommunicated, and only submitted to the Pope under the pressure of the threat of invasion and deposition. Stephen Langton had, meanwhile, in 1207, been consecrated Archbishop in Viterbo, Italy, for Rome was uninhabitable for the Pope. Under Langton and, later, John Pecham, a Franciscan, the clergy became subject to reform. Between these two archbishops Edmund of Abingdon (1233 – 40) made a vain attempt at a reconciliation between King Henry III and Pope Gregory IX. He was canonised by Innocent IV in 1247.

At the end of the century, in 1296, Boniface VIII issued the vehement Bull *Clericis Laicos* which forbade clergy to pay ecclesiastical dues to laymen, and laymen to receive such payments, under threat of excommunication. Boniface appeared to regard laymen 'as notoriously

Sources

- Special acknowledgement is made of the work of Professor N.C.Vincent in respect of the history of the des Roches family, *Peter des Roches, Bishop of Winchester, 'An Alien in British Politics' 1205-1231 (1999) D.Phil Thesis, University of Oxford (St Peter's College).*
- Also in *English Episcopal Acta,* Vol. IX Winchester 1205-1238 Gen. Ed. M.J. Franklin, ed N.Vincent (1994).
- Much used were the Oxford History of England series,Vol III; *From Domesday Book to Magna Carta 1087-1216* by Austin L.Poole 2nd ed. (1955), and Vol IV, *The Thirteenth Century 1216-1307,* Sir Maurice Powicke, 2nd ed.1962. *The Victoria County History of of England,* ed. Doubleday (1903) Vol II. *The Chartularies of Southwick Priory,* ed. K.A. Hanna, Hants. Record Series, 2 Vols; *Cal Selborne Charters* ed. D D.Macray (Hants. Record Series).
- Other sources common to the book, e.g. P. Le Neve, *Fasti Ecc Angl* ed. D. Greenway, London.

hostile to clerics'. The Crusades continued throughout the century but came to an end with the fall of Acre in 1291.

In the sphere of learning, first Oxford, then Cambridge were to be formally established when scholars and masters united in a Guild for protection against the townspeople. In Europe Philosophy, Theology, Science and Art prospered through the works of such as Friar Roger Bacon, St Thomas Aquinas (Doctor Angelicus), Dante and Giotto. St Francis of Assisi died in 1226. William of Occam (of Occam's Razor) was born in 1270.

What is known about archdeacons in those days is fragmentary and depends primarily on the Registers of the Bishops of Winchester. But gradually a picture emerges of their activities in the communities of the diocese and in the affairs of the Bishop.

Ralph (or Ranulph), Archdeacon 1208?–1213 followed Roger I. It is known that in 1208 he was a witness to a Mottisfont charter. It is not certain that he continued throughout the Great Interdict, but such a man was at Wargrave, Berkshire, in November 1211, who stayed at 'Clere (?Kingsclere) at Easter 1212 and at Farnham, Surrey, for Pentecost 1212. He had three brothers, William, Vincent and Andrew who held lands outside Northgate, Winchester.

Masters Bartholomew and Hugh des Roches (de Rupibus) were nephews of the Bishop of Winchester, Peter des Roches (Bishop of Winchester 1205-1238). Originally from Touraine, France, he attracted other nephews, relatives and clergy to come to England. These included Peter de Rivallis (Rievaux) who was groomed for high office in the Country; 'a star' for a time, before being dismissed. Luke des Roches was made Archdeacon of Surrey and Aimery, brother of Hugh was Rector of Preston (?Candover) in 1219. Geoffrey, another brother married a Hampshire heiress and established a line in Fareham, Hampshire (Roches Court) and Boarhunt, but it did not last. Peter des Roches, is buried in the retrochoir of Winchester Cathedral, though his heart was buried in Waverley Abbey, Farnham. He was an able financier, statesman and warrior Bishop, returning a hero from entering Jerusalem in the successful crusade of 1230. He was loyal to King John during the Great Interdict, he crowned the child King Henry III and was his guardian. His name tended to inspire puns, for example:

Peter des Roches: 'the rock upon which the church is founded, and the stones from which the Cathedral of Saints Swithun and Peter is fashioned.'

Bartholmew des Roches was made Archdeacon in 1213. He was presented by King John to the church of North Walsham, Norfolk on 28 May of that year. He held several benefices, canonries and prebends; Canon of Lichfield 1223, Canon of London and Prebend of Ealdstreet c.1209 - 1230, Canon of Exeter, Rector of Martock, Somerset, (being promoted by the abbey of Mont St Michael sometime before 1226), also Canon of Salisbury with the Prebend of Burbage, Wiltshire. He was to have been Dean of York in April 1214 but the appointment was quashed September that year due to local opposition. Yet he retained the prebend into the 1220s. Except for York he does not appear to have been resident in any of these places, and he was, in fact, fined in 1227 by Salisbury for non-residence. Evidence of his various activities in administrative duties is recorded, such as appearances in the Winchester estates 1213-1219; handling money payments at Southwark, London, Farnham, Surrey, and being deputed by the Crown in November 1219 to oversee payments to Bolognese merchants who claimed to have loaned money to King Richard I before 1199. In legal matters he was engaged between 1221 and 1227 in a dispute with the Prioress of Nuneaton over presentation rights for the churches at Catherington and Clanfield, Hampshire, and at one time (after 1216) he was appointed papal judge in a dispute involving Peter FitzHerbert deputing responsibilities to a Master Nicholas de Vienne. In 1227, when Bishop Peter des Roches went on crusade ('took the Cross') he is described as being bishop's procurator working with his cousin Luke des Roches, the Archdeacon of Surrey in order to control episcopal patronage.

In his work he was assisted by some very able dignitaries, the officials of the Bishop, particularly Master Alan of Stokes. Finally in his role as Canon of Salisbury he was involved in a prolonged dispute with the Crown over the right to present to the church of Hurstbourne, Hampshire, and for this cause he set out in 1229 to appeal to the Pope but never returned. It is thought be that he met up with his uncle, Bishop Peter, who on returning from his crusade was involved in a reconciliation between Emperor Frederick II and Pope Gregory IX in 1230. It was Bishop Peter des Roches who reported Bartholomew's death on 12 December 1230.

Roger II, appointed 1230, is thought to be the one who accompanied Bishop Peter on his crusade, and he may have returned with the Bishop in August 1231. He is said to have 'died a pilgrim' March 1232. It is also said that at one time he was a supporter of Richard Poore (Poer) who was Peter des Roches' rival for the See of Winchester in 1205.

Hugh des Roches was active on the Bishop's behalf long before he was appointed archdeacon in 1232. He appears to have been a trusted courier of money, appearing first 1218-1219, possibly as Bishop's almoner, receiving two pence from the Bishop's Marshal *ad elemosinas*. He delivered money from the Royal Treasury to the garrison of Montgomery in the Welsh campaign of 1223, and in that year delivered ten marks to the Bishop's bailiff at Southwark, London. In 1224-5 he carried large sums of money from Taunton, Somerset, Farnham, Surrey and St Albans, Hertfordshire for delivery at Southwark, (the Bishop's house in London). In 1226-7 he succeeded Denis de Bourgueil as *de facto* Bishop's Treasurer, probably serving until the Bishop's return from the Crusade in 1231. It is fairly certain that Hugh was appointed archdeacon in September 1232 after the death of Roger II, although it is not until 1237 that his name appears as witness to the deeds and charters of Southwick Priory. This was an Augustinian Priory originally located in the grounds of Porchester Castle at Portsmouth harbour which was transferred to Southwick in 1145. Nothing remains today; the estate itself was Supreme Allied H.Q. at the time of the invasion of Normandy 6 June 1944.

An example of one of the settlements that Hugh presided over is of interest since it gives an indication of the life and tensions of the times in respect to alien clergy:

> AGREEMENT between Southwick Priory and Robert de Watevyle [rubric, Watevile] concerning a dispute over tithes, obventions and oblations from the demesne of *Stenebir'in, Preston Candover (Prestekandeu')* and all the household *(familia)* there, and from the chapel situated in the court of *la Stenebir'* and its chantry. At the request of Sir H[ugh] de Rupibus, Archdeacon of Winchester, the priory conceded to Robert that if any foreign priest from overseas *(presbiter extraneus ex transverso),* not maliciously brought in, wishes to celebrate divine service in the said chapel, he should be allowed to do so for one, two, three or eight days, provided he receives nothing from the tithes, obventions and oblations; nothwithstanding the principal agreement made beforehand between the aforesaid parties by which no priest was allowed to celebrate divine service in the said chapel unless he had first pledged his word to the mother church that he would receive nothing from the tithes, obventions and oblations to the detriment of that church, and that no foreign preist should be maliciously brought into the aforesaid chantry to the detriment of the

mother church, nor receive anything. Robert promised, on behalf, of himself and his, to keep faith, and undertook to preserve unharmed in these matters, the mother church and its rector. Both parties sealed the chirograph. Witnesses: Sir Geoffrey de Rupibus and Emeric, his brother; and many others.

The benefices which Hugh enjoyed included the church of (Thames) Ditton, Surrey, Canon of Exeter, Rector of Brading, Isle of Wight (before 1238, but advowson disputed). In 1239 he succeeded William de Ralegh (Bishop of Winchester) as Rector of Kings Somborne, Hampshire, and later in 1248 secured the right to patronage of the subject chapel of Little Somborne. But he had to resign the living in 1249 when Bishop William (below) appropriated it to Mottisfont Priory, Hampshire. In 1240 the King petitioned that Hugh, his brother Aimery and cousin Luke be excused from the papal tax on alien clergy, as were all the des Roches immigrants.

These three were engaged in promoting the Royal choice of Bishop to succeed Peter des Roches. First there was William of Valence, but he had died in Italy in 1239. It appears that King Henry had tried to persuade the monks at Winchester to elect him, but they preferred the very able Devonshire judge, William de Ralegh. The King then wanted to have Boniface of Savoy as Bishop and the three des Roches travelled to Italy in the King's cause and with his protection, but to no avail. The monks got the man they wanted. Boniface was appointed Archbishop of Canterbury, arriving in England 1244. Luke des Roches lost his post as Archdeacon of Surrey, but Hugh managed to hold on to his, and was still in post when, in 1250, the under-age Aymer de Valence (Lusignan), half-brother of King Henry, was elected Bishop of Winchester. Hugh des Roches died on about 9 October 1253.

Of the other Archdeacons of the thirteenth century even less is known. There are some unnamed: P—— appears once only and is likely to be Hugh (above) owing to a scribal error. Another P—— has two entries, 27 June 1254 and Nov 1256:

A return, dated 22 Nov. 1256, by P. Archdeacon of Winton to A. the Bishop elect, certifying that Thomas de Wynton, rector of Great Wordlam; died on the morrow of St Martin last (12 Nov.),that had been presented by Sir John de Venuz, but that the Prior and Convent of Selburne are now the patrons by the gift of the said Venuz ; that the person now presented was born in wedlock, and is not in Holy Orders *non est in sacris ordinibus constitutus*, and that the value of the church is commonly reckoned at 16 marks.

Yet another unnamed archdeacon is evident 24 October 1258, 28 May, 31 May and 1 June 1260.

Amaury Guiscard was Prior of Winchester in 1257, and Archdeacon in 1261.

Henry de Helingeye is noted, without title, after October 1263. His name would suggest that he came from Hellingly, East Sussex, near Hailsham and Herstmonceux rather than from Hilgay, Norfolk as previously suggested. He is identified as archdeacon in March 1274 in respect of a writ concerning the benefice of Great Worldham, Hampshire:

> '1274, 13 Jan *die S Hillaire episc* at Duntone. Copy by H[enry de Helingeye] Arch Deacon of Winchester of a return by his official to N[icholas] Bishop of Winchester (Nicholas of Ely) in pursuance of a writ from the King certifying that upon an enquiry made by the rectors of Farendone and Gretham , the vicars of Froyle, Seleburne and Yabesete, and the chaplains of Aultone and Benstead, it was found that the rectory of Worldham was not vacant but was held by John of Brideport who had been instituted by the Bishop on St John's day 1262, on the presentation of the Prior and convent of Seleburne the true patrons.'

Four of the villages around Seleburne (Selborne) may easily be identified; Farringdon, Greatham, Froyle, Binsted and Alton (town). Duntone is difficult to identify but may be Downton in Wiltshire, Yabesete, might be East Tisted. Great Worldham (variously spelt) was sited at today's East Worldham. It was at Worldham Major, that King John had a hunting lodge which he visited in 1204. The advowson of the little church of St. Mary was originally associated with the de Venuz family but eventually transferred by Bishop William of Waynflete to his foundation of Magdalen College, Oxford, c.1484. Worldham Parva is West Worldham, the church of St. Nicholas, established by Richard of Annecy, (the advowson belonged to Tiron Abbey, near Chartres) was later taken over by Bishop William of Wykeham and passed to Winchester College. The Augustinian Priory of Selborne, founded by Bishop Peter des Roches flourished at first, but discipline slipped in the fourteenth century to it becoming 'a society of worldly gentlemen living carelessly and very much at their ease'. William of Wykeham delivered a disciplinary mandate to it, with papal approval. Things improved for a time but by the

1480s it was hardly functioning and had to be closed by William of Waynflete, who transferred the muniments to his Oxford foundation, Magdalen College.

In 1276 there was an un-named Archdeacon of Winchester (Reg. Pontissara II 615-17) doing duty as an assessor:

> '27 Dec 76. Henry de Derngate appears before Nicholas of Ely Bishop of Winton sitting with the Abbot and Prior of Hyde (Abbey, Winchester) and archdeacons of Winchester and Surrey as assessors, craving absolution from sentences of excommunication in which he had been involved for maliciously defaming Bishop of Winton and many other vexatious suits against the church in Winchester in the King's Court. Receiving absolution, Henry was bound over for the sum of 1000 marks to refrain absolutely from such attacks in future. The Rector of Stonham (near Southampton) Martin de Rupibus Kt. (a des Roches) and two citizens of Winchester joining him in suretiship with regard to his penalty'.

Richard de la More is of interest with reference to the undesirable practice of a cleric holding more than one benefice (a plurality), a practice that Archbishop John Pecham tried, unsuccessfully, to stamp out. Richard de la More was already the sub-Dean of Lincoln appearing as Archdeacon of Winchester 11 Sept 1280, and becoming Bishop elect of Winchester by Royal Assent 15 Nov 1280. The Archbishop refused to confirm the election and 'When they appealed to the Pope he maintained the complaints against them and forced them at last to submit to his sentence and drop the cause'.

Richard de la More resigned (by) 9 June 1282. He appears to have continued in his post as archdeacon at least until 19 June 1283, and also as the sub-Dean of Lincoln.

Philip of St Austell alias Cornwaleys began as Bishop's clerk. He was appointed archdeacon in the Spring/Summer 1285 and was in post by 28 Oct 1285. An extract of the respective (later) entry Reg. Pontissara II pp. 456-7 reveals an archdeacon in the role of Proctor:

> *'Bishop had fully intended to go to London at the Arch Bishop of Canterbury's summons – but because of ill health keeps him at Farnham –- asks to be excuse (apologies) – sends as his proctors Archdeacon of Winchester and Ralph de Staunsford, his chaplain – he will come if he can.'*

The Bishop wrote on 29 Oct to Master Philip archdeacon explaining his position (dysentry and throat). However, 'he is willing to travel to Rome'.

Some years later, on 4 May 1293 *in crast. Inv. S Crucis* (the day after the feast of the Invention of the Holy Cross) at Seleburne , an entry in the Chartularies of Selborne Priory runs:

'Mandate from P[hilip Cornwaleys], archdeacon of Winchester, to the dean of Aultone, in pursuance of a mandate from J. Bishop of Winchester' (John de Pontissara) dated at Suthwerk, 12 Maii 1293, in which the appropriation of the church of Great Worldham to the Prior and convent of Selb[urne] is notified, for giving corporal possession of the said church to the said religious.'

Philip of St Austell (Cornwaleys) saw out the end of a very turbulent century and he died shortly before 10 June 1304.

14th-Century Archdeacons

The Kings of England in the fourteenth century were Edward I (1272-1307), Edward II (murdered 1327), Edward III (d., 1377) and Richard II (deposed by Bolingbroke (Henry IV) in 1399). It was a century of tumult and war, marked by campaigns in Scotland, Wales and Ireland and the beginning of the 'Hundred Years War' with France. History records the battles of Crecy and Poitiers, the capture of Calais, the valour of the Black Prince and the power of the Welsh longbow. In 1349, plague (Black Death) spread from Europe to Britain and almost one third of the population died of this disease. In 1381 came the Peasants' Revolt led by Wat Tyler.

It was a time of development in the Arts; the Universities of Oxford and Cambridge expanded and English became the official language (1362). It was the time of Piers Plowman (Will Langland), John Gower, Geoffrey Chaucer, Julian of Norwich, John Wyclif and the Lollards, the publication of *The Cloud of Unknowing*, and in Italy, of Dante (d.1320), Boccaccio and Petrarch.

Resentment of the presence of foreign clergy led to the closure of the Alien Priories and the expulsion of the monks. The Papal (Avignon) influence on eccesiastical appointments was restrained by the Statute of Provisors 1351 and of *Praemunire* 1353, 1365 and 1393. Of the ten Bishops of Winchester during the fourteenth century two were to hold office over the last 55 years, Edington

Sources

- Merton Wood and Loggan *Histoire et Antiquitates Univ. Oxon*. Vol 2 (1695) Oxford
- Botte A. *Monuments of Merton College* (1977) Oxford.,
- Garrod H.W., ed. Highfield J.R.L. An Indenture between William Rede, Bishop of Chichester and John Bloxham and Henry Stapilton,Fellows of Merton College, Oxford, 22 October 1374 in '*Bodleian Library Record*' (1978-1982).
- Martin.G.E. and Highfield J.R.I., *A History of Merton College* 1977 Oxford.
- Lowth.R. *The Life of William of Wykeham*,1777 3rd ed. Oxford.
- *St Cross Hospital History and Buildings*, ed. Warren.W.T. (1899) Warren.Winchester.
- Blomfield F. *History of Norfolk*.
- Common. DNB. ODCC. Le Neve, *Fasti Anglicani*, 1974, London.
- Greatrex J. *Biographical Register of the English Cathedrals and Priories in the Province of Canterbury 1066-1540*, Oxford, 1997
- *Oxford History of England*, ed. Sir George Clark, 3rd edn. Vols 2-15(A.D. 550 -1945) 1971 Oxford.

and Wykeham (the first and second Prelates of the Order of the Garter, established in 1348). Both were involved in the remodelling of the nave of Winchester Cathedral.

The Synodial Statutes of John de Pontissara (Bishop of Winchester 1282 – 1304)

Master Philip of St Austell alias Cornwaleys was Archdeacon 1285-1304 at the time these Statutes were being drafted and subsequently adopted at Diocesan Synod. The Prior of St Swithun's monastery at that time, Henry Woodlock de Merewell, has also been identified as being principally involved. A fine and, dedicated man, Henry succeeded John as Bishop (1305-1316) and is remembered in the Cathedral for commissioning the fine woodcarvings in the choir (1308 by William of Lyngwode).

The Synodial Statutes, in translation, bear close examination, because the tone of reform expressed in the instructions reflects the existence of ecclesiastical malpractice by extortion and intimidation. By way of introduction the Bishop is styled as 'A keeper in the vineyard... thwarting foxes... rooting up weeds, so that the vines may be fruitful and answer their Lord's expectations'. The long document deals with Baptism, Confirmation, The Sacraments of the Altar, Penance, Extreme Unction, Matrimony, Ordination, Churches, Holy Places and their Ornaments, The Life and Conduct of the Clergy, Wills, Archdeacons, Officials, Deans and their Apparitors, Veneration of Saints, the Celebration of Festivals and Excommunication. The section on the Archdeacons is of burgeoning interest and the restrictions are most revealing:

> *ON ARCHDEACONS, OFFICIALS, DEANS, AND THEIR APPARITORS*
>
> *As greater causes by their nature require greater judges, we inhibit Archdeacons, their Officials, or Deans from presuming to handle matrimonial or civil causes which tend to deposition or deprivation of a benefice, whether the action is criminal or civil, or those which belong in any other way to our jurisdiction. Let them not claim or receive procurations from Churches in our collation and exempt, or in any way take upon themselves to visit them.*
>
> *And, moreover, let them not venture without our special licence to increase old procurations, or to accept those increased, or to impose new procurations on poor Churches from which on account of their poverty none were payable in our predecessors' times, or to extort any so imposed.*
>
> *Let not the Archdeacons visit several Churches on one day, and let not them nor their men dare on any pretext to claim gifts from those whom they visit.*

Also, we enjoin that Archdeacons do not presume to demand or receive procurations from Churches which they do not visit personally, or when they visit that they do not exceed the amount of profits laid down by the Lateran Council, but behave in their household and among all others quietly according to the tenor of the new Constitution.

Moreover, we strictly forbid Rectors and Vicars of Churches in our gift, in which the Archdeacon has no place, either themselves, their Chaplains, or Parishioners to follow suit at the Archdeacons' Chapters or answer before them against the ancient custom of the Church of Winchester.

But, allowing the correction of lesser offences and cognizance in lesser causes to the same Rectors or Vicars in their Parishes according to ancient custom, we strictly forbid them to concern themselves with matrimonial or other greater causes, or with the correction of greater offences, or even that they handle the lesser through unlearned and unskilled Chaplains or farmers.

We enjoin that Priests unknown and of foreign ordination whom we will have examined by ourself or our Official be not admitted to celebrate without our special mandate.

Moreover, to the Archdeacons themselves, their Officials, and others having ordinary jurisdiction, we enjoin and command that, in assigning fines and amercements on their dependents, they show themselves so moderate that the receiver may not be considered greedy nor the giver too much burdened, so that for the future no clamour or complaint may din in our ears.

Nevertheless, we forbid the same under pain of canonical distraint to extort any money from our clerical or lay dependents by malicious evasions of our statutes or precepts.

Moreover, we firmly inhibit any Archdeacon, Official, Dean, or Apparitor from summoning anyone to a Chapter unless he be first accused by good and weighty persons.

In fixing a period of expiation for persons thus accused, let them not exceed a term of five years for a light charge or ten or twelve for a greater and detestable crime.

Moreover, greatly desiring to study the quiet of our subjects, we enjoin that the general Chapters of Archdeacons be held in the middle of each Deanery and not unless at intervals of four weeks. At which let Rectors, Vicars, Parish Priests, private persons, but not all be compelled to attend; only those who are nearest, and others who may have their own or their parishioners' business to see to there. And then we enjoin that they should be set free as soon as possible, lest they linger on outside their own Parishes to the peril of souls.

And let none be vexatiously dragged from one Deanery to another, or to distant spots.

But Chaplains of Parish Churches engaged about the burials of their Parishioners or other lawful business, provided they may be reasonably excused by their clerks or other messengers if they fail to come to any Chapters, we will not have adjudged contumacious on this account.

Let no Archdeacon's clerk except the Official venture to publish sentences of excommunication or suspension against any dependent of the Archdeacon, or in any way to practise jurisdiction unless a commission by letter has been given him by the Archdeacon or his Official for a lawful reason.

And as it is right that both we and our Official should often receive information by the assertions of the Rural Deans and Apparitors about citations and other things, we appoint that for the future as well Deans as Apparitors be chosen by us or our Official, the Archdeacons or their Officials in common, and likewise be removed in common by the same persons. But there should be in each Deanery only a single Apparitor without a horse, except in the more scattered Deaneries in which we allow their Apparitors to be mounted, since they could not on foot accomplish with due speed all that we, our Official, or the Archdeacons and their Officials shall enjoin on them.

Let them not entrust citations to Parochial Chaplains outside their own Parishes, lest meanwhile the cure of souls be left in danger.

Also, since it is a grievous sin to hinder the blessing of peace, we decree that provided the cause is one which can be duly terminated by a composition, the litigants can retire from a suit whenever they wish without penalty, and let no amercement be exacted from them on this account, unless there be clear proof of excessive injury and evil-doing on one side or the other.

Further, since the remedy of an appeal has been set on foot for the defence of innocence, we enjoin that Archdeacons, their Officials, and Deans, when appeals have been lodged for our audience, accept them reverently, giving no trouble to the appellants or to their own people on this account, nor threatening them at all so as to make them withdraw their opposition. But when we or our Official can be easily approached, let a convenient term be fixed for such appellants, within which they can appear to prosecute their appeal.

Since every man ought to bear his own burden, we forbid the Archdeacons, their Officials, or the Deans on account of the crimes of Rectors or Vicars to suspend Churches from divine services, but let them restrain and curb such delinquents by sentences of suspension or excommunication against their persons, or by the compulsion of sequestration and distraint of their goods, if necessary.

But concerning the goods of those who die intestate, which, according to the custom of the Church of England are known to be at the Bishop's disposal, we do not wish that without our special licence anyone should interfere with them.

And since many ignorant and illiterate persons to the peril of their own souls usurp the pastoral office, we enjoin both our Official and the Archdeacons, by the sprinkling of the Blood of Jesus Christ, that personally they make frequent and anxious inquiry whether any Rectors or Vicars are greatly deficient in learning ; and concerning sacerdotal and parochial matters let frequent trial be made whether they know the decalogue and the ten precepts of the Mosaic law, the seven Sacraments moreover, and the seven deadly sins, and whether they have at least a simple understanding of the Faith ; and whether they know how to explain all these to the laity in the vulgar tongue, and to instruct the people committed to them thereon.

We decree, moreover, that if any layman has been convicted of a heinous crime, for which, by right, public punishment ought to be inflicted or a solemn penance, it should by no means be commuted for another, unless perhaps for greater fruit of penance, or if, considering the person of the offender, he who has jurisdiction in the case considers it better to dispense otherwise.

Clergy also convicted of, or confessing to, similar crimes, we will to be suspended, and that the suspension should not be relaxed without our knowledge; and we enjoin that such, both Clergy and Laity, should be sent to our penitentiars to receive condign penance for their sins, and that they should return to their own Priest with the penitentiars' letters containing the penance enjoined them, that he may be able in due course to bear witness that the penance has been carried out.

But Archdeacons, their Officials, and Deans who permit Clergy thus suspended or repeatedly convicted of incontinence, on payment of money, to carry out their office, we will to be ipso facto *suspended from the execution of their office.*

Archdeacons also and their Officials or Deans who in regard of cupidity, by occasion of gain, commute corporal penances justly due into others, or enjoin corporal penances where they are not due, that for fear of them they may be able to extort money, if convicted of this, must from their own purse restore double, and, notwithstanding, submit to another heavy punishment.

Moreover, we inhibit the Archdeacons (by reason of a custom by which from some time back they have extorted twelve pence yearly from the several Churches of their Archdeaconry, which, to conceal the vice of simony inherent in it, some call a present, others a pork-butcher's gift, others by a feigned name the Archdeacon's pig) from daring to extort any money, or the Rectors or Vicars from paying the exaction, until the Archdeacons themselves have clearly shown us their right to receive this payment, and the Rectors and Vicars have other instructions from us hereon.

Clearly, the post of Archdeacon was not to be enjoyed as before.

Michael (Nicholas) de Hellestone held the post for 52 days (10 June – 31 July 1304). He appears to have been an official of the Diocese, for in 1296 he had presented accounts of expenses incurred on a visit to Rome on behalf of the Bishops of Winchester and Lincoln. This is followed by a claim of 50 shillings expenses incurred in returning from Cambrey (?Chambery) the home of Amadeus, Count of Savoy, and then another request – for his salary! In 1299 he acted as a representative of the Bishop in cases and suits in the Consistory Court of Winchester. In 1301 and 1303 he received instructions by letter from the Bishop who was on business in Viterbo and Rome. He enjoyed the benefices of Martyr Worthy (Hants.) and the rectory of Meonstoke (Hants.), retiring to that rectory on his resignation as Archdeacon.

For the next 39 years the Archdeacons of Winchester bore Italian names. Master James Sinobaldi de Florentia (de Pulcis) filled the post 1304-1325. He was Papal Nuncio, Vicar General, and a member of a syndicate of Florentine merchant bankers who collected papal dues ('one tenth') for, say, funding Crusades. There is a record in 1293 as his being in receipt of £13,967–17s–8½d. He is likely to have been an unpopular visitor to the benefices (he might well have been nicknamed 'The Flea' (Pulce means Flea). There is an unusual record that on the very day of collation to the archdeaconry 'the clergy and the laity within the archdeaconry are admonished to show reverence and obedience to the new archdeacon and those who act under him. Already enjoying the benefice (rectory) of Brightwell (Berks) from 1298, he was in 1324 admitted to the prebendal portion of St Lawrence in the conventual church of Romsey, to which he was presented by the Abbess and Convent with the chapels annexed to it.

Little is known of the other Italian-named Archdeacons 1325-45. **Philip Sapiti** (1 April 1325) died sometime in January 1328, to be followed by **John de Podio Barzaco** (17 Feb 1328) who died at Curia before Sept 1343. **Stephen de Malo Leone** enjoyed a royal grant during the lifetime of Podio Barzaco and he probably continued until 1345. **Ayguelmino Guillelmi de Sparra** was also provided Archdeacon on 9 Sept 1343 but does not appear to have gained possession of the archdeaconry.

Robert de Burton (1345-1361) followed the above by royal grant 7 July 1345. William of Edington, already Treasurer of England, became Bishop of Winchester the following year. Previously Robert was canon of Bishop Auckland and prebendary of Kirk Merrington in the diocese of Durham. He exchanged this benefice on 3 June 1359 with John Bretteull for the rectory of Kempshott (Basingstoke). He appears to have survived the plague years and died sometime before 18 June 1361.

John de Wolveley (1361 June – October) was another who had been active as an official and whose tenure as Archdeacon was brief. He seems to have excelled himself in collecting benefices. On 10 April 1349 he exchanged Arreton I.O.W. for North Waltham, Hants. and on the next day obtained Edington Wilts. in the diocese of Salisbury but under the patronage of William of Edynton (Bishop of Winchester) who had established a collegiate church there. John became a canon of Salisbury. In September the same year he acquired Brightwell, Berks – with the title of Bishop's Chancellor. He exchanged the rectorship of Michelchurch, Hants. for Calbourne, I.O.W. which he exchanged immediately for Alverstoke, Hants. In September 1356 he was collated to the vicarage of Twyford in exchange for Itchen, which he had at first held. On 16 October 1352, acting as canon of Salisbury and Bishop's Chancellor he inducted the new Prior to the Hospital of St Thomas Southwark (Fr John de Ivingho). He was Archdeacon for four months, resigning before 18 Oct 1361, presumably to continue to enjoy his plurality.

However, it should be pointed out that Canon Law in those days allowed the collection of any number of benefices but without the cure of souls. But in such a collection only one benefice with the cure of souls was allowed save for papal dispensation.

Robert de Wykford Sch.C.L. 18 Oct 1361 – 1372 was already rector of Winchfield, Hants. (31 July 1361). Scarcely two years passed before he was given a licence (9 Nov 1363) for three years' study leave in a University in England on condition he provided suitable officials and staff for the work in the diocese, and that he paid his annual dues (£20). One is surprised to learn from an entry (1365) that he is referred to as the Constable of Bordeaux 'there being a writ of Account against him'. At that time the post of Constable of Bordeaux carried considerable administrative and financial responsibilities with special relationship to the Treasury in Westminster. He is heard of again in 1369 giving absolution to one who had died excommunicate so that his remains might be given a Christian burial, 'the Archdeacon ordered to absolve the corpse if it should appear that the deceased exhibited any symptoms of penitence before death'. On 23 May 1371 he wrote to the Bishop (William of Wykeham) praying him to certify excommunicate certain clergy, namely Richard Grene of Bridlesford, William of St Lawrence, I.O.W., John of Bramdean, Hants., and John Basynge of Eremuth (Yarmouth I.O.W.) for 'contempt'. The certification requested appears to be for 40 days. Robert resigned his post before 19 October 1372 on promotion, possibly as abbot, to the monastery at Wearmouth, Durham founded by Benedict Biscop in A.D. 674.

By now a new breed of men began to arrive on the scene, the first being:

Nicholas de Wykeham (?-1404). Archdeacon 1372-1381.

Ordained 1383.
Prebendary of Bosham, W. Sussex 1370
Sequestrator, Hospital of St Cross, Winchester 1374-1382.
Rector of Witney, Oxford. 1378
Warden of New College, Oxford 1379-89
Archdeacon of Wiltshire 1381-

The services rendered by Nicholas in Winchester and Oxford to his Bishop William of Wykeham are of particular interest. As to kinship, Nicholas was among the *consanguinei incertum quo grado* (of doubtful pedigree).

St. Cross Hospital, Winchester. The Hospice of St Cross was founded in 1136 by Bishop Henry of Blois 'for the poor of Christ'. The care of 13 poor men and the feeding of 100 poor of Winchester was in the hands of a Master, and by then, under the overall care of the Bishop. In 1372 Bishop William of Wykeham had to deprive the Master, Roger de Cloune, of his post on account of 'Dilapidation, Dissipation and Subtraction, public and notorious', selling off corn and cattle, while keeping the proceeds, dismissing the poor brothers and turning away the poor. A long-drawn-out and expensive dispute followed, with final judgement given by the Pope in favour of William of Wykeham who was himself already enduring much hardship on account of being removed from the Chancellorship of England 1371, and being put on trial 1376, forfeiting his temporalities. In his kinsman archdeacon Nicholas he had an administrator able to undertake the management of recovery. On the death of de Cloune 8 Sept 1382 John de Campenden, Archdeacon of Surrey, was appointed Master, completing with great dedication the restorations for which he is venerated to this day.

New College, Oxford. In 1379 William of Wykeham founded his *Seinte Marie College of Wynchestre in Oxenford* ('vulgarly called New College' according to Lowth). Nicholas was warden with a salary £40 *per annum* until 1389, the year William of Wykeham returned to Royal favour.

In 1382 when Nicholas inducted his successor as Archdeacon, John Bloxham, he was being cited prebendary of Timsbury near Romsey, and (incorrectly) as archdeacon of Norwich. He was in fact already archdeacon of Wiltshire by 1381. Later, in 1388, he held the prebend of Bedwyn, Berkshire, in Salisbury Cathedral and was a canon of Salisbury. There is a mandate to him dated July 1401 as Archdeacon of Wiltshire and warden of the *Domus Dei* church in Portsmouth to enforce repairs to the chancel there.

On 4 Jan 1403 on account of the age and ill health of the Bishop he was nominated, by papal Bull coadjutor along with John Elmere, D.C.L., Official General and judge of the Consistory Court. They with John de Campenden were amongst his executors. It is deduced that these three are portrayed in the three figures seated at the foot of the effigy of the Bishop in Wykeham's chantry chapel in Winchester Cathedral.

William of Wykeham's executors at the foot of his effigy in his chantry chapel, Winchester Cathedral.

Nicholas was ordained by the Bishop on 16 May 1383 at Esher. He died in 1406, two years after the Bishop.

Bloxham, John (? – 1387) S.T.B. (B.D.) Oxon.
Fellow 1361 and Warden (1375-87), Merton College, Oxford
Archdeacon of Winchester (1382-87)

In the *Biographical Register of the English Cathedrals and Priories of the Province of Canterbury (1066-1540)* Oxford, (1997) there is an entry to a John Bloxham (Blocksham, Blokesham, Bloxam) of Bath Cathedral Priory who on 1 March 1346 was appointed Prior to the hospital (cell) of St John the Evangelist at Waterford, Ireland, with custody of their lands and possessions. He was also appointed Proctor 3 March. He held the post until 1360.

There appears to be no record linking this man with the Archdeaconry of Winchester, but the association is likely. The Dictionary of National Biography identifies a John Bloxham who was said to be employed frequently by Edward III on business in Scotland and Ireland. He was elected Fellow of Merton College, Oxford in 1361, was Bursar several times and became Warden in 1375. In 1382 he was called, together with a number of theologians and mendicants, to attend a Council at Blackfriars, London, under Archbishop William Courtney in order to pass judgement on the 24 'erroneous' propositions of a former Fellow of Merton (1356) John Wyclif (not named in the proceedings). The four-day council was styled the 'Earthquake Synod' because it was interrupted by an earthquake (variously interpreted by those present).

Bloxham, Merton College Library, William Rede of Chichester and William Wykham. There is an indenture between William Rede, Bishop of Chichester and John Bloxham and Henry Stapilton, Fellows of Merton College, Oxford, London 22 October 1374, witnessing Rede's gift of *£100 ad referacionem libraria* (for the reference library) and 100 books *in dicta libraria . . . cathenandos* (in the said chained library). Bloxham visited Rede in his London Hospice 1373 – 74. In Rede's Will (1382) was also £100 for a loan chest. Earlier in 1370, through the generosity of Simon Bredon, a new library was under construction. Bloxham, then Fellow and Bursar, was Clerk of Works and he brought the master mason, William Humberville of Taynton, Nr. Burford, to London to consult with Bishop Rede, and also to inspect the fine library of the Dominicans (perhaps at Blackfriars, London). They made similar visits to Salisbury, Sherborne and Winchester.

The developments at Merton ran parallel with William of Wykeham's foundation of the *College of Sainte Marie at Oxenford* (New College, 1379). Wykeham was much influenced by the example of Walter de Merton (Bishop of Rochester). It is of note that Wykeham wished Bloxham to be Archdeacon of Winchester at a time when the cathedral nave was undergoing the transformation begun by Bishop Edington. Also there was the creation of the *College of Sainte Marie at Winchester* (Winchester College). Bloxham was a witness to the Foundation Charter in 1386.

Bloxham held his posts at Oxford and Winchester concurrently until his death in 1389. He was buried *in medio choro* of Merton college chapel. Curiously a colleague John Whitton (d. c.1390/1400) was subsequently buried beside him. To a large ledger stone of Purbeck marble (551/2" x 120") was affixed a brass, which was partly restored and moved to a new matrix in 1849. The brass bears an inscription:

> *'Hic iacent magist' Joh'es Bloxham Baculari' sacre theolo-*
> *gie quonda' Custos hui'*
> *Collegii, et Joh'es Whytton' Rector eccle'ie de Wodeton'*
> *& hui' Collegii Benefactor*
> *qui lapide' istu' fecit suis p'priis sumptibus ordinari. quor' a'i'abus p'piciet' d's Amen.'*
>
> 'Here lie Master John Bloxham, B.D. former Warden of this College and John Whytton, Rector of the Church of Wodeton and Benefactor of this College...'

There are two 20" high full-length effigies of John Bloxham and John Whitton. Bloxham is tonsured and is wearing a *supertunica* and *cappa clausa* with two side slits, a white fur hood and shoulder piece. It has been described as the best early example of the dress of a B.D..

Bloxham and the Forrester Provision. With the Avignon Popes 'in Babylonish Captivity' controlled by the French Kings, Edward III and Richard II contested the Papal provision (grant) of ecclesiastical appointments by means of the Statutes of Provisors and *Praemunire* (finally repealed in 1967). Any contempt incurred arrest, payment of compensation, and in further default, banishment. In 1386, when Bloxham had held the archdeaconry for four years, William Forrester appeared with Papal provision of the post. This was 'opposed by royal mandate that persons bringing Papal bulls etc., prejudicial to Crown and to M. John Bloxham, archdcn. of Winchester to be arrested'. It appears that Forrester did not answer the charge of contempt, neither paid damages to Bloxham, and was outlawed. He was pardoned 1 July 1388, a year after Bloxham had died, the King having appointed Roger de Walden 22 July 1387. Forrester finally renounced his claim to the archdeaconry 23 February 1389.

Roger de Walden Archdeacon 1387 - 1395
Treasurer of England, Dean of York, 1395
Archbishop of Canterbury 1398 - 1399
Bishop of London 1405-1406

It is said, without firm foundation that Roger was the son of a butcher in Saffron Walden, Essex. His brother, John, 'Esquire of St Bartholomew's, Smithfield' accumulated much property in Essex. Nothing is known of Roger's education, the first record being his collation to the benefice of St Helier, Jersey, 6 Sept 1371. He lived in Jersey 1378 –79 and in 1383 was custodian of the de Carteret estates, and sometime *locum tenens seu deputatus* (Deputy) of the Channel Isles. He became King's Clerk in 1385.

During the time he was Archdeacon of Winchester he was engaged in some extraordinary secular employment, '...better versed in things of the Camp and the World than of the Church and Study'. He was Captain of Mark, near Calais October 1387, the High Bailiff of Guisnes 1391 and Treasurer of Calais 1387-92. He had joined in the Captain of Calais' cattle raid into French territory 1388.

In 1395 he resigned his Archdeaconry to become the King's secretary and the Treasurer of England.

By this time he had accumulated a number of Prebends – Lincoln, Salisbury, Exeter, Lichfield, St Andrew's Holborn, and Willesden in St Paul's.

When Archbishop Thomas Arundel was banished in 1397 King Richard II, by Papal Bull, invested Walden as Archbishop in January 1398. But when Arundel returned with Bolingbroke Duke of Lancaster (deposing Richard in the following year) the Bull was quashed and Roger had to return all the goods that he had appropriated from Arundel. Yet it was at Arundel's instance that his life was spared. Then a year later in January 1400, he was committed to the Tower of London on the charge of complicity in a plot (the Epiphany plot) against Henry IV. After acquittal he lived in much reduced circumstances 'in the dust and under the foot of man' (notwithstanding a present of two barrels of wine from the King in 1403). It was on his behalf that Thomas Arundel persuaded the King to make Roger Bishop of London, providing he swore allegiance. He was installed in St Paul's Cathedral 30 June 1405, 'the canons in procession wearing garlands of red roses'. But illness followed and he died in his episcopal residence at Much Hadham, Herts. 6 January 1406.

A curious sequel is recorded. Both Roger Walden and John de Waltham, Bishop of Salisbury (Walden's predecessor as Treasurer of England) had previously held the post of rector of Fenny Drayton, Leics. In his will of 1456 a certain John Drayton goldsmith, founded chantries in St Paul's and in the church at Tottenham for the souls of Waltham, Walden, his brother John, and John' s wife Idonea.

It was said of Walden that he was 'modest in prosperity, patient in adversity'. He was popular; all spoke well of him. Indeed Thomas Arundel gave testimony to 'his honest life and devotion to the priestly office'.

Walden, when Archbishop of Canterbury, instituted the commemoration of St David on 1 March.

15th-Century Archdeacons

On the positive side the fifteenth century was one of voyages of discovery and the development of culture. The greater voyages are associated with names such as Henry the Navigator, Bartholomew Diaz, Christopher Columbus, John Cabot, Vasco da Gama and Amerigo Vespucci. The development of the Renaissance conjures up the name of the Medici family in Florence with Cosimo the Elder and Lorenzo the Magnificent. The use of movable type for printing was introduced by Gutenberg in 1454 and, in England, by John Caxton in 1476. A paper mill went into production near Stevenage in Hertfordshire in 1490. King's College, Cambridge and Eton College were founded by Henry VI. Bishop Waynflete of Winchester was both Provost of Eton and Founder of Magdalen College, Oxford.

On the negative side the century was scarred by acts of sheer brutality. Through the act of *De Haeretico Comburendo* in 1401, the burning of heretics in England was made legal. This was the fate of the Lollards, and abroad, the fates of Joan of Arc in Rouen, John Huss in Constance and Savonarola in Florence. The Inquisition was formally established.

The Hundred Years War dragged on and despite Harfleur ('Once more unto the breach, dear friends,') and Agincourt in 1415, the English were finally defeated. There were crusades against the Hussites (followers of Wyclif) in Bohemia. Rural England was torn apart by

Sources

- Greatrex, Dr Joan *Humanistic Script in a Monastic Register. An Outward and Visible sign.* Studies in Church History, XIV, 1977
- Procacci, G. *A History of the Italian People*, London, 1970
- Radford, L.B. *Cardinal Beaufort*, London 1908
- Ed. Joan Greatrex, *The Register of the Common Seal of the Priory of St Swithun, Winchester* Hampshire Record Series, Vol. II, 1978
- *Renaissance* 1961, American Heritage Publishing Company Inc.
- *The Canons of Salisbury. A Record*, Compiled by Christopher Ross

the bloody battles of the Wars of the Roses, there was treachery against the meek King Henry VI, the murders of the Princes in the Tower of London and finally, after the battle of Bosworth Field, England came under what Churchill described as the Tudor dictatorship.

Individual Biographies from 1395 ~ 2000

Robert Broun B.Th. & Nicholas Daniel (Danyel)

1395 ~ 1404

At the turn of the century these two names are recorded. Broun was to be collated to the archdeaconry if found fit after examination in Latin, but there is no further record of him.

Daniel was collated by the Bishop at Esher 16 October 1395. The deanery of York was reserved for him from 31 October 1397 but he never took office.

The only record of Daniel concerns his absence from the important election of a successor to Wykeham in 1404. He was summoned, with John de Campenden, archdeacon of Surrey to be present at 'the hour of Chapter' on 16 October 1404 'for the electoral proceeding'. Campenden personally 'was apprehended and ordered to appear' but 'Danyel could not be found within the realm'. A solemn Mass to the Holy Spirit was sung at the high altar, there being 42 monks present. After the homily and the singing of *Veni Creator Spiritus* a letter was read certifying that 'M. Nicholas Danyel had been duly cited to appear, whom the Prior then pronounced contumacious'. The Prior Thomas Neville was then elected Bishop by those present. However, the election was not ratified by the Pope, who instituted the Bishop of Lincoln, Henry Beaufort, half brother to the King.

Due to the loss of the Bishop's records, the names of the archdeacons between 1404 and 1428 are not known.

Nicholas Bildesten (Billesden)

Archdeacon 1428 ~ 1441

*c.*1420 Secretary to Bishop Henry Beaufort
1426 Chancellor to Cardinal Beaufort
King's Proctor in Curia, Rome
1423 Rector of Bishopstone, Wiltshire
1425 Prebendary of Bedwyn, Wiltshire and Ufcumb (Devon)
1435 Dean of Salisbury, by papal dispensation
1441 Died

The career of Nicholas Bildesten is reflected in the life and times of Beaufort. It is known that the Bishop, an immensely rich and powerful statesman who was twice Chancellor of England, engaged two suffragan Bishops to do the pastoral work of the See, William Solubriensis and John Sewell. Bildesten, the Bishop's secretary appears as Cardinal's chancellor on the Bohemian crusade of 1427 against the Hussites (followers of Wyclif and the Lollards) in Czechoslovakia. He was given the difficult task of conveying to the Pope the news of the rout of the crusaders by the Hussites at Tachau near Pilsen. Thus it is likely that he was with the Cardinal on the planned second Bohemian crusade of 1429. It was a large force, diverted in France to assist the English army which had suffered defeat at the hands of the Maid of Orleans. Thus Beaufort became entangled with her fate. Afterwards, in January 1432 the Cardinal required Bildesten to proceed on a mission to the Pope to urge that any Cardinal used as a mediator in peace negotiations with France should be England-friendly. In the event another, already in Rome, was designated.

In 1435 Nicholas was with the Cardinal in Calais, ready for a large peace conference in Oye, brokered by the Duchess of Burgundy. Three hundred eminent personages from each side confronted each other, armed only with 'swords and daggers'. 'On 6 July Dr Bildesten celebrated mass in the Cardinal's chapel, and soon after six the

Cardinal and the ambassadors rode out to the meeting place.' The talks failed.

Of special note is the record of the award of stipends made in 1429, from an episcopal grant ratified by the Prior and Convent of St Swithun. Bildesten was one of several recipients which included two stewards and four eminent officials of the Crown – Henry, Earl of Northumberland, Richard, Earl of Salisbury, Lewis, Lord of Burghclere and Walter, Earl of Hungerford. The money came in three tranches: £333-6-8 annually during the life of the Bishop, equal amounts payable Easter and Michelmas to come from the castle and town of Taunton and several Somerset manors: £133-6-8 annually from the Wiltshire manors of Downton, Ebbesborne Wake and Knoyle: £200 from Bishop's Waltham, East Meon, Havant, Droxford, Alverstoke and Fareham. It was a huge sum, compared with the average vicar's annual stipend of £6-7-0 in those days.

Nicholas Bildesten has a special place in the history of English Humanism. Beaufort, unlike his great adversary Humphrey, Duke of Gloucester, appears to have had little interest in literature, yet, probably from contact made in the Council of Constance in 1417/18, he invited one Poggio Bracciolini to Winchester. Poggio, who was a papal secretary for fifty years was already renowned in the Renaissance of Humanism, especially for his discovery in the monastery of St Gallen, Switzerland of ancient manuscripts by Quintillian, of Cicero, Lucretius, Vitrullus and Columella. The visit to Winchester, though not a success in terms of discovering manuscripts, nor in securing a good stipend from a benefice, resulted in a special friendship with Nicholas and with Richard Petworth to whom Beaufort left £100 in his will. To Poggio, Nicholas was *homo perhumanus*, a fine compliment. They kept up correspondence and there were requests for books. A humanist circle evolved in Winchester and in time was to include Vincent Clement (below), John Neele and Simon Alyward.

In 1977, Professor Joan Greatrex reported that rare early examples of humanist script (light Italianate as opposed to Gothic) began to appear in the *Register of the Common Seal* of the Priory of St Swithun, 'an outward and visible sign'.

Nicholas died in office 31 May 1441.

Stephen Wilton

Archdeacon 1443 ~ 1450

*c.*1425 Doctor of Canon Law, Cambridge
1427 Archdeacon of Stow
1429 Rector of Long Melford
1433 Archdeacon of Sarum and Canon of Lincoln
1443 Archdeacon of Winchester
1446 Provost of St Elizabeth's Chapel
1450 Prebend, South Cave, York
1457 Died – burial Beverley Minster

Stephen Wilton was Archdeacon of Winchester at the time of Cardinal Henry Beaufort's death on 11th April 1447 and at the beginning of the War of the Roses. Unusually less than one week elapsed between Beaufort's death and the election by the Prior and Convent of his successor, William Wayneflete. No previous election had been effected with such haste. Furthermore, by the end of July, that year, Waynflete had been consecrated as Bishop of Winchester.

Stephen Wilton played a major part in these events. The Prior and Convent had petitioned Henry VI for a licence to freely elect a new pastor (Bishop) on the day after Beaufort's death, that is the 12th April. Incredibly, a Royal congé d'élire was granted by the King on the previous day, the 11th, the day that Beaufort had died; it must have crossed the Prior's letter. The King at Windsor had somehow learned of Beaufort's death on the day that it occurred, and he certainly wasted not a moment in letting the Prior know of his wishes for the succession. The Royal communication requests:

> *'oure right trusty and well beloved clerc and concellour maistre William Wayneflete Provost of oure College Royal of oure Lady of Eton be elected in all haste that ye goodly may...'*

The King was not content to let matters rest at that and on the 15th, another letter was received at Winchester instructing the Prior not to wait upon *'eny lettres under*

Sources

- A. B. Emden, *Biographical Register of the University of Cambridge to 1500* (Cambridge University, 1963).
- *The Victoria History of Hampshire and the Isle of Wight, Vol 2*, ed. H Arthur Doubleday & William Page (Westminster: Archibald Constable, 1903).
- *Register of the Common Seal of the Priory of St. Swithun Winchester, 1345 - 1497*, ed. Joan Greatrex (Hampshire County Council, 1978).

our grete seel for we have in such wise ordeined that ye shal not nede theym'. The King also wrote to Stephen Wilton instructing him to assist in the election. He was to be particularly careful to ensure the canonical legality of the election so as to reduce any possibility of a later challenge. The saintly Henry wanted nothing left to chance over the election of the much favoured Wayneflete. Wilton was to ensure that the Prior and Convent exercised their 'choice' correctly in both meanings of the word. The brethren's election of the new Bishop was enacted with Wilton very much the master of ceremonies.

A detailed record of Waynflete's unsurprising election is given in the *Register of the Common Seal of the Priory of St. Swithun, Winchester*. On 14th April, having received the licence from the King, which was publicly exhibited in the presence of Prior Aulton, Archdeacon Wilton and the brethren assembled in the Chapter House. It was unanimously agreed to hold the election the next day. After a solemn sung Mass at the High Altar and the ringing of bells, the community, the Prior and 36 monks, gathered for the election. Present were Archdeacon Wilton, a representative of the Archdeacon of Surrey and Richard Petworth, the notary. After a homily and devout singing the Register notes that '*all felt themselves immediately inspired by the Holy Spirit to cast their votes for William Wayneflete, a man whose discretion, knowledge and blameless way of life are to be commended*'. Afterwards they sang the *Te Deum Laudamus*, festival bells were rung and Archdeacon Wilton made public, in the vulgar tongue at the Cathedral High Altar, the results of their choice. The news was then sent to Wayneflete at Eton and '*although the elect was reluctant to accept at first, the proctors were ultimately successful, in obtaining his consent*'.

Wilton was Beaufort's Chancellor, as well as Archdeacon, and like Wayneflete can be assumed to be a supporter of the Lancastrian cause. During 1447 Henry's uncle, Humphrey, Duke of Gloucester, who had been during the King's minority Protector of England, was arrested at, it is assumed, the instigation of Henry's Queen, Margaret of Anjou. His subsequent death is the subject of much speculation. Although Henry was obsessively pious it was probably for political reasons that he was so anxious to ensure that the vacuum created by Beaufort's death, after 44 years as Bishop, was quickly filled by someone whom he fully trusted. Wayneflete was the obvious choice. It is likely that Wilton had kept the King fully informed of Beaufort's medical condition and the King was, therefore, fully primed to act when Beaufort died on the 11th April. Wilton's importance at Winchester is underlined by the fact that he had been appointed by

Beaufort as an Executor to his complicated will. Beaufort, the richest man in England (he had once lent Henry V £28,000), had bequeathed a considerable sum to the Cathedral church. In addition to the detailed instructions for his own Chantry Chapel, money was left for a gold and silver altar frontal and for the 'great' shrine of St. Swithun. The Great Screen and new shrine of St. Swithun were the inspiration of Cardinal Beaufort, but needed the abilities of a Wayneflete to ensure their completion after his death. Wilton, in control of Beaufort's bequest, would have played a pivotal role.

Stephen Wilton's early life is unrecorded, but it is known that he was elected a Doctor of Canon Law at Jesus College, Cambridge in 1425 and began his ministry in East Anglia, he was Rector of Long Melford in 1429. After being appointed Archdeacon of Stow in 1427, he was both a Canon of Lincoln and Archdeacon of Sarum in 1433. A year later we find him appointed to the first of a number of livings and appointments in the North of England, including a Canonry of Beverley, and a Prebendary of St. Martins, York, which he was to hold until his death. Already Beaufort's Chancellor, he was elected to the Archdeaconry of Winchester on the 12th March 1443. The previous year the King had granted Beaufort a Charter to assign manors, lordships, and advowsons of churches to the value of £500 per year to the Hospital of St. Cross. This was to ensure the financial future of the Hospital and to enable the Cardinal to establish a second foundation of alms houses for those of 'Noble Poverty'. Wilton was fully engaged in these appropriations, including the church of Crondall.

In 1446, Wilton was elected Provost of St. Elizabeth's Chapel, founded by Bishop Pontoise in 1301. This chapel situated near the gate of Wolvesey, had been founded as a Chantry for the souls of Bishops and Kings and Queens, past and present, and for the general assembly, especially the Prior and Convent of St. Swithun. Seven chaplains were to live together at common table for these purposes. By Wilton's time the post of Provost had become non-residential. The chapel was granted to Thomas Wriothesley, Henry VIII's commissioner at the Dissolution of the Monasteries and sold by him for £360 to Winchester College who demolished it within a year, presumably for the reuse of the building materials.

As was the custom of the time, Wilton was much used by Beaufort and the King as a foreign envoy. In 1433 he treated with the Scots, in 1435 he was sent on a mission to firstly, the Duke of Bavaria, and secondly, the Emperor and Archbishop of Cologne. He was chosen to treat with the French at Calais for much of 1439 and 1440 and again with the Duke of Orleans the following year. The loss of the French possessions had had a profoundly depressing impact on the populace and a pronounced effect on the exchequer; by 1453 England retained only its toehold at Calais itself.

Wilton resigned in 1450, probably to settle in the North, where he still held a living at Barton, Yorks, and his Canonry at Beverley, York. In 1450 he acquired a Prebend at South Cave, York, and a Canonry at Southwell, North Muskham. He relinquished the Southwell Canonry in 1453 when he became Archdeacon of Cleveland which he held at his death in July 1457. He was buried in Beverley Minister where he had founded a Chantry in 1455. Amongst his last acts, in 1455, was, together with others, the foundation of St. William's College, York.

John Pakenham

Archdeacon 1450 ~ 1459

Vincent Clement

Archdeacon 1459 ~ 1475

Very little is known about these two Archdeacons, who served during the largest portion of Waynflete's time as Bishop of Winchester. The only mention of John Pakenham, a Doctor of Canon Law, during his nine years as Archdeacon is in the *Register of the Great Seal* for 1457, where the involvement of the Winchester Archdeaconry in the appropriation of Fordingbridge church to the Royal College of Blessed Mary and St. Nicholas is noted. This had been founded by Henry VI and the King had decided to annex the church to the College. The fact that the formal presentations of this appropriation were handled by Packenham's proctors and not by him personally are not in themselves significant, but as this is the only mention of him at all, it may indicate a low level of commitment by him to his duties as Archdeacon. In any event Packenham resigned in 1459. It is possible that he was related to Hugh Packenham who was Wayneflete's Treasurer in 1455 and a close confident of the Bishop.

We do know a little more about Vincent Clement (Clemente), Doctor of Theology, who was Archdeacon to Bishop Waynflete for 16 years during the most

Sources

- *Register of the Common Seal of the Priory of St. Swithun Winchester*, 1345-1497, ed. Joan Greatrex (Hampshire County Council, 1978).
- Thomas Gascoigne, *Loci e Libro Veritatum*, ed. J. E. Thorold Rogers (Oxford,1881).
- Virginia Davis, *William Wayneflete Bishop and Educationalist* (Woodbridge: Boydell Press, 1993).

turbulent period of the Wars of the Roses, culminating with Edward IV's accession in 1461. Waynflete was a loyal supporter of the Lancastrian King, Henry VI, and his Lord Chancellor from 1456-60 but was, through his discretion and judgement, able to gain the respect and approval of King Edward and as a result probably saved Winchester from the worst ravages of the Civil Wars. Clement held office as Archdeacon during what must have been a particularly testing period. We do not know whether he was sympathetic to Waynflete, or whether he was well regarded by the Bishop, but probably not, as he was a Papal choice as Archdeacon and Waynflete would have had no say in his appointment. This was a time when criticism was growing over the behaviour of the clergy. Thomas Gascoigne was a severe fifteenth-century critic of the church hierarchy and in particular, of plurality and unlicensed absences. In response to this, Waynflete had taken a moderate stance, granting the clergy dispensations which allowed them to hold only two or three incompatible benefices; generally there were few abusers of this system. However, Clement apparently was a notorious exception, with a record of long absences and many pluralities. He was Aragonese by birth and had received letters of naturalization only in 1439. Like Bildeston, Archdeacon until 1443, and Richard Petworth, the notary, who had been present at the election of Waynflete in 1447, Clement was the member of the small circle of English Humanists. It is likely that Winchester became their common meeting ground. The implication is, therefore, that Clement was living within reach of Winchester long before he became Archdeacon in 1459. Clement died in 1475 whilst still Archdeacon.

John Morton

Archdeacon 1475 ~ 1478

*c.*1420 Born in Dorset
D.C.L Balliol College, Oxford
1448 Fellow of Peckwater Inn, Oxford
1450 Sub-dean of Lincoln
by 1453 Principal of Peckwater Inn, Oxford, and incumbent of Bloxworth, Dorset
1458 Prebendary of Lincoln and Salisbury
1472 Rector of St. Dunstan's-in-the-East and Prebendary of St.Paul's
1473 Master of the Rolls
1475 Archdeacon of Winchester (other preferments, including 5 archdeaconries about this time)
1479 Bishop of Ely
1486 Archbishop of Canterbury
1487 Lord Chancellor
1493 Cardinal
1495 Chancellor of the University of Oxford
1500 Died, Knowle, Kent

Although John Morton was Archdeacon of Winchester for only three years, more is known about him than other holders of that office in earlier centuries, for he became Archbishop of Canterbury, Cardinal and Lord Chancellor. Morton was born about 1420 in Dorset, in Milborne St. Andrew, near Bere Regis. He was the son of Richard Morton, a member of a Nottinghamshire family who had migrated to Dorset. John was educated at Cerne Abbey, a Benedictine house near his home and then at Balliol College, Oxford. Qualified as D.C.L., he moved to London where he practised mainly as an ecclesiastical lawyer in the Court of Arches. Here he came to the attention of the Archbishop of Canterbury, Thomas Bourchier, under whose patronage Morton became a Privy Councillor, Chancellor of the Duchy of Cornwall and a master in Chancery. Preferments over the next few years made him Sub-dean of Lincoln, Principal of Peckwater Inn, Oxford, incumbent of Bloxworth near his home in Dorset and Prebendary of Lincoln and Salisbury.

However, national events soon intervened. The disputes which became known as the Wars of the Roses led to open conflict in 1459-61 between supporters of King Henry VI and those of the Yorkists. Following the capture of King Henry at Northampton in July 1460, a Lancastrian army led by Queen Margaret and her young son, Prince Edward, swept down from the North early

Sources

- *Dictionary of National Biography*
- A.B.Emden, *Biographical Register of the University of Oxford to AD 1500* (1958)
- R.I.Woodhouse, *Life of John Morton* (1895)
- K.Feiling, *History of England*
- R.Neillands, *The Wars of the Roses*
- J.D.Mackie, *The Earlier Tudors* 1485-1558
- J.Crook (ed), *Winchester Cathedral – Nine Hundred Years 1093-1992*

in 1461. Meanwhile, the young Edward of March, now Duke of York after his father's death in battle, had marched on London where at the age of almost 19 he was proclaimed king as Edward IV on 4 March 1461. John Morton continued to support the Lancastrian monarchy, with whom he was now closely associated. After a victory at St Albans on 17 February 1461, he took part as chancellor to the young Prince Edward in the ceremony of making him a knight. He was present at the battle of Towton in March, and accompanied Queen Margaret and Prince Edward in their subsequent wanderings after that defeat.

As for many of his contemporaries, the Yorkist victory meant an accusation of treason for John Morton; he was attainted and lost everything. Queen Margaret with her son Edward, Prince of Wales, spent some time in Scotland and then fled to France in April 1462 into the care of her father, Count René of Anjou. John Morton was among those involved in an unsuccessful plot between Margaret and the King of France to dispatch a force to the north and join King Henry in Scotland. In July 1465, Henry VI was captured again and this time was imprisoned in the Tower where he remained for the next five years. Meanwhile Margaret was back in Anjou with the young Prince Edward and some 200 supporters of whom John Morton was one.

In the later 1460s a rift developed between King Edward and his powerful ally and cousin Richard, Earl of Warwick. This gave hope to the exiled Lancastrians who saw an alliance with Warwick as the only chance of restoring Henry VI or his son to the throne. Morton was involved in the negotiations with Warwick and the French King, Louis XI. He left Angers on 4 August 1470, landed at Dartmouth with Warwick on 13 September and was sent on in advance with Sir John Fortescue to London. When the Queen and Prince Edward landed at Weymouth in the following spring, Morton met them and escorted them to his old school at Cerne and thence to Beaulieu. At first the move was successful and Henry VI was restored to the throne but by late May in the following year Edward IV had regained control. Henry VI died in the Tower soon after his son Edward, Prince of Wales, was killed at the battle of Tewkesbury on 4 May 1471 and this was effectively the end of the Lancastrian dynasty.

From this time King Edward IV was securely in control of the kingdom. Anxious to stabilise the government, he was willing to accept the service of those who had opposed him, especially able men like Morton with a knowledge of the law who would help to restore order. Morton lost no time in making his submission to the King; he was pardoned as from 17 June 1471 and the attainder was withdrawn. In March 1473 he became Master of the Rolls, a position which he vacated in 1479 in favour of his nephew Robert Morton. He had also begun to accumulate ecclesiastical preferments. Archbishop Bourchier was still his friend and collated him in 1472 to the rectory of St. Dunstan's-in-the- East and in the same year he became a Prebendary of St Paul's. He became Archdeacon of Chester in 1474, of Winchester and Huntingdon in 1475, of Berkshire in 1476, of Norfolk in 1477 and Leicester in 1478. Perhaps these and other appointments were a way of providing an income for a man whom the king found increasingly useful; it is unlikely that Morton could have taken an active interest in all of them. In 1479 he vacated most of his other positions on being consecrated Bishop of Ely.

It is clear that King Edward IV trusted John Morton. In 1474 he was sent on an embassy to the Emperor Frederick III and the King of Hungary in an attempt to secure their support for an alliance against Louis XI of France. In the following year he was one of the counsellors who arranged the Treaty of Pecquigny signed between England and France; at the same time he was involved in negotiations for a ransom paid by the King of France which enabled Queen Margaret to leave England. On the death of Edward IV in 1483 Morton assisted at his funeral.

Subsequent events soon brought him into trouble again. Morton was associated with those who had tried to have the young King Edward V crowned as soon as possible. Thus Richard III saw him as a threat and had him arrested; he was entrusted to the care of the Duke of Buckingham who, before long, had himself turned against Richard and led a revolt which Morton supported. When this failed, Morton fled across the Channel to join Henry Tudor, Earl of Richmond, who claimed the throne as a descendant of John of Gaunt through his mother, Margaret Beaufort. When rumours became rife that the young Edward V was dead, many of his party gave their support to Henry. John Morton was instrumental in the negotiations to make Henry king and marry him to Elizabeth, daughter of Edward IV, so uniting the houses of Lancaster and York. By the end of August 1485, Richard III had been killed at the battle of Bosworth Field and Henry proclaimed King as Henry VII.

Morton was summoned back to England in November 1485 and was soon established as one of Henry VII's leading councillors. On 6 October 1486 he succeeded Thomas

Bourchier as Archbishop of Canterbury and in the following spring became Lord Chancellor. As Archbishop, he tried to introduce reforms among monastic and secular clergy. He had already been known for building works when at Ely, and now he engaged in construction and restoration at Canterbury, in the Cathedral and in the city, at Lambeth, Knole, Oxford and elsewhere. In 1493, at the King's request, the Pope made Morton a Cardinal. In 1495 the University of Oxford made him Chancellor although he warned that he could not carry out the duties. Morton died at Knole in Kent on 15 September 1500 and was buried in Canterbury Cathedral.

During John Morton's period of three years as Archdeacon of Winchester he may not have been seen often in the diocese, perhaps not at all. It should however be noted that a detailed account appears in his Archbishop's Register of the removal of St. Swithun's shrine to its new position in the retrochoir. This had taken place in 1476 while Morton was Archdeacon; the description reads like that of an eye witness so it may be that he was present on that occasion.

John Morton has been variously described as 'shrewd humorous Morton', 'a wily cleric', 'silver tongued Morton' and in other ways, favourable and unfavourable, but his ability has never been denied. Perhaps the verdict should be left to Sir Thomas More who had served in Morton's household when a boy and whose account of Morton in *Utopia* translates thus – 'his conversation was easy but serious and grave. He spoke both gracefully and weightily. He was eminently skilled in the law, had a vast understanding and a prodigious memory; and those excellent talents with which nature had furnished him were improved by study and experience'.

Robert Morton

Archdeacon 1478 ~ 1486

*c.*1435 born
by 1458 M.A.
by 1480 Lic.C.L.
1462 Canon of York
1469 Rector of Houghton, Huntingdonshire
1471 Canon of Lincoln
1473 Rector of St. Pancras, Axmouth, Devon
1475 Rector of South Molton, Devon
1478 Canon of St. Paul's (other appointments about this time)
1478 Archdeacon of Winchester
1479 Master of the Rolls
1481 Canon of St. George's Chapel, Windsor
1482 Archdeacon of Gloucester
1486 Bishop of Worcester
1497 died

A nephew of Cardinal John Morton, Robert Morton benefited front his uncle's prominence in public affairs. Little is recorded of his early years except that he was the son of William Morton and that he had graduated as M.A. at the University of Oxford by the year 1458, and later held the qualifications of Lic.C.L. and LL.D.

From 1462 to 1467 Robert Morton was a Canon of York and he held a canonry at Lincoln from 1471-73. He was Rector of Houghton, Huntingdonshire in 1469, Rector of the Free Chapel of St. Pancras, Axmouth in 1473 and of South Molton, Devon in 1475. In 1477 he obtained a papal dispensation to hold three 'incompatible benefices'.

It seems that Robert Morton was building a reputation as a lawyer during these years for on 30 May 1477 his uncle secured for him the reversion of the office of Master of the Rolls in the event of his own death or resignation. Robert was appointed to the position by a new patent of 9 January 1479. His tenure of the office was interrupted during the reign of Richard III when his uncle was in disgrace, but when John Morton was once again established in royal favour under Henry VII, Robert was reinstated. He was named as one of the commissioners to perform the office of steward at Henry's coronation. Other tasks must have followed for he soon claimed that he needed help as Master of the Rolls because of his

Sources

- *Dictionary of National Biography*
- A.B.Emden, *Biographical Register of the University of Oxford to AD 1500*
- C.Bailey, *Transcripts from the Municipal Archives of Winchester (1856)*

activity in the King's service. A coadjutor, William Eliot, was appointed in November 1485.

During the years 1478 -1482 a number of ecclesiastical preferments had been heaped on Robert Morton. He became Archdeacon of Winchester, Canon of St. Paul's and of Salisbury in 1478, Rector of Southmere, Norfolk and Canon of Beverley in 1479, Rector of Hollingbourne, Kent, in 1480, Prebendary of Knaresborough and Canon of St. George's Chapel, Windsor in 1481, Archdeacon of Gloucester and Prebendary of Wherwell in 1482. These positions were vacated when in 1486 he was appointed to the Bishopric of Worcester; he was consecrated at Canterbury on 28 January 1487 and was enthroned by proxy on 22 July.

On at least one occasion Robert Morton is recorded as having been in Winchester. This was in 1486 when Prince Arthur, the eldest son of Henry VII and Elizabeth of York, was born at Winchester Castle on 22 September and baptised in the Cathedral a few days later. The event was celebrated with great splendour; the building was elaborately decorated and a special font of silver gilt erected upon a 'Stage of 7 Steppes'. The ceremony was conducted, during a vacancy in the see of Winchester, by the Bishop of Worcester (whom Robert Morton was to succeed a few months later) and Peter Courtenay, then Bishop of Exeter but soon to be translated to Winchester. There was a large attendance of nobility, courtiers, royal officials and others, one of whom was 'Mayster Robert Morton, the Maister of the Rowles'. His name occurs amongst the 'many noble Doctors in rich Copes and grey Amys'.

Robert Morton died in May 1497. In his will he directed that he should be buried in the cemetery of the place where he should die and he was interred in the nave of St. Paul's Cathedral. In view of the number of his appointments at the time when he was Archdeacon of Winchester, it is unlikely that Robert Morton was able to make any notable contribution here. Perhaps a deputy was appointed to act for him but arrangements of this kind have not been recorded. Suffice it to say that here was another prominent figure in public affairs who was briefly connected with Winchester.

William Smith or Smyth

Archdeacon 1487 ~ 1492

*c.*1460 Born
1487 Archdeacon of Winchester from February 1487 until 1492
1514 Died

Smith was believed to be the son of a country squire at Prescot, Lancs., and to have been educated in the household of Margaret Beaufort[(1)], Countess of Richmond and Derby, the mother of King Henry V11. He was probably educated at Lincoln College, Oxford, becoming B.Cn.L. The D.N.B. records that he had some responsibility (as tutor?) for the care of the two daughters of King Edward IV.

He seems to have made the most of his royal connections, and perhaps his talents were recognised early on.

In 1485, he was made Keeper of the hanaper of the chancery – a 'very lucrative office' – he resigned from this 1493. Shortly afterwards, still in his mid-twenties, after Henry's victory at Bosworth, and coronation, Smith became a member of the King's Council. He also received the living of Combe Martin, North Devon, and shortly afterwards, was appointed Archdeacon of Winchester (1487-1492), these dates coinciding exactly with those of Bishop Peter Courtenay. Whether Smith ever lived at Winchester seems unlikely, in view of his other commitments. The D.N.B. even fails to mention his holding of the Winchester Archdeaconry.

His upward career continued, as he became Dean of the Royal Chapel of St. Stephen, Westminster, and two years later, was appointed Bishop of Coventry and Lichfield (1493). Very shortly, Smith went to Lincoln as Bishop (1495-1514). The D.N.B., however, notes that he was

Sources

- *Dictionary of National Biography*
- Emden, *Biographical Register, University of Oxford, up to 1500*

[1] Emden disputes this latter

usually absent from that diocese, having become a member of the Council of Wales in 1491, and becoming Lord President of that Council in 1501. He officiated at Prince Arthur's funeral at Worcester Cathedral in 1502.

Smith became Chancellor of Oxford University for a few years (1500-03), and went on to found Brasenose College (rebuilt on the site of Brasenose Hall) in 1509. He sponsored a fellowship at Oriel College, and is noted as having differences with Bishop Richard Fox (Winchester) over the importance of the revival of Greek studies, which Fox actively supported.

In 1509, Smith was an executor of the King's will, having earlier been, with Richard Fox, a co-trustee of Lady Margaret Beaufort's will. Smith is recorded as having '10 palaces', and to have been noted for nepotism. In 1505, he was fined 'for erecting mills and weirs on the Trent', and also for 'export misdemeanours'. His career seems a typical example of ecclesiastical posts being used as royal rewards for loyal servants of the crown. He died in 1514 at Buckden, Huntingdonshire, and is buried at Lincoln Cathedral.

Robert Frost

Archdeacon c.1492 ~ 1502

1480 King's Hall, Cambridge
1482 Rector, Thornhill, Yorkshire
1486 Chancellor to Prince Arthur
1491 Prebendary, York Minster
1492 Archdeacon of Winchester
1497 Archdeacon of Stow
1500 Prebendary of Lichfield
1511 Vicar, Sandal Magna, Yorkshire

Frost was probably the second son of Thomas Frost of Aketon, Pontefract, Yorkshire. He was for a time Chancellor to Prince Arthur, the King's eldest son, who was born in Winchester in 1486, and died in 1502.

The records indicate that Frost was educated at both Oxford and Cambridge. He studied as a scholar at King's Hall, Cambridge from 1480, gaining a B.Cn.L. He became a fellow in 1481.

He became a D.Cn.L in 1506/7.

He held a series of benefices, mainly in the midlands and the north. He was rector of Thornhill, Yorkshire 1482-98 and became rector of Tankersley, Yorkshire in 1486. He was a prebendary at York Minster 1491-1507, and also Archdeacon of Stow, Lincs. 1497-1506. These were the years when he was Archdeacon of Winchester, probably 1492-1502. Nothing is recorded of his Winchester activities, or whether he even lived here, which on balance seems improbable.

Frost is listed as a prebendary at Lichfield 1500-1507, becoming vicar of Sandal Magna, Yorkshire 1511-34. He was buried at Wakefield Church.

Sources

- Venn, *Cambridge Biographical Register*, Vol 1, pre 1500.
- Emden, *Cambridge Biographical Register to 1500*, (1963 edn).

John Frost D.D.

Archdeacon 1502 ~ 1511

1502 Archdeacon of Winchester
1511 Resigned as Archdeacon of Winchester

Little is known of this Archdeacon's life; details of his birth, education and benefices before installation as Archdeacon at Winchester, have not been traced. The first surviving record appears to have been made in the Register of Richard Fox, Bishop of Winchester, who was translated from Durham to Winchester in October 1501. A few months later, Frost was to benefit from his patronage when he was collated as the next Archdeacon. At his installation on 29 April 1502, his qualification as a Professor of Sacred Theology, or Doctor of Divinity, was duly noted.

Bishop Fox was a clever and gifted man and highly respected by King Henry VII. When the King died in 1509, Richard Fox was appointed one of the executors and was largely responsible for all the arrangements. At the funeral service, the executors were allowed extra servants and a larger entourage and it is easy to speculate on whether John Frost was of their number, but no evidence has been found. If he met others in his patron's circle of acquaintances, amongst them would have been the rising Thomas Wolsey, recently introduced to the court by Richard Fox.

Two years later, on 8 October 1511, Frost resigned as Archdeacon and when his successor was installed, a footnote in the register recorded that the annual income from Frost's benefices had totalled £66.13s.4d, a considerable sum. It is not known where, or in which diocese these interests lay and with this entry, he disappears from the records.

Sources

- HRO 19M54/6, Alchin's Index, vol IV, pp 126-131
- HRO 21M65/A1/17, vol 1, f. 4b, Register of Richard Fox
- *Cal.S.P. For. & Dom. Henry VIII*, vol 1 part 1, 1509, (reprint 1920)
- J A Lipkin, *Institutions in the Diocese of Winchester 1487-1528*, (1979)

SG

Hugh As(s)h(e)ton

Archdeacon 1511 ~ 1519

- ✣ Born Lancashire
- ✣ Comptroller of the household of Lady Margaret Countess of Richmond and Derby

1507 13 Oct: Oxford and then Cambridge Universities

1509 28 May: Prebendary at St Stephens Westminster

1509 Temporal Chancellor of the County Palatine of Durham

pre 1511 Incumbent at Grasmere, Ambleside and Barnake, Lincoln and Prebendary at Lichfield Cathedral

1511 Archdeacon of Winchester

1515 Prebendary of Strensall at York

1515 Archdeacon of Cornwall

1516 Collated Archdeacon of York (admitted 5 Sep 1516)

1522 Rector of Burton Latimer, Northamptonshire

1522 Died, buried at St John's College, Cambridge

Sources

- ✣ *Al Oxford 1500-1714*
- ✣ *Ath Cantab*, pp 26, 526
- ✣ *D.N.B.*
- ✣ Thomas Baker, *History of the College of St John the Evangelist, Cambridge*, 2 vols (1864), ed J E B Mayor
- ✣ Letter from Peter Young, Archivist at York Minster with copy of page from Torre Ms (YMA.L.1.7), held by SG.

✧ Note that the records of the counties palatine, held in the Public Record Office, have not been investigated.

Recognised mainly for his appointment as Archdeacon of York, Hugh Ashton was born in Lancashire, at a date unknown, the son of a landed family. He went up to study at Oxford in October 1507, but shortly afterwards transferred to Cambridge, to study canon law.

At a young age, he had been fortunate to meet Lady Margaret Beaufort, great-granddaughter of John of Gaunt and mother of King Henry VII; it is probable that he had been born close to her Lancashire estates. She was a devout and pious lady and spent much of her fortune in charitable ways and founded professorships of divinity at both Oxford and Cambridge. She appointed Hugh Ashton comptroller of her household and, as his patroness, appears to have had a considerable influence on his life.

His early benefices included Grasmere and Ambleside in Cumbria and also Barnake in the Diocese of Lincoln, whilst at Lichfield he was installed as a canon. In 1509, he was appointed Temporal Chancellor of the Palatine of Durham, charged with working on behalf of the powerful Prince Bishop. In the same year, he was presented by the new King Henry VIII to a canonry in St Stephen's Westminster.

It was at this time that Lady Margaret died and Hugh Ashton was appointed one of several executors. In this role, he helped to implement her wish that much of her wealth be used to build and endow St John's College, Cambridge. Foremost amongst her executors were Richard Fox Bishop of Winchester and her chaplain John Fisher, the ill-fated Bishop of Rochester and together with Ashton, they were responsible for founding the college in her name. In order to help fund the new college, two nunneries were suppressed on the grounds of misconduct and it has been said that the foundation owed more to Bishop Fisher, assisted by Hugh Ashton and one other cleric, than to Lady Margaret.

The Oxford and Cambridge colleges owed much to the influence of their founders, who were some of the most powerful bishops in the land. Eventually, John Fisher would remodel St John's on the system established by Bishop Fox at Corpus Christi Oxford. Ashton's involvement is sometimes questioned, but he certainly founded four fellowships and scholarships at St John's for the benefit of inhabitants of Lancashire, Chester, Durham and York and spent much of his life, working on behalf of the college.

After Lady Margaret's death, Hugh Ashton enjoyed rapid advancement in the Church and in 1511 was installed Archdeacon of Winchester. Bishop Richard Fox, who was a close associate of both the late King Henry VII and his son Henry VIII, was already installed at Winchester where he was building his chantry chapel and it seems logical to assume that he had been instrumental in Ashton's appointment. Thus it was that the new Archdeacon was meeting the highest churchmen in the country. However, if indeed he ever visited Winchester, nothing is known of Ashton's activities whilst in The Close or Cathedral.

He continued to advance his career and in 1515, as Richard Fox's power began to decline, Ashton was installed a prebendary at York. He was introduced there by Wolsey, who was now rapidly replacing Fox in the King's councils. In the same year, Ashton was installed Archdeacon of Cornwall, but resigned soon after and was collated and admitted as the Archdeacon of York; by 1516 his ecclesiastical interests stretched nation-wide. It is not surprising that three years later he resigned as Archdeacon of Winchester and concentrated his interests in Cambridge and the north.

At York, he gave a stained glass window to the Hospital of St Leonard's and endowed his own private chapel at St John's. His was the fourth and last chapel to be built and was hung round with red and green hangings, decorated with a form of white and green lace. It was surmounted by his rebus, a highly fashionable feature at the time and represented an ash tree issuing from a tun, or large cask. It was later suggested that he should be forgiven for this 'humour of the age'. There was general approval of the architecture, although some thought it had a 'greatly too big' upper structure, but the figures with which it was adorned, were less popular. There was probably a window with painted glass, but at the Reformation the altar was pulled down and the chapel converted for use as a chamber. Early in the next century, it was restored at considerable expense and a further window inserted, probably towards the east end, so that the furnishings inside could be placed in a better light. When the Puritans arrived at the college, it was again desecrated, the furniture was removed and the walls painted white, before the chapel was again used as an apartment.

Whilst in residence at Cambridge, where he probably lived with a colleague at Peterhouse, Ashton took a close interest in all the business affairs of St John's, but his other duties forced him away for much of the time, which was a cause of some concern. It was in order to make up for these absences that he had founded the four fellowships, the holders of which also acted as his chaplains.

Hugh Ashton was to be introduced to one more benefice and in July 1522 was presented to the Rectory of Burton Latimer, Northamptonshire, but died shortly afterwards. Authorities differ on his exact date of death and interment. His will was made on 7 December 1522 and proved the following March. He left instructions to be buried before the altar [in his own chapel] at St John's Chapel and an obit was to be kept for him there and at York. However, it has been suggested that instead of Cambridge, he was buried at the Minster where he had served as archdeacon. An inscription on his 'tomb' there, was copied in Queen Mary's reign by the then master of St John's, who wrote that Ashton died on 23 November 1522, which seems improbable, given the date of his will. In addition, there is no known record of a tomb or memorial for Hugh in York Minster, even before the repaving of the church was undertaken in the eighteenth century.

It seems more probable that he was buried on 4 January 1522/3, in his chapel at St John's College, 'in the wall of [his] tomb with his similitude in two images, one lively and the other deadly.' It also had a further long Latin inscription, similar to the one copied at York Minster. He left instructions for his four chaplains together with his four scholars, to sing a funeral hymn there on the day of his interment and to observe a dirge for him, including his friends and Lady Margaret, annually on 4 January. The master or his deputy was to receive 2s, each fellow 1s and each scholar 6d, provided they remained throughout the service.

Besides founding the fellowships and scholarships, he also directed that 88s per annum should be expended on York Minster and Westminster Abbey. A eulogy and verses were penned in his honour and his portrait was eventually bequeathed to the Master of St John's by Thomas Baker, the author of the history of the college and a future holder of one of the fellowships. In his will, Baker especially requested to be buried close to Hugh Ashton, whom he had greatly admired.

St. Mary's Church, Southampton ~ *c.*1850

John Fox(e)

Archdeacon 1520 ~ 1527

1511 Canon of Wells & Prebendary of Henstridge, Somerset
1520 Archdeacon of Winchester
1530 Died

Information about Fox is sparse. His parentage, and date and place of birth, are unknown and, to date, no family link is known with either Bishop Richard Fox of Winchester (1501-1528) or with John Foxe (1516-1587) author of *Actes and Monuments (the Book of Martyrs).*

The records suggest that Fox's higher education came some time after he began his clerical career. His first listed post is in 1511 as a Canon of Wells Cathedral and Prebendary of Henstridge in Somerset. At some point, Fox simultaneously became Archdeacon of Surrey (a part of the Winchester Diocese) until 1519. He then became Rector of Wroughton, Wiltshire, and also a Canon of Salisbury, and Prebendary of Ruscombe (near Sonning, Berkshire), all three posts being held until his death in 1530.

His Oxford college appears to have been Corpus Christi, newly founded in 1516 by Bishop Richard Fox, and which had pioneered the first Oxford professorship in ancient Greek. Fox was admitted to both a B.C.L. and a B.Cn.L. in February 1523.

He was appointed Archdeacon of Winchester on 27 March 1520, presented by Bishop Richard Fox. He accumulated several Hampshire livings, including Cheriton, Overton and Wonston. He is also recorded as Sacrist of Bosham, near Chichester, for a time. Where he lived during this period has not come to light. He does appear to have maintained a formal link with Corpus Christi right up to the time of his death.

[1] Possibly 'Blachford' = Blackford. There are two such livings or curacies in Somerset, Diocese of Bath & Wells (Nat. Gazeteer, 1868)

Source

- Biographical Register – University of Oxford, 1501-1540, Emden 1974.

Finally, the record states that Fox exchanged the Winchester Archdeaconry in 1527 for a Canonry at Lincoln and the Prebend of Cropredy (Oxon), his successor being Richard Pates. He is also recorded as being Rector of a 'free chapel' of Blachford[1] in Somerset until his death.

Fox is recorded as being formally excused attendance at funerals and assemblies in 1528, so possibly was disabled, or in poor health by then: it rather appears he died in his 40s. At his death in August 1530 he left eight books to Corpus Christi.

Richard Pates

Archdeacon 1527 ~ 1529

1504 Born
1527 Archdeacon of Winchester
1528 Archdeacon of Lincoln & Canon of St. Paul's, London
1533 Ambassador to Court of Emporer Charles V
1541 Consecrated Bishop of Worcester
1560 Imprisoned in Tower of London
1565 Died

Source

∻ *Biographical Register, University of Oxford, 1501-1540*, Emden, 1974

Richard Pates was the son of John Pates, and through his mother, Elinor, was a nephew of John Longland (Bishop of Lincoln 1521–1547 and Henry VIII's confessor). Pates, like his Winchester predecessor, John Fox, studied at the newly-founded Oxford college, Corpus Christi, from 1522–1525. The record states, intriguingly, that at some stage during this period Pates was 'industriously engaged in study at (?) Bruges, in company with Anthony Barker'. The date of his ordination is unrecorded.

From 1523 to 1527, Pates held various posts as Rector: at Crowcombe, Somerset, at Wheathampstead, and at Great Haseley, Oxon, becoming Prebendary of Cropredy, Oxon in 1525.

In March 1527, Pates exchanged the parish of Cropredy for the Archdeaconry of Winchester, which John Fox had held. His time at Winchester was, however, short. In 1528 Pates became Archdeacon of Lincoln, and a Canon of St Paul's in London, together with various other canonries: he formally vacated the Winchester post in 1529.

His subsequent career is of interest, illustrating the effect of the English Reformation on a man of ability, high connections and ambition. In November 1533 (after Thomas Cranmer had succeeded William Warham as Archbishop of Canterbury, and King Henry had married Anne Boleyn), Pates was appointed by the King as ambassador to the court of Emperor Charles V (the nephew of Queen Catherine of Aragon).

The record states that Pates was recalled to England in 1537, when the break with Rome was complete. However, in April 1540 he was re-appointed to the Imperial Court, despite Henry VIII's alleged comment that he was 'trop inepte' as an ambassador.

The record continues – 'Pates being out of sympathy with Henry's religious policy, he terminated his embassy by taking flight with his chaplain's secretary, a master Seth Holland, by way of the Rhine valley into Italy'. The following year, 1541, Pates was consecrated Bishop of Worcester by Papal provision on 8th July.

At this point, Cranmer and King Henry took action. Pates, in January 1542, was deprived of all his posts and, together with Cardinal Pole, was attainted of high treason for not taking the Oath of Supremacy, and other grave misdemeanours. Pates remained in exile and attended several sessions of the Council of Trent (1545-63), being recorded as a close associate of Cardinal Pole.

Some time after Queen Mary's accession in 1553, when Papal links were restored and the traditional religion was revived, Pates returned to England. His temporalities were restored to him on 5th March 1555. He was confirmed as Bishop of Worcester. After the death of Archbishop Cranmer, burnt at the stake at Oxford in 1556, Cardinal Pole became Archbishop of Canterbury.

Two years later, Queen Mary died, and Pole died also, within a few hours of her death. Pates declined to take the Elizabethan Oath of Supremacy in 1560, and was imprisoned in the Tower of London for probably two years. He was then released into the custody of Canon John Jewel of Salisbury, for three years, and was subsequently set free in 1565 'subject to producing sufficient sureties' and 'returned to Louvain'.

On his death in October that year he left a bequest of 20 marks annually, for scholarships for four scholars at 'Glocester College', Oxford (now Worcester College) for Worcestershire men, or if they lacked, for Oxford men.

William Boleyn

Archdeacon 1530 ~ 1551

1516 Rector of St. Peter's, Cheapside, London
1529 Canon of St. Paul's, London
1530 Archdeacon of Winchester
1534 Rector of Holt, Norfolk
1551 Died in Norfolk

William Boleyn was the fourth son of Sir William Boleyn, and was an uncle to Anne Boleyn (whom King Henry VIII married in 1533 and who was one of Queen Catherine's ladies-in-waiting). William's brother, Thomas, Anne's father, was Lord Privy Seal from January 1530-1536.

William's appointment to the Winchester Archdeaconry was at the height of the political debate on the King's 'great matter' – *his determination to get his marriage with Queen Catherine annulled, so that he could marry Anne and, hopefully, produce a legitimate male heir.*

Wolsey died in 1530, having been deprived of the bishopric of Winchester the previous year. Stephen Gardiner, who was to succeed Wolsey at Winchester in 1531 was still a supporter of the King's cause in 1530, as was Reginald Pole.

Boleyn appears to have studied at both Oxford and Cambridge between 1503 and 1507, receiving degrees in civil law in both places. After a spell as Rector of Rowner, Hampshire, and subsequently, from 1510, as Vicar of Portsmouth, he is recorded as a university preacher at Cambridge in 1511 and, probably, living at Gonville Hall, 1512-1515.

In 1516, he went as Rector to St Peter's, Cheapside, London, until the later 1520s. (There are indications that this post was in Wolsey's gift.) In 1529 he became a canon

Sources
- Venn = Cambridge Register. Pt.1
- Emden = (1963) Biographical Register of Cambridge

of St Paul's Cathedral and also Rector of Winwick, Lancashire, holding the latter post until his death in 1551: the living of Chiddingstone, Kent, close to Hever Castle, Sir Thomas Boleyn's home, also came his way, in 1528, for 6 years.

Boleyn subsequently, in 1530, became Archdeacon of Winchester, holding this post until his death in 1551. As the bishopric was vacant in 1530 it would be interesting to know who recommended him for appointment, and whether he was active in a temporary role, representing the Bishop during the interregnum. Undoubtedly the Boleyn star was in the ascendant for his first few years as archdeacon, until Anne's disgrace and execution in 1536.

At the dissolution of the monasteries, 1536-39, William would have known of the closure of St Swithun's monastery, of which the Cathedral was an integral part. Careful negotiation enabled the last prior, William Kingsmill – from a well-known Hampshire family – to become the first Dean of the Cathedral in 1541. Bishop Gardiner, by this time, was one of the leading conservative bishops, but is not known to have resisted the Winchester dissolution: Thomas Cromwell's immense powers were virtually irresistible, until, when in 1540, he too fell from grace.

William Boleyn would also have seen the reformation changes brought in on the accession of the young king, Edward VI, from 1547.

Boleyn appears to have retired to Norfolk towards the end of his life. Without further detailed research it is impossible to know where he lived during his time as Archdeacon of Winchester. He became Rector of Holt, Norfolk in 1534, and of Postwick, Norfolk, in 1543, until his death and burial at Stiffkey, Norfolk, in October 1551.

John Philpot

Archdeacon 1550 ~ 1554

1516 Born at Compton, Hampshire, the third son of Sir Peter Philpot.
1534 Elected a Fellow of New College, Oxford
1541 Lived in Italy
1547 Returned to England and took Holy Orders
1550 Archdeacon of Winchester
1554 Deprived
1555 Burnt at the Stake as a Heretic

John Philpot came from a distinguished and ultra-Catholic family, his father, a knight of the Bath, was twice Sheriff of the County. John went to Winchester College in 1526 as a scholar, aged ten, and even as a young boy was fierce in debate and ready for a row with anyone. Also at the College at the time was John White, later to be Headmaster and Warden of the College and later still Bishop of Winchester and with whom Philpot had a long standing dispute.

Philpot is remembered at the College for making a wager of twenty pence with his contemporary and friend, John Harpesfield, that he would make two hundred verses in one night and not make more than three mistakes; he won the wager! He was especially gifted in his knowledge of languages, Latin, Greek and in particular Hebrew. He went up to New College, Oxford, to read civil law and was made a Fellow in 1534 and remained so until 1541, when his fellowship became void on his move to Italy. Although a student of the law, Philpot's ease with the languages of theology had inevitably brought him into contact with early Christian writings, and this, given his inquisitive, incisive mind, had led him to a self-questioning of some of the tenets of Roman Catholic doctrine.

It was in 1534 that papal supremacy was annulled by Parliament and the supremacy of the King, Henry VIII, recognised. In the same year a compete edition of

Sources

- Frederick Bussby, *Winchester Cathedral 1079 – 1975* (Ringwood: Paul Cave, 1979).
- Owen Chadwick, *The Reformation* (London: Penguin, 1990).
- *Winchester College: Sixth Centenary Essays*, ed. Roger Custance (Oxford: University Press, 1982).
- A. G. Dickens, *The English Reformation*, (London: B T Batsford Ltd, 1989).
- R. W. Dixon, *History of the Church Of England* (London: George Routledge, 1891).
- *The Examinations and Writings of John Philpot*, ed. Rev Robert Eden for the Parker Society (Cambridge: University Press, 1862).
- J. Foxe, *Acts and Monuments* (1597).
- J. D'E Firth, Winchester College, (Winchester: P. G. Wells, 1936).
- T.F. Kirby, *Annals of Winchester College* (Winchester: P.G. Wells, 1892).
- *The Lisle Letters*, ed. Muriel St. Claire Bryne (Chicago and London: Chicago University Press, 1981).
- A. L. Leach, *History of Winchester College* (London, 1891).

Luther's translation of the bible was published. Philpot, although now an anti-Papist, would have been equally unhappy with the King's assumption of authority. Matters came to a head in 1539 when parliament enacted the six articles, which coupled with Philpot's increasingly 'enlightened' interpretations of the ancient gospel writings led him to leave England for Italy, thus avoiding the religious turmoil at home. Also his increasing distrust of the Roman Catholic religion had probably brought him into open dispute with his family. Never a man to avoid controversy it is likely that he wanted both to observe the Papacy at first hand and give himself an opportunity to develop his own beliefs. It not being in his nature to keep his own counsel, he soon found himself in serious trouble, whilst on his travels he so irritated a Franciscan Friar, that he threatened to denounce Philpot as a heretic.

He returned to Winchester, probably in 1547, when persecution over the Six Articles had ceased and free exercise of conscience was allowed. About this time he took Holy Orders and began to make a nuisance of himself with his zealous preaching of the 'pure truth' in various parts of the County in a manner obnoxious to the Bishop, Stephen Gardiner. Famously he delivered a lecture in the cathedral upon St. Paul's Epistle to the Romans in which he asserted that the epistle is 'justification for the meritorious obedience of Christ, exclusive of any work of man', ie. directly contradictory of the Romish notion of human merit.

An indication of both Philpot's irritability and his stubbornness is given in a letter written by Stephen Gardiner to Somerset, the Lord Protector, in March 1548. Gardiner writes:

> *'Amonge my gentle wordes I told in dede Philpot that I would ex communicate hym, not for that he wold wishe, but bicause withowt any occation givin of me, being called for other purpose by suche as had charge of the musters, he untrewlie reported my sermond made a fortnight before, in suche matter as I thinke to be my trade of teaching.'*

Gardiner concludes;

> *'He will nedes call himself heretique and therefore I blamed hym gentely. For mye self I call hym onelie unlerned and it angreth hym more then any other name I call hym.'*

In 1550, with Edward VI on the throne and Gardiner deprived of his Bishopric, Philpot became Archdeacon of Winchester. Philpot had held an advowson from Gardiner but the latter, in view of their differences, had held back from appointing him to the Archdeaconry. Bishop John Ponet (Poynet), unlike Gardiner, had at first found in Philpot, 'all he desired'. The two soon fell to squabbling over Philpot's disputes with the registrar, Cook, a man who hated 'pure religion'. The main dispute between them concerned a yearly pension that Cook claimed was his due. Whether Cook had been badly treated is not clear, but Philpot did not approach the problem with either tact or sympathy and their dispute aroused so much ill feeling in the diocese that, 'even so good a man as Ponet could find in his heart to vex his brother so conspicuous both for learning and for life'. So Philpot found himself seriously at odds with his former mentor Ponet.

Matters came to a head when Cook, seeking revenge, waylaid Philpot between Winchester and Philpot's sisters home, three miles away, and set his men upon him and 'sore beat him'. Philpot sought to take remedy in the Spiritual Court but found not only Cook, as Registrar, against him, but Ponet as well. The Bishop no doubt had concluded that Philpot had got all he deserved. That Philpot was difficult and quarrelsome is without doubt true, but this invariably stemmed from a sense of conviction and his inability to compromise his beliefs. This had led him as Archdeacon into an acrimonious dispute with his old school, Winchester College, and in particular with the Warden, John White, the last of the Catholic Wardens. Their differences of view over ritual led to Philpot taking proceedings in the Arches Court and to the excommunication of John White. The Bursars of the College paid 6s 8d for a copy of the process entering the item in a way that implies that as a Wykehamist he should not have put his old College into the Spiritual Court. This is the first usage of the term Wykehamist for an old boy of the College. Later during his examination as a heretic by Bishop Bonner he sought to belittle the evidence given by White, by then Bishop of Lincoln: 'White was known to be my enemy, for that I being Archdeacon did so excommunicate him for preaching naughty doctrine'. During Edward's reign Philpot was able, in spite of the controversy he inevitably engendered, to fulfil his duties as Archdeacon and of course continue his zealous preaching of the 'pure truth', jealously observed by Gardiner, the deprived Bishop of Winchester, who had, after his release from the Fleet prison, been allowed to retire to Winchester.

When Mary came to the throne in 1553 all this changed, and Philpot predictably soon attracted attention. A fervent Catholic, Mary, moved swiftly to restore the Catholic faith and the authority of the See of Rome. The five deprived Bishops, including Gardiner, were restored, followed shortly by the appointment of Gardiner as Lord Chancellor. Mary commanded the Convocation to meet at St. Paul's on 6 October 1553. The first two questions considered, by the Convocation, were on the 42 Articles and the Book of Common Prayer. It was stated that the Catechism was 'pestiferous and full of heresies' and had been 'foisted upon the last synod fraudently'. Philpot refused to sign the document which branded the Catechism. On the 20th of October, all the clergy were required to sign a declaration asserting the real presence, Transubstantiation. All did so bar six led by John Philpot who argued that the question should be debated before settling it and that the leaders of those opposed to it should be released from prison to do so. In spite of his protestations, not surprisingly, the Convocation declared the doctrine of Transubstantiation to be true. After being told he was mad and to hold his tongue, Philpot was excommunicated as 'contumacious', illegally deprived of his Archdeaconry and sent to the King's Bench prison.

After over a year in prison without trial, Philpot was examined by sixteen commissioners. He soon lost what sympathy there was for him. White described him as a 'frantic fellow and a man that will have the last word'. Philpot still claiming to be legally Archdeacon, refused to answer their questions as they were not his 'ordinary'. He was transferred to the coal cellar of Bishop Bonner's residence which was conveniently furnished with stocks. Much of the examination centred around the authority of the church of Rome and in particular in respect of Transubstantiation. Philpot did not move from his conviction that the exact form and substance of Christ's words must be used for – 'by the law it is forbidden to add or take away from God's word'. Philpot was unrepentant and made no concession to his accusers who it seems were seeking a means of accommodation for him. He made it clear that he was ready to yield his life in Christ's cause – 'I look for none other than death at your hands and I am as ready to yield my life in Christ's cause as you be to require it'. A modern reading of the examinations of Philpot might seem to some to illustrate religion at its most self righteous and obstinate. On the other hand one cannot fail to be impressed by Philpot's self possession and his unwavering faith.

Without some compromise on Philpot's part and some evidence of humility it was inevitable that Philpot should be found guilty. Frustrated beyond measure the commission pronounced their condemnation, Philpot responded: 'I thank God that I am a heretic out of your cursed church, I am no heretic before God. But God Bless you and give you once grace to repent your wicked doings: and let all men beware of your bloody church'. He was burned at the stake, suffering with heroism, on 18 December 1555. He was unrepentant to the last as Foxe tells us.

We would probably say of Philpot today that he did not suffer fools gladly. He clearly was a man of deep intellectual strength, one of those rare human beings whose beliefs are founded entirely on the results of their own researches and investigations, a man of towering conviction who faced death rather than compromise with what had become to him the self evident truth. A. G. Dickens sees evidence of Calvinistic emphasis in Philpot's writings, with his assertion of the total sovereignty of God, and the total corruption of man and Philpot vigorously defended Calvin during his examination. He recognised a justification by faith alone tempered by the belief that each man's predestination to bliss or damnation is by the sovereign will of God alone. This for Philpot was immutable, thus it was for him 'a man of learning and integrity' impossible to alter opinions merely because England had a different government. What a difficult man he must have been to deal with: in his paper *Apology for spitting upon an Arian* he wrote:

> *'Let the ground O Lord, open and let them go alive into hell... let their bowels issue out behind, as Arius's did and let them die in their own dung.'*

It is not surprising that Gardiner, White and Bonner found him impossible, and that even the Protestant Ponet lost sympathy for him. Philpot, a magnificent giant of a man with an unshakable steadfast conviction or an arrogant self opinionated stubborn maverick?

Stephen Cheston

Archdeacon 1553 ~ 1572

John Ebden

Archdeacon 1572 ~ 1575

Stephen Cheston
1572 Died

John Ebden
1562 Canon of Winchester Cathedral, Rector of Headbourne Worthy, also Rector of Chilbolton and Canon of St. Paul's Cathedral
1573 Master of the Hospital of St. Mary Magdalene, also Rector of Wonston, until 1614

Stephen Cheston and John Ebden were Archdeacons of Winchester during the first years of Elizabeth's reign, a difficult period for the Church; a time when the reformation was being consolidated following England's reversion to Catholicism under Mary Tudor. Stephen Cheston, a sound Catholic, was collated to the Archdeaconry of Winchester by Bishop Stephen Gardiner on 12 March 1553, and survived the accession of Elizabeth to the throne and the translation of Robert Horne as Bishop of Winchester, remaining in office until his death in 1572. John Ebden, was installed as rector of Headbourne Worthy and collated to a stall in Winchester Cathedral on 7 December 1562, the year after Robert Horne's appointment as Bishop. He succeeded Cheston as Archdeacon in 1572. Both Cheston, a Marian priest, and Ebden, with Protestant credentials, were members of the lower house of convocation during the defining debates of 1562 that settled the reformation, correcting the articles of religion passed during King Edward VI's reign. The pro Catholic delegates resisted change during the heated debates and the motion for amendment failed by just one, Cheston voting against and Ebden in favour of Protestant Reform.

Sources

- Rev. R. F. Bigg-Wilkes, *Historical Notes on the Parish of Wonston* (Winchester: Warren, 1915).
- A. W. Goodman, 'The Cathedral Church and the Archdeaconry of Winchester' in *Hampshire Field Club Proceedings, Vol 14* (1938).
- John Hare, *The Dissolution of the Monasteries in Hampshire, Hampshire Paper* (Hampshire County Council, 1999).
- Sarah Lewin, 'The Visitation Injunctions of Bishop Horne' in *Winchester Cathedral Record, No. 60* (Friends of Winchester Cathedral, 1991).
- John Paul, ' Recusants' in *Hampshire Field Club Proceedings, Vol. 21* (1959).
- *The Victoria History of England, Hampshire and the Isle of Wight, Vol 2*, ed. H. Arthur Doubleday & William Page (Westminster: Archibald Constable, 1903).
- Rev. T. Luthbury, *History of the Convocation* (London: J. Leslie, 1853)
- Wavell, *History and Antiquities of Winchester Vol 2* (attributed to Richard Wavell by Wilkes, 1773).

The Protestant reformer, Robert Horne, had returned from exile in Germany at the beginning of Elizabeth's reign to his appointment as Dean of Durham. Translated shortly afterwards to be Bishop of Winchester, it seems that it was his intention to rid his new diocese of the remaining practices and outward displays of the, 'superstitious religion'. To this end he conducted regular and thorough visitations within the diocese and to the Dean and Chapter at Winchester in 1562 and again in 1571. It is from the records of these visitations that his reputation, perhaps somewhat unfairly, as a Philistine iconoclast stems. The historian, Sarah Lewin, rightly reminds us that his injunctions, following the visitations to the Dean and Chapter, show that Horne was as much concerned with godly reform and in improving learning and morals, as in removing papist display and practice. In addition, Horne was faced with the practical problems arising from a large shortfall of priests within the diocese, stemming from both Mary's and Elizabeth's deprivations; Mary deprived 20 clerics of their livings in Hampshire and Elizabeth in the first eight years of her reign about 30. Horne was also faced with a Chapter of whom only six out of twelve Canons had taken the oath of supremacy.

Although Winchester in the reformation period was regarded as a Catholic bastion, and indeed was described by the future Cardinal Allen, in 1576, as one of the most Catholic towns in England, generally speaking many of the clergy were not energetically opposed to Queen Elizabeth and her Church. Horne had written that the clergy were – 'conforming themselves as it was req'd of them: but the state of the laity was unsatisfactory'. Many of the Marian clergy managed to remain in office during the reigns of both Mary and Elizabeth. In May 1562 five of the Marian Chapter were still in office, including Stephen Cheston. Sarah Lewin suggests this probably indicates a career orientated clergy with a more accommodating nature than their Bishop, but it also seems to indicate a pragmatic side to the Bishop who, on his part, faced with the shortage of priests, was prepared to overlook those not actively causing trouble. Furthermore, the early years of Elizabeth's reign were marked by a relative tolerance of Catholics. However, Horne did not shrink from taking action against the most militant Catholics.

The records of the 1562 visitation show that the Bishop had little regard for the Dean, Francis Newton, who he accused of neglecting his duties as well as favouring superstitious religion. However, in addition, both Cheston and Ebden were named and singled out for particular criticism by the Bishop. The 1562 proceedings show that

Archdeacon Stephen Cheston was reviled for frequenting inns in the town, behaviour that led Horne to include in his injunctions – 'that they ne anie of theim ... be common haunters of taverns or alehouses, or anie of theim be common rangers and walkers aboute the towne'. In Stephen Cheston's case Horne's criticism of him had to do with his personal lifestyle rather than his Catholic past. John Ebden was criticised for failing to preach at the cathedral in person in 1563. In this he was not alone, four other Canons are mentioned for this omission, including Michael Reniger, later to be Ebden's successor as Archdeacon. Ebden was one of a number of Prebendaries who held senior preferments elsewhere, in Ebden's case as a Canon of St Paul's; it is not therefore surprising that he was often absent from Winchester.

The proceedings of Horne's second visitation in 1571 show that the Dean and Chapter had made little progress in implementing the injunctions of 1562 and this led Horne to produce a new set of 31 injunctions, again mostly concerned with deficiencies in preaching, and teaching. He was even more incensed on the second occasion by evidence of bawdy behaviour, adding the offence of 'the playing at unlawful games and admitting suspect wemen or persons to ther howses or chambers' to the previous one of 'resorting to taverns and alehouses'. This time no one was singled out by name and so we do not know whether Cheston was still offending.

Cheston was unmarried and resident in the Close; other than this we know little about him except that he enjoyed three livings in addition to his Archdeaconry, namely, Overton, West Meon and King's Worthy, the latter presented to him in 1563 by Lady Jane Wriothesley, Countess of Southampton, the living having been alienated by Henry VIII to the first Earl in 1545. Interestingly, the records of Horne's 1562 visitation shed a light on another Marian Cheston, Thomas Cheston, Vicar of Romsey, who confessed to a papistical burial, bringing the corpse to the church with candle and tapers and celebrating 'our lady's even which was no Holy Day'. Was this Cheston a relative of the Archdeacon? In any event, like Stephen, it seems he retained his living during Horne's bishopric.

We cannot tell the strength of the patronage, if any, that the Chestons may have received from the Wriothesleys, but both families were Catholics. Thomas Wriothesley, Henry VIII's Chancellor had died in 1545 long before Cheston was made Archdeacon. Wriothesley had been a vigorous supporter of the religious changes, as Royal Commisioner he was responsible for the wanton destruction of St. Swithun's shrine and the cathedral high altar: he was the major financial beneficiary from the dissolution in Hampshire, but his son, the second Earl, was a secret Catholic who was imprisoned from 1569-1573 for his apparent connection with the plot to marry Mary Queen of Scots to the Duke of Norfolk. Like the Dean, Stephen Cheston died the next year in 1572, at a relatively young age. By this time, with the Queen's excommunication in 1570, action against recusants was gaining momentum, as their numbers in the country and Winchester increased. Had Cheston lived longer his survival as Archdeacon might have been more problematical.

Cheston's successor, John Ebden, lived to the great age of 98. However, he served only for three years as Archdeacon, resigning in 1575 to make way for the reforming Protestant, Michael Reniger, but keeping his Prebend. Ebden had been appointed Master of the Hospital of St. Mary Magdalen in 1573, originally a leper hospital which by this date was an almshouse for the poor and elderly, and was one year later to be Rector of Wonston. He had been collated as Rector of Chilbolton in 1566. The Hospital of St. Mary Magdalen had gradually declined in size and importance and by Ebden's time held a total of just eight poor brothers and sisters. Ebden was Master for many years and by indenture dated 2 September 1611, gave £10 annually to be used for a new gown to each brother and sister at Christmas together with 4d each per week.

John Ebden died on 16 November 1614 and was buried in the hospital chapel, a memorial, in brass, was placed on the South side. The inscription, even allowing for sentiment, leaves no doubt about the goodliness of Ebden:

He that God and good men fear'd and lov'd,
Which by example cherish't or reprov'd,
Heer lyes enter'd. He living was, dead is,
A preacher whom the church lov'd, the people mys,
His life for length, learning for truth was great.
His doctrine pure, his deeds without deceite.
And in his life time was, and att his ende,
To rich and poore a father and a friende.

The hospital was destroyed during the civil war by Royalist troops who ate all the livestock, vandalised the buildings of wood for fires, including the high altar, and left damage so severe that after the war it was impossible to repair it within the financial means of the poorly-endowed hospital; thereafter the chapel and the other buildings were demolished and the stone from the ruins was used to erect six almshouses at Water Lane, in Winchester. What happened to Ebden's remains is not known. However, the Time Team TV programme in October of the year 2000 investigated the original site and found the skeleton of a wealthy and elderly member of the community, maybe Ebden's, alongside a number of more simply buried remains.

So what are we to make of Cheston and Ebden, colleagues at Winchester from opposite sides of the religious divide during the final phase of the reformation? Although both were the subject of criticism by Bishop Horne, it seems they were no better or no worse than the rest of a Chapter, regarded by Horne as idle and negligent of their duties. Like many clergymen of the period they held multiple livings. They lived in dangerous times, Cheston appointed Archdeacon by Stephen Gardiner, at the beginning of Mary's reign, managed to survive the early years of Elizabeth's rule and Horne's bishopric, perhaps with the protection of the Wriothesleys. Ebden, a Protestant, had survived Mary's reign; he was aged 46 when he was made a Prebendary at Winchester and we know little of his life before then, other than that he seems to have been Canon of St Paul's. We have only a tantalising glimpse of their characters. It seems Ebden was a much loved, generous and conscientious Master of the Hospital of St. Mary Magdalen. How far was Cheston addicted to worldly pleasures is not clear, but it would seem unfair to judge his character merely on the evidence of Horne's injunction of 1562.

Michael Reniger

Archdeacon 1575 ~ 1609

1530 Born, probably at Basingstoke, Hants
1544 Magdalen College, Oxford
1545 BA
1546 Fellow Magdalen College until 1553
1549 MA
1548 Lecturer in Greek until 1550
1551 Lecturer in Natural Philosophy
1552 Rector Broughton, Hants
1553 Exile on the continent until 1558
1559 Rector Crawley Hants
1560 Prebendary Winchester Cathedral
1566 Chancellor Lincoln Cathedral
1567 Prebendary & Precentor Lincoln Cathedral
1568 Sub-dean Lincoln Cathedral
1573 BD & DD
1575 Rector Chilbolton Hants
1575 Archdeacon Winchester
1583 Canon St Paul's Cathedral
1592 Re-presented a Prebendary Lincoln Cathedral
1597 Ecclesiastical Commissioner for Winchester
1609 Died and buried in Crawley Parish Church

Sources

- HRO Probate Records AD 1609/57 B 1626/102
- *Al Ox* 1500-1714
- F W Pledge, *Crawley*, (1908)
- *DNB*
- *Fasti Ecc Ang*, 1541-1857
- J E Millard, … *Accounts of the Wardens of the Fraternity of the Holy Ghost in Basingstoke 1557-1654*, (1882)
- F J Baigent & J E Millard, *A History of … Basingstoke*, (1889)
- *VCH Hampshire*, vols iii, iv, v.

A Hampshire man, Michael Reniger was probably born at Basingstoke in 1530 and retained his interests in the county throughout his life. He was born into a well-known local family of mainly mercers, tailors and saddlers who lived there for several generations, both before and after his time. There is evidence that in 1556, almost a generation later, a John Reniger of Basingstoke was appointed an Alderman of the ancient Fraternity of the Holy Ghost in that town, an honour bestowed on him by Cardinal Reginald Pole, who was soon to succeed Cranmer as Archbishop.

The Fraternity of the Holy Ghost was an ancient, benevolent association whose members undertook the religious and educational care of boys and young men living in the Basingstoke area. It was dissolved early in the sixteenth century, but revived in 1556/7. An Alderman and two Wardens were elected annually and John Reniger 'the elder' was the first to be elected under the revised constitution and appears to have been highly regarded. Michael Reniger and the Cardinal held firmly opposing views which would have a significant effect on both their lives.

Following a period of study at Cambridge, Reniger went up to Magdalen College Oxford and must have witnessed the effects of the Dissolution of the Monasteries. King Henry VIII died in January 1547 and was succeeded by his son Edward VI who advanced the second stage of the Reformation. Meanwhile at Oxford, Reniger was appointed a lecturer in Greek and then in Natural Philosophy. In 1552, a kinsman Robert Reniger, who had recently purchased Broughton Manor, Hampshire, presented Michael to the local rectory, but he did not have long to enjoy his move to a rural parish.

Whilst the young king reigned, Michael Reniger's reputation grew as a distinguished preacher and upholder of the reformed religion. It must have been at about this time that he married his wife Margery, possibly one of the earliest clerics to wed; they had several sons and at least one daughter.

Queen Mary succeeded her brother in 1553 and life changed for the adherants of the new religion. The Bishop of Winchester Stephen Gardiner, now newly restored to office, was a strong supporter of the Roman Catholic religion and took an active part in the persecution of the Protestants. Reniger was one of the many who were stripped of their offices and exiled to the continent, being forced to leave his wife behind in England. He lived mainly at Strasbourg, but it is known that he also had contact with the English exiles in Zurich from where he sent a letter, describing his poor financial state. He appears to have had sufficient funds in this country, but possibly was unable to gain access to them from abroad. John Po[y]net, a fervent Protestant who had briefly replaced Stephen Gardiner as Bishop of Winchester in 1551, also fled to Strasbourg and died there in 1556. Both Reniger and the Bishop have been credited with a Latin translation of *A Defence for Mariage (sic) of Priestes,* which was probably written whilst they were in exile in Strasbourg.

Meanwhile, Bishop Gardiner died in 1555 and Reginald Pole continued the persecution of the protestants. It was then that Reniger's kinsman was honoured at Basingstoke. Queen Mary died in November 1558, followed by the Cardinal's sudden death just twelve hours later. Elizabeth I came to the throne and the exiles returned home. Almost immediately, Michael Reniger was appointed one of the chaplains to the new queen and now, all his efforts went into advancing the Protestant religion. Soon, Elizabeth presented him to the rectory of Crawley, Hampshire, which he retained for the rest of his life and shortly afterwards was installed a prebendary at Winchester Cathedral. Quietly, his new parish was persuaded to accept his Calvinism and strongly-held ultra-protestant views, but his arrival was remembered for many years afterwards.

It was in his role as a Proctor for the Chapter of Winchester that he attended the

Convocation of Canterbury held in February 1563. There, he signed a petition against the use of the Cross in Baptism, the wearing of copes, surplices, gowns and caps and also the observance of Saints' days. When the petition was put to the vote, there were 58 in favour and 59 against. These customs and practices had been retained by a majority of one vote and Reniger and his colleagues lost the day.

In 1566, he was introduced to Lincoln Cathedral, due largely to the intervention of the Queen, for it was her wish that they should appoint him as their next Chancellor. He enjoyed rapid advancement within the cathedral and the following year was installed precentor and prebendary and then in October 1558 was inducted as Sub-dean. He then resigned the precentorship, but appears to have retained the prebend, although not without some opposition for he was installed a prebendary again in 1592. There is evidence to suggest that at least one child was born at Lincoln and so it is probable that he was at times resident there, but his activities within the Chapter have not been investigated.

Meanwhile, he continued his connections with Oxford and in 1573 was awarded his doctorate. Back in Hampshire, he was presented to the wealthy rectory of Chilbolton, which was in the gift of the Dean and Chapter and a coveted benefice; a later incumbent would remark upon the good fishing and hunting to be had in the vicinity. On 20 May 1575, he succeeded as Archdeacon of Winchester.

It was at around this time that he acquired some large tracts of land at Overton and Church Oakley, both near Basingstoke, probably totalling about 300 acres; at the same time, he purchased the Manor of Quidhampton which formed part of the manor of Overton. Two years later he was installed a prebendary at St Paul's, London and finally in 1597, was appointed one of the Eccesiastical Commissioners for Winchester.

When he died in 1609, in his 79th year, Michael Reniger was still Sub-dean at Lincoln, Archdeacon of Winchester and Rector of Crawley. He was a man of some wealth, which he is said to have left to his son Michael, but little of his will survives, only the grant of probate in the Archdeacon's Court at Winchester, remains. However, it can safely be assumed that all his possessions lay within the jurisdiction of that court and he left nothing in the Diocese of Lincoln.

He was buried in the parish church at Crawley, where he had served as rector for over

51 years and was commemorated by a long Latin inscription on the ledger stone. To the right of the altar on the south side, a brass tablet on the wall also recorded his passing. He was survived by his wife who died many years later in 1626 and also by some of his children. Margery Reniger's will has survived in the Bishop's Court, which might indicate wider interests and in it she gave instructions to be buried in the chancel of Crawley church, close to her husband.

Michael Reniger was a prolific writer and amongst his many titles was, *A Treatise against Treasons, Rebellions, and such Disloyalties*, (1587). In his role as chaplain to Queen Elizabeth, he probably met some of the most famous men of her reign, amongst them Drake, Raleigh, Burleigh and Shakespeare. Despite this, he does not seem to have desired great power and with the exception of Lincoln, his interests appear to have been in his local community; at Crawley he is remembered as:

> *A pious and learned man who upheld the reformation and leaving country and dear wife was exiled ... till Queen Elizabeth recalled him to be her chaplain and Rector of Crawley ... for 51 years ... And as an ever vigilant shepherd by word and example brought back the sheep to the fold of Christ.*

Ralph Barlow

Archdeacon 1609 ~ 1621

1574 Born
1594 Matriculated, BA in 1596 at Oriel College Oxford, MA and Fellow of Pembroke College in 1599
1606 Bachelor of Divinity at Corpus Christi College
1609 Archdeacon of Winchester
1610 Prebendary of Winchester
1621 Dean of Bath and Wells
1631 Died

Ralph Barlow was born in 1574 the son of Henry Barlow from, it is thought, Cheshire. After graduating from Oxford he was, in 1601, presented by Queen Elizabeth to the Rectory of Woodmanstern. The next year he resigned to study for a Bachelor of Divinity at Corpus Christi College. In 1606 he became the incumbent of Radnage, Berks. Three years later in 1609 his career took a favourable turn, and he became Archdeacon of Winchester, and gained the livings of Farthingstone, Northants, and Yaverland on the Isle of Wight. In common with the practice of the day this improvement in his affairs probably stemmed from patronage. About that time he had courted Dorothy Wolridge, the niece of Thomas Bilson, who had become Bishop of Winchester in 1597. He married the young Dorothy, as far as we know, before 1613 when she would have been 18 years of age. In 1610 Ralph Barlow had become a Prebendary at Winchester and had added the living of Fawley to his portfolio. Dorothy's mother, Thomas Bilson's sister, Faith, had married secondly the Rev Lawrence Washington amongst whose benefices was included Fawley in Hampshire. When Lawrence died in 1610 the living was passed to Ralph Barlow, keeping it within the family.

It is clear that Barlow's connection with the Bilson family must have substantially aided his progress within the Church. Thomas Bilson, a member of a prominent Winchester family, whom claimed kinship with the

Sources

- W. H. Challen, 'Thomas Bilson, Bishop Of Winchester' in *Hampshire Field Club Proceedings, Vol 19* (1955 -7).
- Peter Hopewell, *Saint Cross, England's Oldest Almshouse* (Chichester: Phillimore, 1995)

Duke of Bavaria, was an influential Bishop of Winchester having preached the sermon at the Coronation of James I in 1603. He had famously been instrumental in the final revision of the translation of the Authorised Version of the Bible. He died in 1616 and was buried in Westminster Abbey. Little is known of Ralph Barlow's 12 years as Archdeacon and Prebendary as there is a serious gap in the Cathedral records between the years 1600 and 1622; no Chapter Books exist for that period. However, in addition to the influential Bilson, the Dean was Thomas Morton who rose to be Bishop of Durham. The well-educated Barlow would have had the benefit of stimulating colleagues.

He must have been well thought of because, in 1621, he was elevated to be the Dean of Wells, where he served until his death in 1631. Barlow had lost his first wife, Dorothy, in 1620 at the young age of 25 (she was buried at Winchester Cathedral) and had married again shortly afterwards to Christian Marsh a widow with children. Barlow's move to Wells no doubt was influenced by the Bishop of Bath and Wells, Arthur Lake, who would have been well acquainted with Ralph Barlow.

Bishop Lake had even greater access to patronage than Bilson, for his brother was Secretary of State to James I. A Wykehamist, he was Archdeacon of Surrey as well as a caring Master of St. Cross, at the time when Barlow became Archdeacon of Winchester. In 1613 he became Warden of New College and in 1616 Bishop of Bath and Wells. There is a difference of view as to the extent to which he himself benefited from his brother's patronage. Certainly his brother, Thomas, had by stealth, including bribery, prevented the Mastership of St. Cross going to James I's favourite, the layman James Hudson and acquired the post for Arthur. However, Lake was a man of considerable ability, of liberal view, a scholar and a conscientious priest – 'to his city an oracle, to scholars a living library, to the whole church a priest whose lips did preserve knowledge'.

When Ralph Barlow died in 1631 he desired to be buried in the South Choir aisle of Wells Cathedral near Arthur Lake's tomb (he had died in 1626). From this we can, perhaps, safely assume that not only was there a mutual regard between the two men, but that they shared common religious and social views. Although there is no direct evidence available, it seems Ralph himself was a substantial man with commendable attributes. Whilst his family clerical connections would have been of value to him, we know he was well educated and have no reason to believe he was without merit. Both of his likely mentors were themselves considerable men and outstanding churchmen of their time.

Edward Burby

Archdeacon 1631 ~ 1653

*c.*1600 Born
1616 Matriculated, aged 16, Lincoln College Oxford
1619 BA
1622 MA (incorporated at Cambridge 1625)
1636 DD(Oxon)
1627 Vicar of Canewdon, Essex
1629 Rector of East Woodhay, Hampshire
1630 Married Frances Neile. Prebendary of Winchester
1631 Archdeacon of Winchester and Rector of Wonston
1633 Rector of Chilbolton
1638 Prebendary of Southwall
1653 Died on 2nd June and was buried at Wonston on 6th June

Sources

- Chapter Book
- Oxford Alumni Book
- *Victoria County History*
- Wonston Parish Register
- Two letters from The Herriard Collection in The Hampshire Record Office

Edward Burby, a gentleman from London, was educated at Lincoln College, Oxford. His entry states that he matriculated on 12 April 1616 aged 16. Therefore his date of birth was about 1600. He was awarded a BA degree on 25 October 1619, MA on 26 June 1622 and he became a Doctor of Divinity in 1636.

Burby's first appointment was as Vicar of Canewdon in Essex in 1627. He then moved to be Rector of East Woodhay in Hampshire in 1629. He married Frances Neile on 14 January 1630 and the wedding took place at St Margaret's Westminster.

Their first child, Elizabeth, was born in 1631 and was baptised on 21 June at St Andrew Undershaft in London. Their other eight children were baptised in Winchester. Two died in infancy, Sarah, their second child, was baptised and buried in the Cathedral on 18 October 1632.

On 18 November 1630 Burby became a Prebendary of Winchester and in 1631 he was collated Rector of Wonston on Monday 7 February. In the same year he was appointed Archdeacon of Winchester and was installed on 24 September. When Burby was resident in Winchester he lived at No. 1 The Close. In 1633 he also became Rector of Chilbolton. The extant Parish Registers of Chilbolton date from the end of the seventeenth century; they mention that 'the living was a sinecure for Deans and

Prebendaries of Winchester giving them good fishing on the Test and good hunting on the Downs'. The same situation probably obtained 40 years earlier. In 1638 Burby became Prebendary of Southwell.

In 1639 a gunpowder store was being made in Hampshire and on 25 April William Neale in Portsmouth wrote to Edward Burby stating that 'according to the advice from the Lorde Lieu[ten]ante, here is order come downe, for the supplying the County, w[i]th such a quantitie of powder, as shal[l] be required, not exceeding three Hasks, and the price is eighteen pence the pound, if a whole barrel be bought, but if a lesse quantitie be required then nineteen pence must be paid for every pound', he goes on to say that the powder will be given if it is collected. Burby replied by saying that 'he had commande from my grace of Canterbury, – the Clergie – should be freed from sending either men, armour, or horses out of the County. And had not the extremitye of this wet weather pr[e]vented me, I should have attended you in p[er]son' So no contribution was made.

In 1640 the Chapter wrote to Bishop Walter Curle, asking if he could settle a difficulty about which stall in the Choir should be occupied by the Mayor and which by Archdeacon Burby. The Bishop replied directly to Edward Burby and stated that it was up to the Chapter to decide a convenient stall for the Archdeacon of Winchester and he concluded by saying that he hoped 'so small a matter may be ordered without further trouble of me, or breach of unity among yourselves'.

Edward Burby appears to have lived in Essex during part of the Civil War. He was in Woodford for three months in 1646 and probably owned property there. In 1645 the County Committee for sequestration ordered him to appear before them, but he did not do so and his estate was sequestered. Subsequently the funds were refunded for false sequestration. (The Seqestration Ordinance of 1643 placed the estates of known Royalists under the control of local commissioners and diverted their rents to the rebel Government, Parliament. Both sides needed finance and both had their systems of raising it.)

There appears to be no record of Burby's whereabouts from the mid 1640s until his death.

Burby died on 2 June 1653 and was buried in Wonston on 6 June. The burial entry in the Parish Register states 'Edward Burby Dr of Divinitie sometime Rector of this parish was buried June 6' His will, as of The Close Winchester, mentions his wife Frances, sons Edward and Charles and five daughters. He had property in London and

Walthamstow, Essex and household items in Wonston. Forty shillings was to be paid to the overseer (executor) L. Hinton and to Barnabas Love, Rector of Wonston, for the funeral sermon. Barnabas Love was Burby's son-in-law and had served as a soldier in the Royalist army.

St. Mary's Church, Southampton ~ *c.*1900

George Roberts

Archdeacon 1660 ~ 1661

&

Thomas Gorges

Archdeacon 1661 ~ 1666

GEORGE ROBERTS
1661 DIED

THOMAS GORGES
1603 BORN
1667 DIED

These two Archdeacons were the first to be appointed after the restoration of the Monarchy on 29 May in 1660. When on 8 August that year the Cathedral, once more, passed into the care of a Dean and Chapter, the previous Dean, John Young, and seven out of the twelve Prebendaries were dead. Little is known of Georges Robert's early career or his whereabouts during the Commonwealth period. However, it was the King, as patron, who presented him to be Archdeacon on 3 August 1660 and he was installed on 9 August. Understandably, in view of his legal responsibilities, his was one of the earliest appointments made. By 10 September the new Dean, Alexander Hyde, a cousin of the Lord Chancellor (later to be the Earl of Clarendon), was in a position to call a Chapter meeting to elect the King's choice as the new Bishop. Brian Duppa, who had been tutor to the young Charles II, was duly elected. By this time in 1660, Duppa was over seventy, but following legal precedent the Chapter had to elect the King's choice. As important, was the need for the Chapter to express its loyalty to the Crown which was accomplished by the gift of the large sum of £1,500 to Charles II. The problems facing Bishop Duppa and the Cathedral Chapter were

Sources

∴ Barbara Carpenter Turner, The Return of the Church, Cathedral and Close, 1660 - 1662, *Winchester Cathedral Record* No 29 (1960).

enormous. The Bishop's Palaces were in ruins as were the Close houses; of thirteen, nine had been demolished or nearly completely destroyed. There was no certainty as to how much money could be raised in a timely fashion from the church estates.

The speed of the regeneration of the Church in Winchester and the total of monies collected, £8,175 in 1660 and £14,303 the following year, is astonishing. In 1662, Archbishop Juxton held a Visitation of the Cathedral and by the actual date of his visit, May 1663, was able to report that the restoration of the Cathedral was complete. George Roberts' contribution to this remarkable turn around is difficult to judge, for he was to be in post for less than a year, dying on 16 March 1661 and being buried at Hambledon, Bucks.

Thomas Gorges was collated as Archdeacon on that day, 16 March, and installed by proxy on 19 March. Thomas was the son of Sir Edward Gorges of Wraxall in Somerset. He was born in 1603 and had matriculated from Queen's College Oxford in 1621 at the age of 18. He was an accomplished scholar, becoming a B.A. in 1621, an M.A. from St. Albans Hall in 1624 and a Fellow of All Souls in 1629. He had been elected as a Prebendary at Sarum in 1643, at the start of the Civil War, and held that post until his death in 1667. At the time of his appointment as Archdeacon of Winchester, he was also made a Prebendary of Westminster. He was appointed Sub- almoner to the King at the same time. Again it is difficult to judge the scale of his contribution to the recovery at Winchester. He resigned in April 1666, possibly through ill health and died on 12th December 1667, after just five years as Archdeacon, a short period for that time. He was, as a Prebendary at Westminster, buried in Westminster Abbey.

Walter Dayrell

Archdeacon 1666 ~ 1684

1610 Born
1628 Matriculated, Jesus College, Oxford
1631 BA, Fellow of Christchurch College, Oxford
1634 MA
1647 Ejected by Parliamentary Visitors
1660 DD, restored to Fellowship
1661 Prebendary of Winchester
1662 Rector of Crawley
1666 Archdeacon of Winchester
1684 Died 29 March

The Dayrell family came from the parish of Lillingstone Dayrell in Buckinghamshire where they had been the lords of the manor since the twelfth century. The father of the archdeacon, also named Walter, was the fourth son of Paul Dayrell who was then the head of the family. Walter was a lawyer, a barrister of Gray's Inn and later in life Recorder of Abingdon where he died in 1628 at the age of 62.

Walter Dayrell the elder had three sons. Paul was born in 1606 and, like his father, became a lawyer. Towards the end of his life, he was living in Oxford; he died in 1698. The second son, Thomas, became a Fellow of All Souls but was ejected from his Fellowship by the Parliamentary Visitors in 1648. He also lost his Rectory of Easington in Oxford where he was ordered to be sequestered because 'he has resided at Oxford since it was a garrison for the King'. He did not live to be reinstated at the Restoration, having died in 1655.

The youngest brother, Walter Dayrell, was born in 1610. He entered Jesus College, Oxford, matriculating at the age of 17, and graduating B.A. in 1631. He became a Fellow of Christchurch in the same year. Like his brother Thomas, he was ejected by the Parliamentary Visitors, but Walter was restored and the degree of D.D. conferred on him in 1660. It is not known where the two brothers lived during the years of the Commonwealth. Perhaps they were accommodated on the family estates in

Sources

- Will and Inventory of Walter Dayrell (Hants R.O. 1684 B25)
- J. Crook, *The Wainscot Book, Chapter Minutes 1660-95*
- *Buckinghamshire Victoria County History*
- Hampshire Hearth Tax Assessment 1665, ed E.Hughes and P.White (H. Record Series 1991)
- Foster, Oxford Alumni
- F.W. Pledge, *Crawley* (1907)

Buckinghamshire, though that may not have been the safest possible refuge as Peter Dayrell, who had inherited in 1628, took part in the Civil War as an ardent Royalist for which he was fined £788 in 1646.

There is no record of Walter Dayrell's having any connection with Hampshire until after the Restoration of King Charles II in 1660. The first Bishop of Winchester to be appointed when the diocese was reinstated was Brian Duppa, formerly Bishop of Salisbury, a leading royalist who had been prominent in negotiations for the revival of the Church. Bishop Duppa had become Dean of Christchurch, Oxford, in 1629 and Vice-Chancellor of the University in 1634. When he was translated to Winchester in 1660 he had the task of appointing clergy to vacant livings in the diocese and to those from which unqualified ministers had been ejected, and it seems likely that he would have remembered those men he had known in Oxford and who had been removed from their posts. Walter Dayrell became a Prebendary of Winchester and Rector of Crawley, Hampshire. His name first appears among the Canons in the Chapter Minutes of November 1661, but he was not collated to Crawley until September 1662 after the Rev. Samuel Tomlyn was ejected under the Act of Uniformity passed in that year. Crawley was one of the richest livings in the diocese and was in the gift of the Bishop. A number of learned clergy held the living at various times and it was not unusual for the incumbent to be a Prebendary of the Cathedral or Archdeacon. The parish consisted of the village of Crawley and the chapelry of Hunton which had been attached to Crawley since the 10th century and continued to be so until 1910. There was a rectory house at Crawley, listed under the name of Doctor 'Dorrell' in the Hearth Tax assessment of 1665, when it seems to have been the third largest house in the parish, but it is not known whether Dayrell ever lived there. At the end of his life, only a very few items are mentioned in the inventory of his possessions as being at Crawley, but he could have resided there at an earlier time. The parish was served by a curate, John Turner, who had been appointed in 1661. He remained there until his death in 1707, having for most of that time combined the curacy with the Rectory of Lainston.

In 1662 Brian Duppa was succeeded as Bishop by George Morley and it was he who appointed Walter Dayrell to be Archdeacon of Winchester in 1666. For the next eighteen years he continued to serve in this capacity until his death in 1684. In addition to his other duties, Walter Dayrell was Master of the Hospital of St Mary Magdalen.

This medieval foundation on the hill to the east of the town had suffered during the Civil War when soldiers had been quartered there and had burnt the wood from the buildings for fuel. Further damage had occurred during the Dutch war in 1665 when the hospital had been used as a prison. By Dayrell's time the buildings were no longer habitable and the poor people who should have been housed there had to be accommodated in the town. In Dayrell's Will he mentions several houses in Colebrook Street leased from Winchester College, which he left for the use of the poor people of the hospital, the leases to be transferred to his successor as Master. He also left money to be divided between the Brothers and Sisters of the Magdalen Hospital.

When the Dean and Chapter were reinstated at the Restoration, they were soon engaged in an extensive building programme. Some of the houses in the Close had been pulled down during the Commonwealth period, others had been partly demolished and were in a bad state of repair. According to the statutes, it was necessary to provide each of the Canons with a house where he could fulfil his terms of residence. By November 1661 the houses in Dome Alley were under construction. When Walter Dayrell came to Winchester he was at first offered accommodation in No. 11 The Close, (later pulled down - between No. 10 and the present No. 11) the occupant of which was offered No. 8, one of the new houses. By September 1663, it was ordered that Dayrell could continue to live there until 'his owne house' was completed. This was to be constructed on the site of a previous house, assigned during the Commonwealth to a Parliamentary officer, Captain Thomas Bettesworth, who demolished it for the value of the materials. The new house, then known as No. 12 (now No. 11) was said to be habitable by 1663-4. Some idea of the interior decoration of the new house is given in *The Wainscot Book*, a document listing panelling and other items of 'fixtures and fittings'; these were originally installed at the expense of the individual occupant, whose successor then made a payment to him when the property changed hands. Among the original entries for Dayrell's house are 'nynty yardes of wainscott in the Dyning roome' at a cost of £33.15.Od., and £5 for a 'Chimney peice ... the cornish & all the ornament to it' in the same room. *The Wainscot Book* records that the interior painting was completed in 1665.

The twelve Prebendaries of the Cathedral were required to reside for three months of the year, three at a time being responsible for the conduct of services. At other times, they could be living in their parishes or elsewhere. It seems, however, that Walter Dayrell made his home in the Close and by the end of his life the new house had become a comfortable and quite luxurious dwelling. The furnishing in the Parlour included four 'Spanish Tables', nineteen chairs and a 'Turky workd Couch', as well as four 'Turky Carpetts' and other items. The Hall contained a table and twelve 'ioyned Stooles' ie. made by a joiner or cabinet-maker rather than by a carpenter. In the 'Hall above Stares' were a table, a leather carpet, five leather chairs, three 'brass Sconces' and a 'sett of pictures', while at the 'Staires head' there was a clock. There and in 'ye Long Gallery' were twelve maps. In the study, equipped with only a small table, a carpet and a chair, were books valued at £50, worth more than all the furniture in the house. The Archdeacon had his own transport provided by a 'pare of Geldings' and a coach in the stable.

Walter Dayrell's Will and the inventory of his possessions taken at the time of his death in 1684 provide some personal information about him. First of all he asked for his body to be interred 'with as little Cost, Pomp and Ostentation as conveniently may be'. He left £10 to his niece Alice Hall, perhaps a daughter of his brother Paul, and £5 to a god-son Edward Dalby. The beneficiaries he was most anxious to provide for were the family of Benjamin Whitear whom he refers to as 'my servant'. Whitear was one of the Lay Vicars at the Cathedral from November 1669 and became Sub-Sacrist in January 1677. It seems that Whitear and his family were running Dayrell's house for him and were living there. A house in Colebrook Street was bequeathed to Whitear and also all the furniture in the 'best Chamber', all the books in the study and 'all my Pictures'. In addition, he was to receive £20 in money and mourning for himself and family 'of good Cloathe of sixteen shillings a yard' (surely very costly at that time?) and a cloak of the same. To his god-daughter, Susanna Whitear, the Archdeacon left the wainscot money due from his successor which amounted to £69-18s.

Other beneficiaries of the Will included servants who had been with the Archdeacon for a year, as well as the Petty Canons, lay Vicars and Choristers. His brother Paul Dayrell of Oxford was made residuary legatee and executor of the Will, but it is clear that Walter Dayrell was not happy about this; in a codicil to the Will he declared that if the executor failed to make any of the payments or caused any difficulties, then Benjamin Whitear should take over as executor and receive the residue of the estate. Walter Dayrell died on 29 March 1684, at the age of 74, nine months before the death of Bishop Morley on 29 October in the same year. He was buried in the Cathedral and has a memorial stone on the north side of the nave in the sanctuary near the nave altar.

PM

Robert Sharrock

Archdeacon 1684

1630 Baptised at Drayton Parslow, Buckinghamshire
1643 Winchester College
1650 Matriculated, New College Oxford
1654 BCL
1661 DCL
1665 Rector Horwood Magna, Bucks until 1668
1665 Installed Prebendary Winchester Cathedral
1668 Rector East Woodhay, Hants
1670 Rector Bishops Waltham, Hants
1684 Archdeacon of Winchester
1684 Died and Buried in Bishops Waltham

Sources

- HRO 30M77 PR2 Bishops Waltham Original Parish Registers
- Win Cath Lib. Chapter Books 1660-1695, 1696-1739
- *Alumni Oxonienses,* vol iv, (1892)
- T F Kirby, *Winchester Scholars*, (1888)
- *V C H Hampshire*, vols iii, iv (1914)
- *International Genealogical Index*, (1992)
- *Dictionary of National Biography*
- R Sharrock, *History of the Propagation and Improvement of Vegetables* ..., (1660)
- Pickering & Chatto, Notes on: *The Correspondence of Robert Boyle* ..., 6 vols. (2001)
- *Archives of New College Oxford*, (1974) pp 141, 122, 197
- John Crook, *The Wainscot Book*, (1984)
- ed W R Ward, *Parson and Parish in 18th Century Hampshire: Replies to Bishops' Visitations*, (1995)
- Harleian Society, Musgrave's *Obituaries*, vol v, (1901)

Born the third son of the Revd Robert and Judith Sharrock, Robert was baptised at Drayton Parslow, Buckinghamshire on 29 June 1630. In the following years more boys were born until at last a daughter completed the family. Later, his father purchased the advowson of the Rectory of Adstock in the same county, which would pass eventually to his grandson, another Robert, who would bequeath it to the Bishopric of Lincoln.

Robert was at Winchester College by 1643, in the midst of the civil wars and not long after the city had fallen to Parliament. It could be expected that on his arrival, he heard much about the local conflict and the looting that was still taking place. Then, the castle changed hands and for a time a royal garrison was re-established there, but in 1645 Robert and his friends would have learnt of the final fall of the Royalist cause. Soon, he went up to New College, Oxford, a city so lately favoured by King Charles I, where he continued with his education. Cromwell was elected Lord Protector and the full effects of Puritan rule would have fallen on Oxford.

During the Commonwealth, Robert seems to have spent his time writing and lecturing. Several documents in which he had an interest survive in the New College archives. One dated 2 December 1658, was addressed to Richard Cromwell. In it, Sharrock gave his observations and comments on the election of the Warden, but the

Protector's reply is unrecorded. Other letters survive, notably three that he and two colleagues had addressed to the Warden. It was dated shortly after the Restoration, in June 1660, in which they discussed the presentation of plate to King Charles II, but the outcome is unknown. The following year, on 24 May 1661, Robert was awarded his D.C.L.

Meanwhile, he had been followed first to Winchester College and then to New College, by Thomas Ken, (1637-1711). It was probably at Oxford that the two met for the first time, for Robert Sharrock was a Greek lecturer at the College at the same time as Ken was an undergraduate. They would meet again in 1669, when Ken joined Robert Sharrock at Winchester and took up residence in The Close.

Another contemporary was Robert Boyle, (1627-1691). He settled at Oxford, where he set up his laboratory and in 1662 published what has become known as 'Boyle's Law'. He was a prolific writer and carried on an extensive correspondence with over 300 men and women, many of whom were leading figures of their time and including Robert Sharrock. [If any correspondence between Boyle and Sharrock has survived, perhaps it is to be found in *The Correspondence of Robert Boyle* ... 6 vols, (2001)]

In the seventeenth century, many more clergy were ordained than could be provided with permanent benefices and it was only the well-connected who could hope for advancement. During the Commonwealth, Sharrock had remained lecturing at Oxford and thus avoided the sufferings of many of his colleagues. In June 1665 he was presented to the college Rectory of Horwood Magna, Buckinghamshire and three months later, on 13 September 1665, was installed a Prebendary at Winchester.

It was now that Robert embarked on a long correspondence, lasting until 1668 and amounting to 29 letters and memoranda, one of which was signed by King Charles II. It was all in connection with his wish to exchange the Rectory of Horwood Magna with East Woodhay, Hampshire, which was held by his younger brother Edmund. The exchange eventually took place and in 1668 he was able to move nearer to Winchester. Meanwhile, he had married Frances daughter of Edmund West and in 1668 their first child Elizabeth was born and baptised whilst they were still at Horwood.

Robert did not stay long at East Woodhay and the following year was installed as the Rector at Bishop's Waltham, where the advowson, which had been through many hands, was now in the control of the Bishop. By now, Robert was an acknowledged academic and following in the footsteps of an earlier Rector, Dr Robert Ward, who at one time had been Bishop Lancelot Andrewes' tutor. He was fortunate to have moved to a parish church which was in good order, having been newly roofed the previous year.

On 21 February 1669/70 the parish registers clearly show a change of handwriting and almost immediately afterwards, there is an entry recording the baptism of his second daughter Anne. This was the only time his wife's name was recorded in a parish register. Two more children, Frances and Robert, were baptised in 1673 and 1678 respectively, children of 'Docktor Sharrock', but that was the fashion of the time.

Meanwhile, Bishop Morley was keen that Thomas Ken, who was living on the Isle of Wight, should live nearer Winchester and took advantage of these moves. Ken was offered the Rectory of East Woodhay, recently vacated by Sharrock.

When Robert was installed a prebendary in 1665, as the newest member of the Chapter, he was allotted the house at No. 11 The Close. It was the least coveted of all the houses and badly in need of repair; it stood on the west side between the current Nos. 10 and 11 and has since been demolished. In 1668, he was promised that at the next vacancy he would be moved and in April 1669 the transfer took place and he was given No. 1, whilst Thomas Ken replaced him at No. 11. Sharrock probably only stayed in the Close during his period of statutory residence, for his new house was also let to the Cathedral Organist and there is evidence that he spent much of his time at Bishop's Waltham. Meanwhile, as an expert in Canon Law, in 1679 he was responsible for the re-issue of Lyndwood's *Provinciale,* which is still read by students in this field of study to-day.

Following his installation, he took an active part in the meetings of the Chapter and in his turn acted as Vice-Dean and on occasions, signed his name with an impressive flourish. He was present in 1667, when the discussion centred on the nation's 'sudden and imminent danger' and it was agreed to help raise a troop of horse to serve during the emergency. Meanwhile, in The Close there was much turmoil as reconstruction got under way, following the damage inflicted on the buildings in the previous decades.

It was at this time that he was involved in an incident, which is still recalled in Bishop's Waltham to-day, over three hundred years later. There was a feud in 1681, the reasons for which are now unclear, but the outcome was that the Clerk and one of the Church wardens locked Dr Sharrock and his parishioners out of the church. He had to apply to his patron, the Bishop of Winchester, to force the lock and fit a new one and the second key is inscribed with the date of that event. Evidence survives in the massive oak door to the south porch of the church which since that time has had two locks.

On 21 April 1684 he was installed Archdeacon, but died only three months later, on 11 July 1684, aged fifty-four. He was survived by his wife Frances and children, the youngest of whom was only seven. Almost certainly his death occurred at Bishop's Waltham, for he was buried there, just two days later. Frances died in 1692 and lies buried in the same place, but there are no surviving memorials, in either the church or churchyard. Following his death, No. 1 The Close was found to be in a poor state of repair, probably due to the tenant's neglect. In his will, Robert Sharrock left several items to the house, including two tables, kitchen fixtures and importantly a garden roller, for he was a keen horticulturalist. His son Robert, who inherited the advowson of the Rectory of Adstock, remained in the Bishop's Waltham area and with his wife was still there fifty years later and they lie buried in the same churchyard.

Robert Sharrock must have taken a keen interest in the re-establishment of the Cathedral Library, which now 350 years later, holds a copy of one of his books. He was a man of wide interests and published botanical, philosophical and other works, including a *History of the Propagation of Vegetables.* It went to three editions in 1660, 62 & 72 with a further improved edition published in 1694, after his death. He was encouraged in his work by Robert Boyle who made suggestions and observations and clearly had been of considerable help. Measuring about 15 by 10 cm, it is packed with useful horticultural information. It was based on his own observations and experience and his knowledge of the subject is evident throughout. It is easy to understand how his contemporaries were quick to compliment him on his work, for the transcripts of two letters have survived. The book is full of memorable suggestions and when writing of anemones:

> *Within a moneth (sic) after the seed ... is gather[e]d and prepared ... or three days before the full Moon in Septemb[er] it must be sown, for by that means you shall gain a year in the growing... (p 18).*

It is a delightful book and a joy to read.

Thomas Clutterbuck

Archdeacon 1684 ~ 1700

1623 Born Dunton, Buckinghamshire
1639 Matriculated Magdalen Hall Oxford
1639 Emmanuel College, Cambridge until 1642
1643 BA Magdalen College Oxford
1644 Fellow, Magdalen College Oxford, ejected
1645 MA, Magdalen College Oxford
*c.*1653 Sequestered from the living of Great Brickhill
*c.*1660 Rector Leckford, Hants and sinecure Rectory of Llandrillo in Edeirion, Mon.
1662 Rector St Mary's Southampton
1669 DD Cambridge
1684 Archdeacon of Winchester
1700 Died at St Mary's Southampton

Sources

- HRO 45M77 Leckford Parish registers
- HRO 129M71 The Rolle Charity, Deeds for Lockerley Farm
- SRO PR5/1/1 St Mary's Southampton Original Parish Registers
- Win Cath Lib: Chapter Books 1660-1695, 1696-1739
- *VCH, Hampshire*, vol iii, (1910)
- Harleian Society, *Musgrave's Obituaries* . . . , vol. ii (1900-1)
- *Alumni Oxonienses 1500-1714 vol. 1* (1891)
- *Athenae Cantab*
- *International Genealogical Directory* (1992)
- *Calendar State Papers, Domestic, 1655-6*, pp 34, 60(2), 61
- A G Matthews, *Calamy Revised*, (1934)
- www.st-marys-church-southampton.co.uk/history
- ed. W R Ward, *Parson and Parish in 18th Century Hampshire: replies to Bishop's Visitations*, (1995)

Thomas was born in 1623, the first child of the Revd Samuel Clutterbuck. Sources disagree on his place of birth, some suggest Dunton and others Dinton, both in Buckinghamshire and lying about fifteen miles apart. However, the parish registers for Dunton confirm the following baptism: '7 Sep 1623 Thomas son of Samuel Clutterbucke'. In the same registers there are also entries for his younger siblings, Richard, Frances, John and Margaret and when Samuel their father died in 1658, his obituary referred to him as of 'Dunton, Bucks'.

Thomas entered Magdalen Hall Oxford and matriculated in 1639 aged 15 years. He spent three years at Emmanuel College, Cambridge, before returning to Magdalen where he graduated in 1643. Fellowship followed in 1644 and M.A. in 1646. This was at the height of the conflict of the Civil Wars, with all the consequences that ensued, particularly in a Royalist city and two years later in 1648, when the King's cause had at last collapsed, he was expelled from Magdalen by the Parliamentary visitors. It is not known where or how he spent the next five years, but it seems probable that his sympathies lay with the Royalist cause.

In 1653 he was presented by the rightful patron to the Rectory of Great Brickhill, Buckinghamshire, but was unable to gain permanent possession. At the same time, there was a dissenting minister at Stepney who also claimed the living and a long legal battle ensued, lasting at least two years. His patron petitioned the Commissioners and eventually Thomas Clutterbuck obtained a licence at Aylesbury Assizes and was allowed to officiate whilst the case was pending. The dissenting minister took his case to a London court, but failed and then considered applying for a presentation from the Protector, Oliver Cromwell. Meanwhile, the Commissioners began to delay the matter so that new law suits could be initiated. By now, Thomas was getting tired of fighting his case and with costs mounting, he resigned his right and title to the Rectory. The patron offered it to another, who was then ejected by force after a troop of horse was called in from Aylesbury. Thus it was that Thomas Clutterbuck was deemed to have been sequestered from the living and at the Restoration, it was his successor who was restored. (*Lipscombe, 'History of Buckinghamshire', (1847), may hold more detailed information*).

Later, Thomas was offered the Rectory of Leckford, Hampshire, which for a brief time after the Restoration, was in the patronage of King Charles II; at the same time, he was also offered the sinecure rectory of Llandrillo in Edeirion, Monmouth. The Leckford parish registers have not survived prior to 1757 and it is not known when he took possession. However, he did not remain long and by 1662 had been installed Rector of St Mary's, Southampton, which remained his home for the rest of his life.

It should have been a valuable living, in the patronage of the bishop, but there were problems connected with ownership of the tithes that had been included in the terms of a 100 year lease. Under the pretence that they had belonged to a dissolved chantry, an unnamed adversary had tried to carry away the title and alienate them from St Mary's. Thomas Clutterbuck, on being collated to the Rectory, ejected his opponent and quietly enjoyed the tithes and all the lands that went with them and they continued to be held by his successors. Meanwhile, in 1669 a Royal mandate had conferred on him the degree of D.D.

The church to which he had moved was in a bad state of repair, but it would be many years before the start of a restoration programme. In 1686, shortly after he became Archdeacon of Winchester, the work began in a 'niggardly fashion', but a disastrous fire destroyed it all in 1706, just a few years after his death.

Dr Clutterbuck also had interests in the north of the county, for conveyances survive with details of title to Lockerley Farm, dated around 1682. In this he was joined by his unmarried daughter Mary and this is the only reference to his family that has been found.

He did not serve as a prebendary, but in July 1684 was installed Archdeacon of Winchester, a position he held until his death in November 1700. Thus it was that his connection with The Close came at a time when much of the post-Restoration work was over and life was settling down into a regular pattern once more.

It seems probable that in his last weeks he suffered from a terminal illness, for his successor as Archdeacon was installed on the day following Dr Clutterbuck's death. He was buried at St Mary's, Southampton, where some entries in the parish registers are duplicated and others are not in chronological order. Nevertheless, the following entry can be found out of place: '16 Nov [1700] Dr Thomas Clutterbuck R[everend]d of St Maries [was buried]'.

Searches have been made for his will in the Winchester Diocesan Records, but without success. However, reference has been found to it being proved, in an unknown court, on 8 Jan 1700/1, (Clutterbuck, III, 300) and is probably held at the Public Record Office.
[*A reference has been found suggesting that he was a benefactor of Emmanuel College, Cambridge and it is possible that more details may be found in E. Carter, The History of the University of Cambridge' ... (1753)*].

George Fulham

Archdeacon 1700 ~ 1702

1659 Born at Hampton Poyle, Oxfordshire
1676 Matriculated Christ Church, Oxford
1677 Magdalen College, Oxford
1680 BA, Magdalen College, Oxford
1682 Fellow, Magdalen College, Oxford
1683 MA, Magdalen College, Oxford
1685 Praelector of moral philosophy
1685 Rector Compton, Surrey
1690 Rector West Meon, Hants
1691 Rector Droxford, Hants
1692 Prebendary Winchester Cathedral
1694 DD Magdalen College Oxford
1700 Rector St Mary's Southampton
1700 Archdeacon of Winchester
1702 Died and Buried in Winchester Cathedral

George was born in 1659/60, one of several sons of the Revd Edward Fulham of Westminster and Hampton Poyle, Oxfordshire. His father was later installed a Canon of Windsor and Archdeacon of Llandaff and had a colourful career in the church; he was chaplain to both King Charles I and II and in the *interregnum* was deprived of several benefices. Noteworthy also, was Edward Fulham's meeting with the Earl of Clarendon who presented him with a great silver cup which was highly regarded.

At about the age of twenty-five, George Fulham was presented to the Rectory of Compton, Surrey, a village at the foot of the Hog's Back where his father owned the Manor of Eastborough with the advowson of the local church. Edward Fulham had already served the parish as their rector and amongst his gifts to the church were a flagon and paten. Only a few years before George's birth, he had also acquired the manor of Compton Eastbury and it was intended that George should eventually inherit it together with the precious silver cup. Dr Edward Fulham died in 1694 aged 90 and George came into his inheritance, which included all his father's books. However, following George's untimely death a few years later and that of his son soon after in 1710, it all passed out of the immediate family.

In 1690, George Fulham was installed Rector of West Meon, Hampshire, where he had the benefit of a curate's

Sources

- Friends of the PRO Index to PCC Probate records 1701-1749
- Win Cath Lib: Chapter Book 1696-1739
- Robert Boumphrey, Heraldic Index
- A J Jewers, Winchester Cathedral Inscriptions etc 4 Boxes, Box 2 p 207
- B M Kipling, Index to Monumental Inscriptions
- *International Genealogical Index*, (1992)
- *Al. Oxon* vol II, (1891)
- Harleian Society, *Musgrave's Obituaries*, vol v (1900-1)
- Phillimore, *Hampshire Parish Registers*, vol iv (1902)
- *The Lives of the Bishops of Winchester*, 2 vols (1827)
- J Vaughan, *Winchester Cathedral* ..., (1919)
- *Victoria County History, Surrey*, (1911)

help and in the following year was also introduced to the near-by Rectory of Droxford. Both parishes lie in the Meon Valley and the advowsons were in the hands of the bishop; three years later he was installed a Prebendary of Winchester Cathedral.

He did not sever his connections with Surrey and it was at about this time that he must have married Catherine Evelyn, eldest daughter of George Evelyn of Wotton Park, which lies not far from Compton. An heiress and over ten years his junior, she was the eldest daughter of George Evelyn, a nephew of John Evelyn the diarist. It was to be a short and sad marriage; they had two sons and the first was probably born early in 1698 and given his father's name of George. The following year their second son William was born, but Catherine did not recover and died soon after. She was buried in the cathedral and a small white marble tablet in the floor of the south retroquire aisle, is her memorial. The marble slab, now very worn and becoming illegible records: *S.I. / Catharina Conjux / Georgii Fulham / STP / hujus Ecclesiae / Praebendarii / 1699.* It was originally surmounted by the arms of Evelyn of Wotton Park impaled by those of Dr Fulham, but very little now survives. Her infant son lived only two more months and lies buried near his mother. Meanwhile, George Fulham continued to take an active part in the Chapter and served for a period as Vice-Dean.

On 17 Nov 1700, he was installed Archdeacon on the day immediately following the burial of his predecessor. His tenure lasted just two years and he died on 23 November 1702. The General Chapter met for its routine meeting on the same day, after 'those present' had already been listed. It is the habit of many committee secretaries to prepare their minutes of meetings in advance and to correct the mistake, after his name had to be added the simple entry 'mort'. He was only 40 years old and it would seem that he had met a sudden death, for it must have been unexpected by his colleagues. Five days later, he was buried in the cathedral.

He made his will just two days before his death and in it he left almost all his estate to his surviving son George, who was still a minor. George was put into the care of his father's servant Sarah and the trustees appointed to serve during his minority included the Dean of Salisbury and other eminent men of the day. The Archdeacon had been a wealthy man and his estates at Westminster and Chiddingfold were to be sold for the benefit of nephews and nieces. An interesting item added that if his son should die, the residue was to be used for the benefit of widows and orphans of clergymen. Thirty years earlier, Morley College, a charity for the widows of clergy, had been built in The Outer Close and the Dean and Chapter acted as trustees. Dr Fulham had been present at Chapter meetings when the suitability of applicants had been discussed and it seems probable that he had this charity in mind when he made his will, now held in the Public Record Office (PCC: W. Prob 11/467, sig 194 STP).

Unfortunately, his son George outlived his parents by only a few years and died aged eleven in 1710. He was buried near the other members of his family and it has to be assumed that Morley College was then able to benefit from the late Archdeacon's estate.

Ralph Brideoake

Archdeacon 1702 ~ 1743

1664 Born at Thistleworth (Isleworth)
1678 Entered Winchester College
1681 Matriculated Trinity College Oxford
1685 BA New College Oxford
1688 MA New College Oxford
1688 Fellow Winchester College
1701 Rector Crawley Hants
1702 Rector St Mary's Southampton
1702 Archdeacon Winchester
1720 Prebendary Hereford Cathedral
1742/3 Died at St Mary's, Southampton

Born at Isleworth *c.*1665, his father was the Revd Ralph Brideoake who was already in his fifties when his son was born and only one other sibling has been identified: his brother John was born the following year. His father had a distinguished career, notably as chaplain to William Lenthall, (Speaker of the House of Commons 1640-1653) and at the Restoration, chaplain to King Charles II, then Dean of Salisbury and in 1675, Bishop of Chichester. However, the young Ralph soon lost the guidance of his father, for he was only about fourteen years of age when the Bishop died. This sad event must have occurred at about the same time as Ralph's arrival at Winchester College. In time, he moved to Trinity College and then New College Oxford, from where he was awarded his M.A. and from where he returned on his appointment as a fellow at Winchester College.

Having spent twenty years in academic life, Ralph was presented to his first living in 1701 when the Bishop offered him the Rectory of Crawley, Hampshire. However, the following year he resigned on becoming Archdeacon of Winchester and being collated to St. Mary's Southampton. It seems probable that he had not taken up residence at Crawley, for since the Restoration all the duties had been performed by the curate, who served the parish for 46 years. Brideoake's successor at Crawley held it for the next 53 years and is generally accepted as the first resident Rector.

Sources

- Win Cath Lib: Chapter Book 1696-1739, 1739-1776
- A J Jewers, Winchester Cathedral Inscriptions etc 4 Boxes, Box 3 p 219
- HRO 35M48/10/22 Liber Visitacionis or Call Book (1743)
- SRO PR5/1/2 St Mary's Southampton Parish Register Ts
- Friends of the PRO Index to Probate Records 1701-1749
- T F Kirby, *Winchester Scholars,* (1888)
- *Al Oxon vol 1, (1891)*
- *Gentleman's Magazine*, vol xiii p 163 (1743)
- Harleian Society, *Musgrave's Obituaries*, (1900-1)
- F W Pledge, *Crawley*, (1907)
- *Victoria County History Hampshire*, (1914)
- ed. W R Ward, *Parson and Parish in 18th Century Hampshire: replies to Bishops' Visitations*, (1995)
- Letter from Miss J Williams, Hereford Cathedral Librarian, held by SG.

The church of St Mary's at Southampton was in a poor state of repair when he arrived, but it had a valuable glebe and owned tithes locally and in the surrounding district. In 1706, a few years after his arrival, there was a disastrous fire and much of the church burnt down and the registers and other documents were lost. The old chancel survived, but in a poor state and in 1711, he endeavoured to attach a new nave, but it was not a success. Attempts to repair the chancel failed and in 1723 he rebuilt it largely at his own expense. He was highly praised by the bishop for his endeavours, but the new building was considered by some to be 'most unlovely'. However, there were others who agreed with the bishop and thought it a 'fine modern church'. Later in life, he commented that he had been a great benefactor to the parish by building the church and chancel and the parsonage house, all of which had cost him almost £5000. Little, if anything, of his building survives.

Meanwhile, in 1720 he was installed a Prebendary of Hereford Cathedral, a position he held until his death in 1743. Clearly the prebend was an honour and source of income, for it would appear that he had very little personal connection with Hereford.

It is probable that he enjoyed a scholarly life and enjoyed writing. It was common-place for incumbents to reply to the Bishop's visitation queries with one-word comments, but that was not Ralph Brideoake's way. In 1725, he went to considerable trouble to make full and detailed replies to all the questions and has left a valuable account of his parish and parishioners.

His life continued at Southampton and in The Close and one of the most important contributions made by the cathedral clergy at that time, was the foundation of a hospital in the city centre. It was instigated by one of Brideoake's colleagues and was the first to be established outside London and began the spread of hospitals nationwide.

Ralph Brideoake was nearly eighty when he died in 1743. The records of his visitations survive and the final call book, which had been prepared shortly before his death, became the first of his successor's. In it, there is a memorandum of his death: 'The 17th day of March 1742/3 the Revd Ralph Briddoake (sic) ... died at St Maries ab[ou]t 6 in the morning.'

It was his special wish to be buried in his parish church, on the south side of the chancel in a 'handsome compartment not unlike my mother on the north side expressing the titles I carryed and the principle actions of my life in such modest inscription as I shall cause to be prepared for that purpose'. The burial register recorded that on 23 March 1742/3: 'Archdeacon of Winchester and the worthy Rector of this Parish for upwards of 40 years, buried in the Chancel of St Maries to the great grief of all his Friends and of this Parish in general.'

His will, made about four months before his death, survives in the Public Record Office, PROB 11/726 sig 150. He did not approve of giving gold rings, but instead requested that medals be struck to preserve his memory and distributed amongst his friends and relatives.

Robert Eden

Archdeacon 1743 ~ 1749 and 1756 ~ 1759

1701 Born at Newcastle upon Tyne
c.1716 Matriculated from Brasenose College, Oxford
1720 BA Lincoln College, Oxford
1723 MA University College, Oxford
1733 Proctor at Oxford
1734 BD
1754 DD
1738 Rector Headbourne Worthy
1743 1st term as Archdeacon of Winchester
1747 Prebendary Worcester Cathedral
1749 Prebendary Winchester Cathedral
1756 Rector Michelmersh
1756 2nd term as Archdeacon
1759 Died and buried in Winchester Cathedral

Sources

- HRO 21M65/A/2/1 Episcopal Registers
- HRO 169M84W/20, 22 Texts of sermons
- HRO 31M71/T39 Title to Land at Liss 1712-1760,
- HRO 91M72/PZ16/1-3 Michelmersh Parish Records
- Win Cath Lib: Robert Boumphrey, Heraldic Index
- Chapter Books 1696-1739, 1739-1776
- Letter held by SG from David Morrison Librarian/archivist, Worcester Cathedral, quoting
- J M Horn, *Fasti Ecclesiae Anglicanae 1541-1857 VII Ely, Norwich, Westminster and Worcester Diocese, (1992).*
- *Alumni Cantab*, Part 1 vol 2, (reprint 1974)
- *Al Oxon*, (1891)
- *International Genealogical Directory*, (1992)
- ed. W P W Phillimore, *Hampshire Parish Registers*, vol iv, (1903)
- F Bussby, *Winchester Cathedral*, (1979)
- Anon, *St Swithun Headbourne Worthy*, (n.d. c 1970)
- *V C H Hampshire*, vol iii, (1914)
- ed. W R Ward, *Parson and Parish in 18th Century Hampshire: replies to Bishop's Visitations,* (1995)
- J H Slessor, *Notes on the Church of Headbourne Worthy*. (1888), HRO 21M62/PZ10
- B Carpenter Turner, *A History of Winchester*, (1992)

Robert was one of the sons of Robert Eden Snr, a merchant and at one time Sheriff of Newcastle upon Tyne; he was baptised at All Saints parish church, on 26 August 1701. At 15, he matriculated at Brasenose College, Oxford and in 1720 was awarded a B.A. from Lincoln College, followed three years later with an M.A. His studies continued and in 1733, he assumed the role of proctor and became responsible for the enforcement of university regulations. His B.D. followed in 1734/5 and it must have been soon afterwards that he began to look for a suitable benefice.

He achieved this in 1738 when he was installed Rector at the tiny village of Headbourne Worthy, Hampshire, having been presented by University College, Oxford. Despite other moves and advancements, he remained Rector for the next twenty years. The church still retains much of its Saxon heritage, but unfortunately it stands on a high water-table, from which it has always suffered. During the period of Robert Eden's incumbency, little work to the fabric appears to have been done. Indeed, when eventually the church needed a new ceiling, it was the parishioners who forced him to provide one. In 1754, it was agreed '... that he [Robert Eden] may inclose for his own use a piece of glebe land containing about 4 acres adjoining to the Rector's several, on consideration of the said Rector's new cieling (sic) the church at his own expense.' It was also in that year that he was awarded his doctorate.

Meanwhile, he had been installed Archdeacon of Winchester on 14 April 1743. Soon after, he preached on the 'Connexion of Publick and Private Happiness', at the Assize in Winchester and it is one of at least two printed sermons that have survived.

It was now that he probably met his future wife Martha Lowth who was living with her father in Winchester. Martha was the daughter of the distinguished Hebrew scholar and theologian William Lowth, Rector of Buriton and Prebendary of the Cathedral. She was one of at least three children and had been born whilst her parents still lived at Buriton. Two years after his installation as Archdeacon, Robert and Martha were married in the cathedral on 20 June 1745 and a daughter Mary, was born the following year. In November 1747, he was installed a prebendary at Worcester Cathedral, which was an honour and an additional source of income.

Five years after his installation as Archdeacon of Winchester, he resigned and was collated to a prebend that had recently been vacated by the death of one of his colleagues. He served in that capacity for a further ten years, whilst two others fulfilled his former role of Archdeacon. One served for just one year before resigning and the second, Robert Lowth, was the brother of Martha, his wife. Eden continued to participate in the life of The Close and preached in the cathedral at Dr Hoadly's visitation as Chancellor of the Diocese on 24 September 1754. His subject was 'Truth and Love in Matters of Religion' and this is the second of his sermons to have survived.

In 1756, Robert Lowth also resigned as Archdeacon and Dr Eden was once more installed in his place. It was to be a busy year for him. He resigned his prebendal stall at Worcester, but whilst still Rector at Headbourne Worthy, was installed Rector at Michelmersh. It has to be assumed that he resigned from Worcester to allow more time for his life in Hampshire. It has been observed that 'Hampshire clergy were notorious non-residers ... of the 250 parishes responding to the [Bishop's Visitation] inquiry of 1725, 137 had incumbents who at some time during their tenure held other preferments.' (Ward p.xviii).

Robert took his turn as Vice-Dean and at each mid-summer meeting of the Chapter, the prebendaries chose one month in the coming year when they would remain in residence. At their meetings, they were often concerned about the upkeep of the roads and of particular interest to Dr Eden was the annual cost of repairs to the road to Headbourne Worthy. He also acted as the Chapter Treasurer, in which capacity he made the annual payment of £2.0.0 to the County Gaol, for the benefit of the prisoners.

Despite this activity, the decades of the 1740s and 50s seem to have been generally comfortable and pleasant ones for Robert and his wife, with her Lowth relatives living near by. For almost fifty years, both families retained an interest in land at Liss, Surrey, which between 1712 and 1760 generated a large bundle of documents connected with the title. Socially, The Close was a lively and entertaining place, but one seldom entered by the townspeople. Robert's love of music led him to join with Chancellor Hoadly and between them they founded an amateur orchestra of local clerics. It was a pleasant life and indeed, one contemporary wrote, 'The life of a prebendary is a pretty easy way of dawdling away one's time; praying, walking, visiting; and as little study as your heart would wish.'

Robert's second term as Archdeacon ended with his death on 11 July 1759, at the age of 58. He was buried in the cathedral, in the south nave aisle, where the ledger stone is emblazoned with his arms: Gules on a chevron [Argent] between three garbs [Or] as many escallops [Sable]. He was survived by his wife, who outlived him by forty years and when she died on 23 March 1798 was buried beside her husband.

Nicholas Lechmere

Archdeacon 1749 ~ 1750

1700 Born probably London
1718 Matriculated Wadham College, Oxford
1723 BA
1725 MA Merton College, Oxford
1733 Rector Warnford, Hants
1749 Archdeacon of Winchester
1750 Prebendary Winchester Cathedral
1770 Died and Buried in the Cathedral

Nicholas was born in 1700/1, son of Richard Lechmere of London, but nothing more is known of his parents. His famous namesakes, including Lord Lechmere and others, many of whom were born in the Hanley Castle district of Worcestershire, were leading MPs, barristers and judges, but no connection has been proved. Nicholas' baptism, possibly somewhere in London, has not been found, but his given name was popular in the Worcestershire family, which might indicate a collateral branch.

He attended Wadham College, Oxford and later took a B.A. and then an M.A. from Merton College. It is not known what happened to him between his Master's degree in 1725 and arrival as the new rector in Warnford, Hampshire in 1733. This quiet backwater in the Meon Valley seems to have suited him and his life style and he remained there for the rest of his life, leading what appears to have been the life of a typical country gentleman.

His predecessor had lived only two years in the parish, but in that short time had rebuilt the Parsonage House, largely at his own expense. He had admitted that he did not have the patience to await the funding, but it was Lechmere who was to benefit from his industry. The rectory stood in a walled garden, set back from the road and was of a considerable size, having 25 rooms with 15 fireplaces.

Sources

- Win Cath Lib: Chapter Book 1739-1776
- A J Jewers, Winchester Cathedral Inscriptions etc 4 Boxes, Box 2 p 103
- HRO 21M65/A/2/1 Episcopal Registers
- HRO 5M66 Warnford Original Parish Registers
- Ibid. PW4 Warnford Churchwardens' Account and Rate Book
- *Gentleman's Magazine,* vol xl p 487, (1770)
- J Hurst & others, *Warnford* ..., (2nd ed 1970)
- *Al Ox*, 1715-1886, part 3 (1888)
- *D N B*
- Norfolk Record Office, *Virtual Norfolk: Jacobitism,* www.uea.ac.uk/his
- Harleian Society, *Musgrave's Obituaries*, (1900-1)
- Phillimore, *Hampshire Parish Registers*, vol iv (1902)
- F T Madge, *Hampshire Inductions*, (1918)

Until Lechmere's arrival, the entries in the parish registers had been poorly kept, but there was a remarkable change in 1734 and from then onwards the vital events in his parishioners' lives seem to have been accurately recorded. The poor rates were collected and disbursed and he appears to have taken an active part in the life of the village, for occasionally he was called upon to place his signature amongst those of the churchwardens. He also had the administration of a small charity which had been bequeathed to the parish by one of Jane Austen's ancestors.

Twenty years into his incumbency, in 1752, the total income from the parish rates amounted to almost £100.00, but that has to be compared with the Rector's payment of £10.00, which together with the rent from the lord of the manor, raised the income to nearly £150.00 per annum. Also in that year, the church roof had to be repaired. Its last restoration had been in Tudor times, when it was re-covered in lead. Now, in order to pay for the repairs, the lead was sold and slates were purchased as replacements. This proved to be a disastrous decision, for it led to years of recurring trouble, largely due to the low pitch of the roof, which was always intended to carry lead. When covered in slates, the pitch was not sufficient to keep out the rain and the battens beneath slowly decayed. A hundred years later, the whole structure was rotten so that even vibration caused by the singing of the congregation was thought to present a danger.

Nicholas, with his wife Mary, seems to have enjoyed the life of a country parson, spending his time writing letters and attending when required in Winchester. There were no children and except in the mid-1740s, nothing to disturb his quiet life. He was surrounded by about 150 parishioners and there were no dissenting chapels, no school and no curate, but the George Inn, which still stands to-day, was a significant stop on the road south and must have seen some passing activity.

A letter survives in the Norfolk Record Office which not only gives an insight into his daily life, but also has a national interest. The Jacobite uprising in 1745 was causing much concern and there were rumours of French landings on the south coast. At that time, fear of invasion was a daily concern in southern England. It was then that Lechmere addressed a letter to Sir Thomas Drury in London. He acknowledged that his only pleasure was in letter-writing, but the covers that Sir Thomas had franked for him (signed so as to ensure them being sent free of charge), were nearly all used and he was requesting a fresh supply ...

> *... the only amusement I have in a little country village consisting of Farmers only, and what I wou[l]d be sorry to be without at any time, and especially at the present, which is the most critical that I can remember. I live about twelve miles from our coast, between Chichester and Portsmouth, and it is impossible to express the terrors we have been in on account of the intended french (sic) invasion...*
> *14 Jan[ua]ry 1745/6*

He went on to explain that on one occasion, some smugglers had landed with their goods and were met by armed conspirators waiting on shore, but they had been mistaken for French troops. At the same time, the English fleet hovering out at sea, had been interpreted as a French squadron. Nerves were clearly on edge. The farmers to whom he referred in his letter were mainly cultivating wheat, barley and oats, but only a few years after this letter was written, a paper mill started production, which surely must have been of interest to him.

In April 1749, he was installed as Archdeacon, but served for only twelve months. On 10 April 1750 he was admitted to a Prebend left vacant by the death of a colleague and immediately resigned as Archdeacon. He continued in this capacity until his death, twenty years later.

His wife Mary died in 1764 and was buried in the north nave aisle of the cathedral. When Nicholas died in October 1770, at his special request he was buried beside her. The memorial inscription includes his M.A. and service as a prebendary, but his time as Archdeacon was unrecorded. It has to be assumed that by then, his relatives had forgotten a brief interlude of over twenty years before. Aged 69, he had served the people of Warnford, as their Rector, for nearly forty years. His will, made just a few months after his wife's death, survives in the PRO: PCC Jenner 402. Later, two further members of the Lechmere family were interred in the same place: Rebecca (Nicholas' niece) and her husband Thomas G Waller.

Robert Lowth

Archdeacon 1750 ~ 1756

1722 Winchester College
1729 Matriculated St John's College, Oxford; Fellow, New College, Oxford
1733 BA (Oxon)
1737 MA (Oxon)
1739 Vicar of Overton, Hampshire
1741 Professor of Poetry, Oxford
1750 Archdeacon of Winchester
1753 Rector of East Woodhay, Hampshire
1754 DD (Oxon)
1755 Prebendary of Durham, Chaplain in Ordinary to His Majesty George III and Rector of Sedgefield
1765 FRS London; FRS Göttingen
1766 Bishop of St David's; Bishop of Oxford
1777 Privy Councillor; Bishop of London; Dean of Chapel Royal and Privy Councillor

Sources

- An essential basic source is *Sermons and other Remains/Memories of Robert Lowth*, one of 8 volumes of *Robert Lowth (1710-1787): The Major works* (1995) Routledge/Thoemmes Press, with an introduction by David A Reibel. This must be supported by *Critics of the Bible 1724-1873* (1989) ed. J Doury, and Murray Poston's *Prophet and Poet. The Bible and the Growth of Romanticism* (1965) Faber & Faber.
- Other sources include: *The Dictionary of National Biography, The Oxford Dictionary of the Christian Church, The Wainscot Book* (Crook), *Alumni Oxonienses* (Fowler), *Winchester Cathedral 1079-1979* (1979) Bussby, Cave, *Archivist Fulham Parish Church*, G H Blore's *Some Wykehamists of the 18th Century* (1944) privately printed, James Boswell's *Life of Samuel Johnson*; *Natural Supernaturalism* by M H Abrams (1973) Norton, New York, and B Hepworth's *Robert Lowth* (1978) Boston. This last contains an interesting error, requiring the reader's indulgence. He is informed that the river Itchen (Hants) flows into the river Thames at Hampton Court. Doubtless a misinterpretation of Lowth's (Katherine-Hill) line: 'The peaceful Itchen's gentle waters slide;/Thrice happy stream! which visits Hampton's towers . . .'.

Before houses were numbered, No. 5 The Close, Winchester was described as 'The First House on the Left Hand in Dumb Alley (now called Dome Alley)'. This is where the Revd. Prebendary William Lowth and his wife, Margaret, were living when on 27 November 1710 their second son, Robert, was born. He was baptised 7 December 1710.

Prebendary William Lowth (1660-1732) M.A., B.D. (Oxon), Rector of Buriton with the Chapelry of Petersfield, also vicar of Overton, Hampshire, was a distinguished theologian. A Hebrew, Greek and Latin scholar, he was recognised for his *Directions for the Profitable Reading of the Holy Scriptures* and his 'excellent continuation of Bishop Patrick's *Commentary on the Old Testament*'.

The Lowth family originally came from Lincolnshire (Louth?) but had settled in Sawtry, near Little Gidding, Huntingdonshire. Robert's grandfather was an Apothecary in Ludgate, London and in the Great Fire 1666 was 'burnt out'. Robert's great-grandfather, Rev Simon Lowth, was a sequestered Royalist, later Rector of Tilehurst, Berkshire, and another son of his, also Rev Simon Lowth D.D., became a fervent supporter of the non-jurors. Robert's mother, Margaret (née Pitt, with kinship to the Earl of Chatham) was from Blanchford, Dorset.

Robert's eldest brother, the Revd William Lowth M.A.,

was Prebendary of Winchester and Vicar of Lewisham. Of these three sisters, Martha married Revd Dr John Sturges, Prebendary of Winchester, and Rector of Alderstoke. Margaret became the wife of Revd Dr Eden, Prebendary of Winchester and Archdeacon. Elizabeth died unmarried.

Robert entered Winchester College in 1722, where he developed his interest in poetry. His first poem, *On a Thunderstorm by night* was written at the age of 14. *Katherine Hill* (1729) was published in the *Gentleman's Magazine* (1753). Another long poem *The Genealogy of Christ* as it is represented on the East Window in Winchester Chapel (replaced since) (1729) is said to have been written as an imposition.

It is recorded that he matriculated at St John's College Oxford (his father's old college) on 26 March 1729 and was elected Fellow of New College in the same year. Graduating B.A. 1733, elected M.A. 1737, he took holy orders and in 1735 he was instituted vicar of Overton, Hampshire. At the age of 30 he was appointed Professor of Poetry, Oxford, succeeding his friend Joseph Spence (and before Spence, the two Thomas Wartons). Robert had been applying himself to a considerable work on the subject of vice and virtue *The Choice of Hercules* published later (1747). G F Handel used this to compose a serenata of the same name (1749). It was during this Oxford period that Robert delivered, in Latin, his celebrated lectures on Hebrew poetry, published in Latin 1753. In 1748 he accompanied the man to whom he dedicated these lectures, Henry Bilson-Legge, the Ambassador, to Berlin. Another commission followed, as tutor to the Lords George (future Marquis of Hartington) and his brother Frederick Cavendish on their 'grand tour' of Europe, clearly successfully.

On his return to England Robert was appointed Archdeacon of Winchester, relinquishing both his Professorship and Fellowship (1750). Two years later he married Mary, daughter of Lawrence Jackson, a lawyer, of Christchurch, Hampshire. She was the niece of Dean Cheyney of Winchester. They had seven children.

1753 saw Robert's collation of the rectory of East Woodhay, near Newbury, and the publication of his lectures on Hebrew poetry for which, in 1754, the University of Oxford created him D.D., by diploma.

When the Marquis of Hartington (Duke of Devonshire) was appointed Lord Lieutenant of Ireland in 1755, Lowth accompanied him as first chaplain. He was offered the

Bishopric of Limerick, but being disinclined to remain in Ireland, obtained permission to transfer the offer to Dr James Leslie, Prebendary of Durham, thereby receiving in exchange that 'golden prebend' worth some £600 per annum and also the rectory of Sedgefield, Durham. It so happened at that time that another Prebendary was the Reverend William Warburton and it is likely that minds soon began to clash; a bright young scholar versus a man, seven years senior of wide-reading with a 'rough intellectual vigour' and of quarrelsome temperament receiving £100 less *per annum*. Within a year there was sharp correspondence between these two arising from certain passages in Lowth's lectures (1753) which Warburton felt were aired at his own theories concerning the Book of Job in his *Divine Legation of Moses demonstrated* (1737). Upon Lowth's sharp denial there seemed to be an amicable truce, but animosity flared again in 1765 when Warburton, now Bishop of Gloucester, renewed his complaint in a later edition of *Divine Legation*. The contest firmly entered the public domain with Lowth's amusing and sarcastic riposte in *A Letter to the Author of 'Divine Legation' in Answer by a late Professor of Oxford*, which attracted the attention of no less a person than His Majesty King George III. James Boswell records that on the great occasion when Samuel Johnson was received by His Majesty for conversation he was asked what he thought about the controversy; 'Warburton has the most general, most scholastic learning, Lowth is the more correct scholar. I do not know which of them calls names best'. And on Johnson replying to a question said that there 'wasn't much argument in the case', the King made his notable observation 'Why, truly, when it comes to calling names, argument is pretty well at an end.' Both were good men: Warburton, admired by Johnson ('He praised me at a time when praise was of value to me' – *Essay on Macbeth*), was a generous and loving family man. He had once been an attorney. Edward Gibbon observed that 'Warburton retains the habit of an attorney and continually mistakes wrangling for reasoning'. Robert Lowth, a florid and stout man, said by his son to be moody and short tempered had, nevertheless, a refined manner. He was a formidable adversary and his polished sarcasm was exercised in controversy with others.

On 15 June 1766 he was consecrated Bishop of St David's but a few months later was translated to Oxford. In 1777 he was translated to London. A man who showed tolerance to non-conformers (and much compassion to a Dr Harwood), he had as Bishop a notable encounter with John Wesley. Wesley, seven years his senior, had been up at Oxford with him (Christchurch and Fellow of Lincoln College) when after 'conversion' by

William Law's *A Serious Call to a Devout and Holy Life* (1728) he, Wesley, had formed his 'Holy Club' and Methodism (1729). At a dinner Lowth insisted that Wesley sit above him at table. Both deferred as to place, but Lowth settled the matter by saying that he was deaf in one ear and could best hear Wesley if he sat below him. Wesley's journal entry was: 'Lowth's whole behaviour worthy of a Christian bishop.'

The Church of England owes Robert Lowth a debt of gratitude for his stand against an iniquitous practice that had grown up in general resignation bonds. He refused to carry out an institution to a living because the patron had effected a bond from the appointee to resign on demand with a penalty of £3,000 on failure to comply. The patron took action in the Court of Common Pleas and won the case. The Bishop appealed and lost. Then 'He appealed to the House of Lords, and Bonds of Resignation were declared illegal' ('adjudged to be simoniacal'). In a *Letter to the Clergy of his Diocese* 12 April 1784, he explains in detail the pains he went to so that 'this part of the clergy be, as they should be, freeholders in their own benefices, and not tenants at will.'

Like his great-grandfather, Robert was a royalist. It is said that he used regularly to entertain his episcopal brethren on 4 June, King George III's birthday. In 1783 their Majesties visited him several times. Richard Hurd, Bishop of Worcester had recommended that Robert should succeed Frederick Cornwallis as Archbishop of Canterbury. Even though his Majesty tried to persuade him to accept, he had to decline on the grounds of ill-health. He suffered from gout, the painful misery of stones in the urinary bladder, and from stones in the gall bladder (revealed at autopsy). Besides, he grieved much over the loss of five of his seven children: Thomas-Henry the eldest son died June 1778 aged 25; Mary, the eldest daughter died July 1768, aged 13 and was buried at Cuddesdon, Oxford (a monument with epitaph by the father); the second daughter, Frances, aged 25 died suddenly presiding at the tea table in the presence of her parents and friends. 'Take this,' she said 'to the Bishop of Bristol.' Immediately the cup and her hand fell together upon the salver, and she instantly expired' (July 1783). The fourth and fifth daughters, Margaret and Charlotte died in infancy and were buried in St James' church, Piccadilly.

Robert Lowth caused a family tomb to be erected in the churchyard of All Saints' parish church, Fulham (Fulham Palace being included in the parish). Thomas-Henry was interred first; Margaret and Charlotte were reinterred there; Frances in 1783; Bishop Robert, himself who died 3 November 1878 (interred 10 November); Mary, his wife, 1803; Martha 1812, and much later one of his grandsons, George Thomas Lowth of Hinton, Hampshire and Grove House, Chiswick who died 31 December 1893.

'The tomb is tall and rectangular and is close to the east end of All Saints', near the external steps leading down to the vestry cellar. The condition is now somewhat worn and parts of the inscription are not very clear. There is the coat of arms of the Bishops of London and another coat, very worn, which is presumably Bishop Lowth's family coat.'

English grammar and English poetry also owe a debt of gratitude to Robert Lowth. It is said that he regarded himself as the best writer of English prose, and with good reason. His *Short Introduction to English Grammar* published anonymously in 1762 was much praised and became the standard Grammar for many years. His clear and easy-to-read style can be appreciated in his book on *The Life of William Wykeham* (1758) which was dedicated to Benjamin Hoadly, Bishop of Winchester (1734-61) who had helped him so much in his career. The book makes enjoyable reading and deserves to be preserved. Of Lowth's sermons, the *Visitation Sermon* (before the Bishop of Durham) (1758) is frequently cited. It reveals that as a man of his time, at ease with the Enlightenment, Robert Lowth is able to demonstrate clearly that Christianity can, with its Pilot, ride out any storm and continue on its course.

The change from the Neo-classical to the Romantic style of poetry owes something to Lowth's abiding interest in orientalism and the Hebrew of the Psalms, manifest in his 34 lectures, delivered in Latin between 1741-1750 on the *Sacred Poetry of the Hebrews (Praelectiones Academicae de Sacra Poesi Hebraeorum).* Published in Latin 1753, and translated into English by G Gregory 1878, their worth was recognised immediately. J D Michaelis of Göttingen translated them into German in 1763 (Lowth was elected FRS Göttingen and FRS London in 1765).

Lowth, understanding the immense difficulty in translating poetry, had to 'think' and 'be' Hebrew. Becoming sensitive to the ancient use of antiphony ('And the women answered one another as they played, and said, Saul hath slain his thousands, and David his ten thousands' 1 Sam 18.7), he discerned a poetic form, not of metre, that he termed 'parallelism'; 'so that in two lines . . . things for the most part shall answer things, and words to words as if fitted to each other as a kind of rule or measure.' He identified three main species of parallelism:

The Synonymous	'When Israel came out of Egypt; The House of Jacob from a strange people' Ps.114
The Antithetical	'The blows of a friend are faithful; But the kisses of an enemy are treacherous.' Prov.27
Synthetic or Constructional	where sentences answer one another: *'The judgements of JEHOVAH are truth, they are just altogether.* *More desirable than gold, or much fine gold;* *And sweeter than honey, or the dropping of honey-combs' Ps.19*

Twenty-five years later (1778) Lowth published his great work, *Isaiah: A New Translation*, continuing his exposition of the Sublime, the Passion, the Divine in Hebrew poetry. By insisting that the poetry of the Prophets be set out in the Bible as poetry and not as prose, his example has been followed ever since.

What he had revealed soon influenced English poets; Christopher Smart (*Jubilate Agno* – which includes 'My Cat Jeoffrey'), William Blake, S. T. Coleridge and William Wordsworth. Hannah More's (1745-1833) compliment in *Sensibility* is truly justified:

Illustrious Lowth! for him the muses wove
The fairest garland from their greenest grove ...
. . .
Born on the wing of Amos' son
He seized his mantle as the Prophet flew
And caught some portion of his spirit too.

Thomas Balguy

Archdeacon 1759 ~ 1795

1716 Born 27 September
1737 BA St. John's College, Cambridge
1741 MA and Fellowship at St. John's
1748 Prebendary of Lincoln and Rector of North Stoke
1757 Prebendary of Winchester
1759 Archdeacon of Winchester
1771 Vicar of Alton
1795 Died 19 January

John Balguy, the father of Thomas, was a scholarly clergyman who had contacts among the episcopal establishment and took part in the controversies of his time. He and his wife had both come from Sheffield but, by the time his son Thomas was born on the 27 September 1716, the family were living at Cox Close, near Ravensworth Castle, the home of his patron Sir Henry Liddell.

Thomas Balguy was educated at the Ripon Free School and then at St. John's College, Cambridge where he was admitted about 1732. He graduated B.A. in 1737 and M.A. in 1741 when he was elected to a Fellowship at St. John's. In 1744 he became assistant tutor to his friend Dr Powell, later Master of St. John's, and lectured on moral philosophy. He continued to teach in Cambridge, although he gave up his fellowship in 1748 when he was presented to the Rectory of North Stoke in Lincolnshire and a Prebend at Lincoln.

In 1757 Thomas Balguy obtained a Prebend at Winchester. Balguy stated that he owed his preferments to 'the favour and friendship of Bishop Hoadly'. His father, John Balguy, had taken part in the Bangorian Controversy which had caused a storm in the church in 1717 and the following years. He had supported Benjamin Hoadly, then Bishop of Bangor, and published pamphlets in defence of his views. In later years the connection continued and John Balguy was presented to a Prebend

Sources

- G.H.Blore. 'An Archdeacon of the 18th century, *Winchester Cathedral Record*, No. 20. 1951
- *Dictionary of National Biography*
- *General Biographical Dictionary* (ed. 1812)
- Venn, *Cambridge Alumni*
- F.Bussby, *Winchester Cathedral 1079-1979* (1979)
- B.Carpenter Turner, *Winchester*, 1980
- J.Crook, *The Wainscot Book* (1984)
- D.Fairer, *Correspondence of Thomas Warton* (1995)
- F.C.Mather, High Church Prophet (1992)
- J. Milner, *History and Survey of the Antiquities of Winchester*, (3rd Edn. 1839)
- J.Vaughan, *Winchester Cathedral, its Monuments and Memorials* (1919)

at Salisbury in 1728, by which time Hoadly was Bishop of that diocese. In 1734 Bishop Hoadly had been translated to Winchester and in 1757 Thomas Balguy became a Prebendary.

Two years later in 1759 Balguy became Archdeacon and in 1771 was appointed to the Vicarage of Alton, a living in the gift of the Dean and Chapter; at this time he resigned the Rectory of North Stoke. It seems that Balguy settled in Winchester in 1757 and continued to live here in a house in the Close for the rest of his life. For the first two years, he had the use of No. 12 until in September 1759 he moved to No. 9, now the Diocesan Offices. He did not marry and his household was managed by a cousin, Sarah Drake.

Among Thomas Balguy's friends were a number who have left references to him in their writings. Particulars of these and much else that is known about Balguy we owe to the researches of G. H. Blore who wrote about him for *Winchester Cathedral Record* in 1951. The following quotations are taken from this article.

> 'Of his Cambridge associates the most interesting was the poet Gray, who did not lose sight of his old friend when he migrated to Winchester. In one of those holiday tours which revealed Gray as a pioneer in the appreciation of English scenery, he stayed in our Close as Balguy's guest, and evidently enjoyed his company. Gray was fastidious in the choice of his friends, and we may guess that he found Balguy a man not only of wide reading, but also of congenial tastes, and of a caustic humour. He writes to a friend. 'We are as great as two peas'. Gray notes in 1758 that Balguy has already improved since he settled in Winchester - 'is freer and more open, and his heart less set upon the Mammon of Unrighteousness...'. Five years later he reports to a common friend that Balguy 'means to rule the Chapter,' and that he is proposing reforms in the administration of their Charities.'

Another friend was William Warburton, Bishop of Gloucester and a controversial writer, who mentions that Balguy suffered from gout and asthma, that 'he found the air of Winchester 'too sharp', and periodically repaired to Bath in search of a milder climate. We also learn that it was not his way to sit inactive at home. When he talked of returning from a Visitation to his easy chair, this meant only a change of activity, and some new subject of study. 'The chair', says Warburton, 'has a spring that tosses him out whenever a novelty in the literary or political worldcomes across his system.'

Among Balguy's other friends were Joseph Warton at the College and his brother, Thomas Warton, who was elected Professor of Poetry at Oxford in 1756 and became Poet Laureate in 1785. Both were prolific writers and Balguy features in their correspondence as someone they knew well. When Balguy published a volume of discourses and charges in 1785, Thomas Warton wrote from Oxford to Richard Hurd, Bishop of Worcester, that 'Dr. Balguy's Sermons are here most exceedingly liked'. He added that 'the Dissenters never received so sensible and so decisive a Confutation'. This comment indicates Balguy's general standpoint. While not a rigid upholder of tradition, he was concerned to maintain unity, and denounced clergy who attacked the Church. He opposed a move to relax subscription to the Thirty-nine Articles and when in 1776 a General Fast was proclaimed an account of the American war, he supported the government, urging the need for unity in time of crisis. In this last matter he took the opposite view to his friend, Jonathan Shipley, Dean of Winchester, at whose consecration Balguy preached in 1769 when Shipley became Bishop of Llandaff; while Balguy attacked the disloyalty of American rebels, Shipley became friendly with Benjamin Franklin and declared that 'I look upon North America as the only great nursery of freemen left on the face of the earth'.

Balguy had a reputation as a preacher, perhaps due in part to his father who is said to have burnt all his own sermons, wishing to ensure that his son should develop his talents and not be tempted into lazy habits. Among the discourses published in 1785 are several of the charges delivered to the clergy of his archdeaconry. The first, dated 1760, is chiefly about the conduct of the clergy and their way of life. As in matters of church order, he maintains a balanced view devoid of extremes; while warning clergy against shutting themselves up in their studies, he comments 'Love of letters may make us unsociable; love of society may make us illiterate'.

Perhaps this reflects a personal dilemma in a man of considerable learning and wide contacts. That he was widely known and esteemed is shown by the King's wish to make him Bishop of Gloucester after the death of William Warburton in 1779. In a letter of George III to the Prime Minister, Lord North, the king maintained that 'Dr. Balguy is the first man in point of reputation in the republic of letters of either University'. The offer was made but Balguy declined on grounds of health. The King's interest continued, for in the following year he was urging that Balguy should be released from his prebendal duties while continuing to enjoy the emoluments.

That the offer of preferment was of great significance to Balguy is evident from its being mentioned on his memorial in the cathedral. It is clear that he had serious health problems, specifically of failing sight which was mentioned among his reasons for refusal. As this exchange took place in 1780, it seems that he must have been suffering some degree of infirmity during the last fifteen years of his life. It cannot have been too disabling as it did not prevent his being a frequent borrower from the Cathedral Library of books on a variety of subjects including history, the formation of the earth, biography and maps. Nevertheless, his health problems may have caused him to curtail his activities and avoid involvement in local affairs which were demanding the attention of his colleagues at the time. The Roman Catholic John Milner (later Bishop) wrote of Balguy that 'being gifted with natural and acquired talents, which must have ensured him success and fame in any station that he might occupy, had yet the rare moderation of declining the highest dignity of his profession, when it was in his power to have risen to it'. Milner had been in Winchester since 1779, involved in the welfare of French prisoners as well as the local Catholic community and the building of the chapel in St. Peter Street. He must have known Balguy and this mention in a work published in 1798, only three years after Balguy's death, does not give the impression that he refers to someone who had withdrawn entirely from public life. However, it is likely that Balguy was not too actively involved in matters relating to the French emigré clergy, of whom 680 were living in the old royal palace by November 1793, and other matters of local import during the last few years of his life.

Thomas Balguy died on 19 January 1795 at his house in the Close. His monument in the Cathedral, in the south aisle of the nave, has lost some of its original ornament described by Milner as 'grapes and foliage of exquisite workmanship', but remains a dignified memorial to a man of learning and distinction.

Matthew Woodford

Archdeacon 1795 ~ 1807

*c.*1737 Born
1807 Died

Woodford was the son of Matthew Woodford of Southampton. Despite his long life, little is known of him. He was educated at Christ Church, Oxford, gaining a B.A. in 1759 and M.A. in 1762. The next record of him is as Rector of Tedmonton, Oxon. in 1780, the same year that he moved into No. 5 The Close, Winchester and became a prebendary of the Cathedral. He was appointed Rector of Crawley, Hampshire and of Calbourne in the Isle of Wight in the same year.

He became Archdeacon of Winchester in 1795, during the episcopacy of Brownlow North (1780-1820), a half-brother to Lord North. In 1798 he was appointed Rector of Chilbolton, with Upham, Hampshire and in May 1798 he moved to No. 5 The Close where he lived for the rest of his life.

He became Vice-Dean in 1806 and chaired Chapter meetings from time to time. Chapter minutes show that they were concerned with a wide range of financial and property matters, and also with the bestowal of certain benefices, often on sons of the clergy. Two particular items may indicate the minutiae of certain issues: the appointment, in 1806, of a clergy widow as Matron of Morley College (an almshouse in The Close) and, in the same year, the receipt of a written apology by a Mr Hill to the cantor, Mr Newbolt, for failing to keep an appointment.

Sources:

- Alumni Oxonienses 1715-1886
- Wainscot Book, Dr John Crook
- Cathedral Chapter minutes 1805-7
- Hampshire Chronicle, Oct, Nov 1807

Woodford's sister, who died in 1794, is buried in the Cathedral, near the south door, with a fine, simply inscribed tomb slab, with a striking coat-of-arms with three lions, with fleur-de-lys. Woodford's death on 30th September 1807, at age 70, was noted in the Hampshire Chronicle: the only benefices he appears to have held at that time were Crawley and Calbourne. No other obituary notice appeared, and it is not known if he was married or had children. Interestingly, the next archdeacon was appointed within five weeks of the vacancy.

He was buried in the Cathedral but his whereabouts are unknown. A plain memorial slab on a pillar in the north presbytery aisle commemorates both Matthew and his sister, Mary.

St. Mary's, Crawley ~ *c.*1850

The Hon. Thomas De Grey

Archdeacon 1807 ~ 1814

1778 Born 10 April
1779 M.A. St. John's College, Cambridge
1802 Ordained Priest
1802 married Elizabeth North on 12 August
1802 Vicar of Aston Abbots, Bucks.
1803 Rector of Merton, Norfolk
1804 Rector of Bishopstoke and Weeke
1806 Rector of Fawley
1807 Prebendary of Winchester
1807 Rector of Calbourne, I.O.W.
1807 Archdeacon of Winchester
1814 Archdeacon of Surrey
1831 Succeeded as fourth Baron Walsingham
1834 Resigned Prebend and Rectory of Calbourne
1839 Died 8 September

The family of De Grey had held land at Merton in Norfolk since the fourteenth century, though the barony of Walsingham only dated from 1780. In that year Sir William De Grey, who had held senior legal positions culminating in that of Chief Justice of the Common Pleas, was raised to the peerage. His son Thomas the second baron, had been chairman of committees in the House of Lords for twenty years and on retiring in 1814 was granted, by the Prince Regent, a pension of £2000 a year for life. When he died in 1818, he was succeeded by his elder son, George.

The Honourable Thomas De Grey, younger son of the second Baron Walsingham, was born on 10 April 1778 in London. After school at Eton, he was admitted a Fellow Commoner at St. John's College, Cambridge in 1796, where he matriculated in 1797 and graduated M.A. in 1799. He was ordained deacon in Gloucester in 1801 and priest in Winchester in 1802. For a short time in 1802–03 he was Vicar of Aston Abbots in Buckinghamshire, and in 1803 he was instituted to the Rectory of Merton, Norfolk, a living in the gift of his own family, which he retained until the end of his life.

The connection of Thomas De Grey with Hampshire probably began when, on 12 August 1802, he married Elizabeth, the youngest daughter of Brownlow North, Bishop of Winchester. From 1804 to 1807, he was Rector of Bishopstoke and of Weeke, both parishes in the gift of

Sources

Venn, *Cambridge Alumi*
Foster, *Oxford Alumni*
Burke's Peerage, 1839
Clergy List 184 5
Winchester Cathedral Chapter Minutes
John Crook, *The Wainscot Book*
Gentleman's Magazine 1839
M.Gould, *Three Hundred Years in a New Forest Parish* [Fawley]
R.B.Martin, *Enter Rumour*
Fawley, Exbury, Bishopstoke parish registers
White, *Directory of Hampshire*, 1878

the Bishop. He resigned these livings when in 1806 he was instituted to the Rectory of Fawley with Exbury and in the following year to the Rectory of Calbourne on the Isle of Wight, both wealthy livings of which the Bishop was the patron.

In December 1807 De Grey became Archdeacon of Winchester, a position which he held until 1814 when he was transferred to the Archdeaconry of Surrey. Also in 1807, he was appointed to a Prebend at Winchester and began his long connection with the Cathedral. He first attended a Chapter meeting in November of that year, though there must have been some delay in taking up his appointment as he was fined for not keeping his period of residence in 1807. From then onwards he was present at most Chapter meetings and seems to have kept his terms of three months residence each year.

Determined attempts were being made at this time to ensure that both these requirements were strictly adhered to, with financial penalties for defaulters. Bishop North seemed very conscious of this, for he wrote from Bath in 1813 to his son, Charles Augustus, warning him that all who were not present at the first day of Chapter would 'absolutely forfeit the whole of their dividend' and mentioning that 'De Grey who is now here sets out by the night Coach leaving Elizabeth in Bath'. The time of year when each Prebendary was in residence varied. For some years De Grey was there from April to June and then for a period he served for the last quarter from October to December.

During the years from 1807 until 1834 when De Grey resigned his Prebend, he had the use of three different houses in the Close. After ten years at No. 9, he moved to No. 10 in 1817 when he seems to have demanded extensive repairs. The Chapter Minutes record that the members present on 26 June did not feel competent to decide on the 'many Questions upon which Doubts have arisen' in Mr De Grey's application; however, the required work was authorised at the next meeting. In 1831 there was another move to No. 3 The Close. His large family would have needed fairly spacious accommodation. There were four daughters and six sons. The eldest son, Thomas, born in 1804, became a barrister, and succeeded to the title as 5th Lord Walsingham in 1839. The second son, William Brownlow, died in 1819 at the age of 14; the others were Brownlow North Osborne, Frederick, George and the youngest, Francis, born in 1815, who was drowned in 1836 while attempting to save the lives of some people adrift in a boat on the river Medway. One of the daughters, Charlotte Harriet, died in infancy in 1807; her sisters were Elizabeth Augusta, Georgina, and Henrietta Maria who married her cousin Brownlow North Garnier, son of the Rev. William Garnier of Rookesbury whose brother Thomas later became Dean of Winchester.

The parish of Fawley to which Thomas De Grey was appointed in 1806 was extensive at that time, stretching from Hythe down to Calshot and westwards to include the Chapelry of Exbury. Most of the population lived in and around Fawley itself, where the figure of 1,972 inhabitants was recorded in 1845; at that date there were 406 in Exbury and only 300 in Hythe which was still a small fishing village. Entries in the registers with the Rector's signature suggest that he and his family spent a good deal of time in Fawley. There was a resident curate but for parts of each year the Rector was there conducting baptisms and marriages and no doubt Sunday services as well though the records of these do not survive. He also on occasions officiated at Exbury, It seems clear that he was conscientious and precise. When entering a baptism, he always carefully included the date of birth of the child; if there was a divergence from the normal procedure, such as a baptism having taken place elsewhere, this was recorded. His early entries in the burial register include not only the cause of death, if known, but also the position of the grave in the church or churchyard.

Exbury had its own chapel but it was a medieval building in poor condition by this time and was rebuilt in 1827. A church was built at Hythe in 1823 and from then the village had its own curate and became an independent ecclesiastical district in 1841. The curate whom De Grey appointed in 1823 was a cousin, Adolphus Frederick Irby, who remained in Hythe until his death in 1863. Two of the Irby brothers were noted for their part in the naval wars against Napoleon and the parish registers record the baptism in 1813 of a negro boy who had been rescued from a slave ship by Frederick Paul Irby, Captain of HMS Amelia. Perhaps this naval link is connected with a story related about the Rector who is said to have 'driven to church in a coach and four, escorted by footmen with powdered wigs and drawn cutlasses'. The Rectory house at Fawley was an old building, said to be in origin Jacobean and containing stone from Beaulieu Abbey. De Grey added a drawing room and outhouses, but seems to have made no major alterations as his successor found it necessary to make expensive improvements in 1840. In the garden, 'Lady Walsingham built a curious grotto ... lined with shells, coral, and Mica'.

In 1807 De Grey became Archdeacon of Winchester, a position which he held until 1814 when he was transferred to the Archdeaconry of Surrey. In 1831 his situation in life was unexpectedly changed when his elder brother George lost his life in a fire at his London house in Harley Street and Thomas succeeded him as the fourth Baron Walsingham. His new responsibilities no doubt required his attention and his signature - now simply 'Walsingham' - appeared less in parish registers. In 1834 he resigned his Prebend at Winchester and also the Rectory of Calbourne, though continuing as Archdeacon of Surrey and Rector of Fawley. He also continued to hold the Rectory of Merton on his own estates in Norfolk. He died at Merton on 8 September 1839 at the age of 61.

The Hon. Augustus George Legge

Archdeacon 1814 ~ 1819

1773 Born
∻ Educated at Hatton
1794 BA Christchurch, Oxford
1795 Married Honora Bagot
1796 MA Merton College, Oxford
1797 Rector of Wonston
1798 King's Chaplain
1801? Prebendary of Lichfield
1807 Rector of Crawley
1814 Archdeacon of Winchester
1817 Prebendary of Winchester; resigned Rectory of Crawley
1819 Resigned as Archdeacon; became Rector of North Waltham
1820 Chancellor of the Diocese
1828 Died 21 August

As a son of the second Earl of Dartmouth, Augustus George Legge was closely connected with the North family. His father, William, had become the stepson of Lord North, later 1st Earl of Guilford, when his widowed mother re-married in 1736. By his first marriage Lord North had one son, Frederick, later to become Prime Minister, who was born in 1732; the future Bishop of Winchester, Brownlow North, born in 1741, was a child of the second marriage. Thus William Legge, born in 1731, who succeeded his grandfather as second Earl of Dartmouth in 1750, had grown up as half-brother to both the future Prime Minister and the future Bishop of Winchester. This family connection was advantageous when seeking appointments for his sons. Two were ordained; the family living of Lewisham had been given to Edward, later Bishop of Oxford, so it was Brownlow North to whom the family looked for preferments for the youngest son, Augustus George.

Born on 21 April 1773, Augustus George Legge was educated at Hatton by Dr Samuel Parr, a learned Whig and Latitudinarian scholar, known as a member of the Johnsonian circle. After teaching at Harrow and other schools, Parr had established himself at Hatton in Warwickshire where he took a few private pupils while building up a library of some ten thousand volumes. At the age of 17, Legge matriculated at Christchurch, Oxford, in 1790 and graduated B.A. in 1794; M.A. followed in 1796 from Merton College. On 15 December 1795,

Sources
∻ A.G.Legge *DNB,*
∻ *Oxford Alumni*
∻ *Burke's Peerage*
∻ *Victoria County History*
∻ *White's Directory of Hampshire* 1878
∻ AJ Willis *Winchester Ordinations.*
∻ *Hampshire Chronicle*
∻ Diocesan Records, Hampshire Record Office

Augustus George Legge married Honora, daughter of the Rev. Walter Bagot, Rector of Blithfield and Leigh, Staffordshire. Blithfield was the residence of the first Baron Bagot, whose family were connected to the Legges by an earlier marriage. The couple were married by Honora's uncle, Lewis Bagot, Bishop of St. Asaph.

In 1797, Legge was presented to the Rectory of Wonston which he retained until the end of his life. The parsonage house was large and dated back to medieval times and it seems as if Legge and his family always spent much of their time there; he was said to have made it his permanent residence in later years. In a diocesan enquiry about curates' licences in 1810, the return for Wonston had been filled in by the Rector who stated that he was resident and had no curate; With a population of nearly 600, the church could hold about 250. In 1807 Legge also became Rector of Crawley. The 1810 return for Crawley was completed by the curate, Jobn Taylor Lamb, who resided in the Rectory and had a stipend of £70 a year. In reply to a question about the incumbent's normal place of residence, this was said to be Wonston, the adjoining parish of which he was Rector. Crawley had a population of 300 and the church could accommodate that number. The chapel at Hunton was attached to Crawley at that time and was served by Charles Tahourdin, who received £30 annually for taking a service each Sunday; he was the Rector of Stoke Charity, an adjoining parish where he resided. Among the curates who served Crawley while Legge was Rector, there was at least one who later became eminent; Richard Mant, who was licensed to the parish in 1808, went on to become a distinguished bishop, author and hymn writer.

Legge had been appointed a Chaplain to King George III in 1798. In 1814 he became Archdeacon of Winchester, and in 1817 a Canon of the Cathedral; at this time he gave up the Rectory of Crawley. In 1819 he resigned as Archdeacon and was appointed to the Rectory of North Waltham. In the following year, he became Chancellor of the diocese. Augustus George Legge died suddenly on 21 August 1828, aged 55, at the house of his brother Henry at Blackheath. The obituary in the local paper recorded that his loss would be felt by the whole county: 'He was strictly conscientious in the discharge of the duties of the high stations which he filled; the poor have to lament the loss of a kind and charitable friend'. His wife Honora survived him until 1863.

Of their large family of ten children, most had died young and there are memorials to several of them in the church at Wonston. Henry, who was ordained deacon in 1826, was the only one of the sons to outlive his father. Two lived into their twenties; the eldest, George Augustus, died in 1826 and his brother Heneage Walter, a Midshipman in the Royal Navy, died at the age of 22 in 1827 Three daughters survived their father, Charlotte Ann and the two youngest of the family, born in 1816 and 1817, both of whom retained Hampshire connections throughout their lives. Honora Augusta married Lieut. General William Cowper Coles who died in 1867, and Louisa Frances Katherine married in 1866 the Rev. Alfred Caesar Bishop. Property which included Bramdean House had been inherited by Honora Legge, wife of Augustus George, from her brother, the Revd. Egerton Arden Bagot. Later in the century, Louisa Frances and her family were living in Bramdean House, and her sister Honora Cowper Coles at Bramdean Lodge. It was the latter who in 1899 bequeathed £300 for the installation of a stained-glass window to be installed in the Cathedral in memory of her father, Canon and Chancellor, and Honora his wife. The window, by C. E. Kempe was installed in the Langton Chapel.

Gilbert Heathcote

Archdeacon 1819 ~ 1829

1765 Born
1787 BA New College, Oxford
1804 Rector of Hursley and Fellow of Winchester College
1805 Married Sophia Wall who died 1806
1807 Married Ann Beadon
1811 Vicar of Andover
1814 Treasurer of Wells Cathedral
1819 Archdeacon of Winchester
1829 Died 18 October

The landed estate of the Heathcote family was one of the largest in Hampshire, extending for some 14,000 acres in and around Hursley by the early nineteenth century. Gilbert Heathcote, born in 1765, was the fifth son of Sir Thomas Heathcote, the second Baronet, who died in 1787. William, Gilbert's half-brother, succeeded to the title; he took an active part in local affairs and served as MP for the County from 1790 to 1806. After his death in 1819, his son Thomas inherited, but only lived a few years and was succeeded in 1825 by his nephew William, the 5th Baronet, a few weeks before his twenty-fourth birthday. Sir William Heathcote became one of the leaders in county affairs during the next half century as well as being remembered for his friendship with the Revd John Keble and the writer Charlotte Yonge.

Gilbert Heathcote was educated at Winchester College and New College, Oxford, where he graduated B.A. in 1787. He was elected a Fellow and it seems likely that he remained in Oxford for some years, as nothing is recorded of him until 1804 when he was presented to the living of Hursley by his half-brother Sir William. In the same year he was elected a Fellow of Winchester College. At this time he must have resigned his Fellowship at New College which he could no longer hold after his marriage in 1805 to Sophia Elizabeth, daughter of Martin Wall, M.D., Clinical Professor in the University of Oxford. Their first child, Gilbert Wall Heathcote, was born on 5 May 1806 but sadly his mother died a few weeks later on

Sources

- Foster, *Oxford Alumni*
- E.D.Heathcote, *The Families of Heathcote*
- F.Awdry, *A Country Gentleman of the Nineteenth Century: a Short Memoir of*
- *Sir William Heathcote* (1906)
- B.Carpenter Turner, *Winchester*
- R.Foster, *The Politics of County Power* (1990)
- C.M.Yonge, *John Keble's Parishes* (1898)
- S. Himsworth, *Catalogue of Winchester College Muniments*. Vol. I
- *The Gentleman's Magazine* 1829, Vol. III, p. 571
- Hursley Parish Records, 39M69/PB.1-2, and Marriage Registers (HRO)
- Otterbourne Parish Registers (HRO)
- Andover Parish Records, 60M67/PB.1 and Marriage Registers (IHRO)
- Winchester St.Thomas Parish Registers (HRO)
- Winchester City Records, WF3/312/1, 333/5-6 (HRO)
- *Hampshire Chronicle*. 26 Oct. & 2 Nov., 1829
- Diocesan Records (HRO)

2 June. In September 1807 Gilbert Heathcote married again; his second wife was Anne, daughter of the Rev. Edwards Beadon, Rector of North Stoneham. Five children were born to the couple, George Edwards in 1809, twins Dawsonne and Mary in 1810, William Beadon in 1812 and Anne in 1816. The children of this second marriage were all baptised by their father at St.Thomas's church, the address of the family being given as St.Thomas Street.

The parish of Hursley, to which Otterbourne was attached with its own church, was served by a resident curate. John Marsh, who had been licensed to the parish in 1788, lived in Hursley where he continued until 1820; then George Chard was there for a year and James Scott for four years until the young Sir William brought in John Keble as curate, only to lose him soon afterwards when Keble left to assist his father at Fairford. However, it is clear that Gilbert Heathcote took an active part in the work of the parish, though it seems that he officiated at services more often at Otterbourne than at Hursley. In reply to a diocesan enquiry in 1810, he stated that the church at Otterbourne was served by the Vicar. In the Hursley registers for the years from 1813 until Gilbert Heathcote's death in 1829, there is only one occasion when he officiated at a marriage in Hursley, until the last two years when his signature appears more often, while nearly all the baptisms during that time were conducted by John Marsh. On the other hand the Vicar officiated at nearly all the baptisms and marriages at Otterbourne during the same period. Help was also provided sometimes at both churches by another member of the Heathcote family, The Revd Samuel Heathcote.

Various improvements were introduced at Hursley during these years. In 1816 a document was drawn up which, while primarily providing for maintenance of the Heathcote family vault, also made provision for payment to the officiating minister for performing divine service on each of the six days in Passion Week. In the same year a Trust was established at the request of some parishioners who wanted two services on Sundays instead of only one; money was subscribed and the interest was to be paid to the officiating minister if he held two services with sermon. Particulars of this were written up by the Vicar and the comment added that the practice of only holding one service had begun because there were two churches to serve.

The church at Otterbourne was still the old church near the river at Brambridge. Charlotte Yonge records that at that time Otterbourne had one Sunday service, alternately Matins or Evensong, with Holy Communion four times a year, 'and the church bell was rung as soon as the clergyman was seen riding down the lane'. She goes on to relate that Robert Shuckburgh was the first resident curate at Otterbourne; he was appointed by the Archdeacon, and was the first to have two services on Sunday. His name first appears in the registers in 1827. She claims that the Archdeacon 'generally resided there' but it must be remembered that Charlotte Yonge was not born until 1823, so much of what she reports would have been hearsay and she was writing many years later. It seems to be the case that Heathcote's normal place of residence was Winchester. Nevertheless Charlotte Yonge does provide a little personal data about the Archdeacon. 'He was a man of great musical talent, and some of his chants are still in use. The only other fact recollected of him was, that being told that he used hard words in his sermons, he asked a labourer if he knew what was meant by Predestination, and was answered, "Yes, sir, some'at about the innards of a pig"'.

In 1804 Gilbert Heathcote was elected a Fellow of Winchester College and it seems likely that much of his life was centred on the College from then onwards. In response to an enquiry about clerical residence in 1810, when he declared that the church at Otterbourne was served by himself, the Vicar, he wrote from Winchester College; this seems to indicate that he considered the College his main sphere of work. In seven years between 1807 and 1826 he served as one of the Bursars, in 1814 he was acting as Sub-Warden and in 1823 a letter was sent to him as Librarian. In 1808 he compiled 'A Commonplace Book of College Concerns' in which he collected together information about college servants, accounts, meetings, allowances and other matters of concern; for this purpose he must have been well acquainted with the running of the college.

The living of Andover was in the gift of Winchester College and Gilbert Heathcote became Vicar in 1811. An account book survives which he began to compile soon after his induction to record payments and receipts, explaining that earlier books had been handed down to him. Among the items listed are particulars of the curate's stipend which was made up of £60 paid by the Vicar plus Easter offering and fees which together amounted to £100 *per annum*. In Andover Heathcote had an experienced curate in William Pedder, who had been in the parish since the early 1790s and who was evidently highly regarded. On the death of 'my very worthy curate, William Pedder' in 1823, Heathcote recorded that he had 'attended and read the funeral service to a very large congregation of inhabitants who were anxious to testify their respect to a Minister whom they so highly esteemed'. The late curate's son, William Newland Pedder, succeeded to the curacy at Lady Day 1823.

A school was set up in Andover in 1811 and a schoolmaster, Robert Cole, was licensed in the following year. Among other matters of concern were the establishment of a District Committee of SPCK in 1813, and repairs to the chapel at Foxcott, two miles north of the town. A service had been held at Foxcott only once a month until early in 1813 when repairs had been completed. From that time a curate, Robert Evans, was to be paid to conduct a service every Sunday, alternately morning and evening, with the Sacrament four times a year instead of only once.

In 1814 Gilbert Heathcote became Treasurer of Wells Cathedral. This preferment was probably due to his wife's relationship to Richard Beadon, the Bishop of Bath and Wells. Five years later in 1819 he was appointed Archdeacon of Winchester by Bishop Brownlow North. He took an active part in local affairs and mention was made at the time of his death in 1829 of the support he had given to the suits in Chancery against the Corporation of the City in the preceding years; the purpose of these was to investigate the administration of city charities, in particular of St. John's, and eventually reform was brought about. It 'cannot be questioned that the authority of his name added great weight to the proceedings, and mainly contributed to a final and successful issue'.

Gilbert Heathcote died at Great Audley Street in London on 19 October 1829 and was buried in the cloister of Winchester College where both his wives had been interred and also the son who had died as a child. It seems that he may have been in poor health for some time. A letter from John Keble to Sir William Heathcote in June 1827 referred to the Archdeacon's moving house as if this had been a worry for the family; he declared himself to be 'exceedingly glad that it was found possible for the Archdeacon himself to move'. At the time of his death, the obituary in the *Hampshire Chronicle* wrote that he 'united in a singular degree the utmost mildness and sincerity of manners, the soundest judgement, and the most disinterested integrity', As a token of respect, shops in the city and suburbs were closed on the day of the funeral. His eldest son, Gilbert Wall Heathcote, succeeded his father as Vicar of Hursley, was Rector of Ash in Surrey and a Fellow, Bursar and Sub-Warden of Winchester College. The second son, George Edwards, died in Canada in 1886, while the youngest brother, William Beadon Heathcote, became a Fellow of New College, Warden of Radley, Precentor of Salisbury and Rector of Compton Bassett.

Charles James Hoare

Archdeacon 1829 ~ 1847

1781 Born
1804 Ordained as priest
1806 Fellow of St. John's College Cambridge, Seatonian prizeman in 1807
1807 Vicar of Blandford
1821 Rector of Godstone, Archdeacon of Surrey from 1847
1829 Archdeacon of Winchester
1829 Residentiary Canon of Winchester Cathedral
1865 Died

Sources

- *Sussex Express*, 28 January 1865.
- Frederick Bussby, *Winchester Cathedral 1079 - 1979* (Ringwood: Paul Cave, 1979).
- Hennell Michael, *John Venn and the Clapham Sect* (Lutterworth Press, 1958).
- C. J. Hoare, *A Charge to the Clergy of the Archdeaconry of Winchester: Easter 1841* (Winchester: Jacob and Johnson, 1841).
- Mary Alden Hopkins, *Hannah More and Her Circle* (London: Longman, Green & Co, 1947).

Charles Hoare was born in 1781, the third son of Henry Hoare, a banker of Fleet Street, London. He was brought up in a well-to-do family, his mother Lydia being the daughter and co-heiress of the successful merchant, Isaac Malortie, of Hanover and London. His father, Henry, was in 1799 one of the founders of the Church Missionary Society, and the family tradition of support for missionary work and the propagation of the Bible remained with Charles throughout his life. The Hoare family were intimates of the Clapham Sect, that group of Evangelical Christians, prominent in the period from 1790 to 1830, who promoted missionary work both at home and abroad and who worked for the abolition of slavery. The group got their name from the church in Clapham whose Rector, John Venn, provided the focus of their activities. Its members included William Wilberforce, banker and philanthropist, Henry Thornton, Zachary Macaulay, editor of *The Christian Observer*, whose experiences in Jamaica made him a passionate opponent of slavery, the religious writer and educator Hannah More and Charles Simeon a leading Evangelical and founder of the Church Missionary Society. Charles became an intimate acquaintance of these members of the Sect and remained on friendly terms with them long after leaving the family home at Mitcham. Henry Hoare's house at Mitcham must have been much visited by the group and the biography of Hannah More, who was more of Henry's generation than that of Charles', records a visit by her there in 1813, during which she was taken ill and confined to bed, being able to take only one meal with the family during the whole visit.

The Clapham Sect pursued a wide range of interests; including missionary work and propagation of the Bible, prison reform, prevention of cruel sports, and abolition of slavery. They published their own journal, *The Christian Observer*, and gave moral and financial support to a number of Bible Societies, and to Hannah More's schools and pamphlets. In contrast to the Methodists, they were mostly well connected and wealthy conservatives who, whilst they preached philanthropic benevolence, strongly believed in the preservation of rank and order within society. As example, Hannah More believed that the poor should learn just sufficient for servants – 'such coarse works as may fit them'; she allowed no writing for the poor. Their wealth and standing enabled them to achieve great success in mobilising public opinion. They were part of the vanguard for the hundreds of societies and institutions for improvement, moral and philanthropic as well as religious, that dominated Victorian Society in the middle of the nineteenth century.

Charles went up to St John's College, Cambridge in 1799 and had a glittering academic record; in 1803 he was second Wrangler, second Smith's prizeman and second Classical Medalist. A Fellow in 1806, he was Seatonian prizeman in 1807. Amongst his friends were J.W. Cunningham who became curate to John Venn and in 1818 was made Honorary Life Governor of the Church Missionary Society, and Henry Martyn who became a missionary in India. Also a firm friend and mentor was Archdeacon Dealtry, a strong supporter of the British and Foreign Bible Society, and Rector of Clapham after John Venn. Charles was ordained in 1804 and became curate to Dr Thomas Rennell, Dean of Winchester and vicar of Alton, Hampshire. He was a successful and well loved vicar of Blandford, in Dorset, at the early age of 26 and served there from 1807 until 1821. Whilst there he married Jane Holden, of Yorkshire, and they had seven children. In 1821 he removed to the family living at Godstone near Reigate in Surrey where he remained Rector for the rest of his life. He had throughout maintained his interest in religious societies and at Godstone held each year a highly-regarded popular gathering for missionaries.

He was elevated to be Archdeacon of Winchester in 1829 and two years later became a Residentiary Canon under Bishop Charles Sumner who, like him, was a middle of the road evangelical. His old tutor and friend Doctor Dealtry had become Archdeacon of

Surrey in 1830 and they must have made a particularly happy and effective team for the Diocese. This was a time of great debate over ecclesiastical issues and Charles Hoare was an energetic participant. He was amongst the first of the 'modern' Archdeacons in an era when the Church of England began to focus on social problems and in particular the relief of poverty.

He was also a vigorous supporter of the Irish Church, of the integrity and maintenance of Cathedral establishments, and was wary of the aims of the Catholic revival movement, the Oxford Tractarians. In 1836 when legislation was passed for the establishment of Commissioners to administer the revenues of the Cathedrals, a general protest was made by the Cathedrals, and in addition Winchester chose to make its own separate protest; Charles Hoare was a signatory to both documents and an active protester. The Dean and Canons at Winchester whilst allowing the importance of daily services of 'prayer and praise' argued that the 'utility of cathedral institutions were not to be measured by that alone'. They continued 'Cathedrals were retreats of learned leisure, where, free from the anxieties attendant upon a narrow income and from the incessant cares which belong to the cure of souls, they could give themselves more entirely to the higher walks of literature and theology...' a good try, but not surprisingly unsuccessful!

Charles Hoare lived within the Close at No. 3, which was next to the Dean's stables (now part of The Pilgrim's School) and during his time as Archdeacon entered fully into the life of the cathedral and city. In 1841 a booklet was published of his sermons given at Easter that year as *A charge to the Clergy of the Archdeaconry of Winchester*. This gives us a good clue as to the issues which were foremost in his mind at that time. It also shows that Charles, like his Bishop, did not deviate from central evangelical doctrine. He supported the decision by the Chief Justices that parishioners or actual residents within a parish were bound to repair the body of a church whenever necessary and for them to provide all things essential to the performance of divine service. He then stressed the need for further efforts towards education by the Diocesan Board of Education. Charles had overseen good work on education at Godstone and the first report made by the Winchester Diocesan Board of Education (which he included in his booklet) recommended the report of the Godstone Rural Deanery as an example of what might be done in every district of the diocese. Again, Charles was in tune with the Bishop's views, it was Bishop Sumner who had taken the initiative to set up a Diocesan Education Board.

Charles it seems had not lost his concern over 'Romanists' – 'any compromise to meet the wishes of Romanists, is of all other events in the church, the most to be deplored and depreciated'. Bishop Sumner had himself constantly warned of 'the deep corruption of Rome'. He referred to the virtual silencing of Convocation, the loss of Rural Chapters and the suspension (hopefully temporary) of Cathedral Chapters as together representing a serious loss of communication within the church. As an advocate for the Society for the Propagation of the Gospel in Foreign Parts and the Church Missionary Society he hoped to establish 'ere long' an Association in aid of them in every Parish in the Archdeaconry.

There is quite clearly a consistency in Charles' ministry founded upon the beliefs and experiences of his childhood and he never deviated from his evangelical roots. In 1847 he was transferred to the Archdeaconry of Surrey which had been held by his dear friend Dr Dealtry and who had died that year; a white marble tablet on the South aisle of Winchester Cathedral commemorates – 'this distinguished and sound Divine'. Here he entered eagerly into the keen debate over the nature and meaning of Baptism, writing a booklet in 1848 entitled, *Baptism, or the Ministrations of Public Baptism of Infants scripturally illustrated*. However, his energy was largely concentrated on alleviating the burden of parish priests in the highly populated areas South of the Thames, and to providing further church accommodation there. In 1860 he was struck by a serious and debilitating illness and died in 1865 at the age of 83. He was greatly mourned by all who knew him as his obituary in the *Sussex Express* testifies – 'the esteem in which he was held was shown by the attendance at the ceremony, when a greater number of persons were gathered than we can ever remember to have seen on any similar occasion'.

Joseph Cotton Wigram

Archdeacon 1847 ~ 1860

1798 Born 26 December
1819 BA Trinity College, Cambridge
1823 MA
1823 Ordained Priest
1827 Secretary of National Society; assistant at St. James, Westminster
1837 Married Susan Maria Arkwright
1839 Rector of East Tisted
1847 Archdeacon of Winchester
1851 Rector of St. Mary's, Southampton
1860 Bishop of Rochester
1867 Died 6 April

A member of a large family, Joseph Cotton Wigram was a son of Sir Robert Wigram, of Wexford, who was an important London merchant and was created a Baronet in 1805. Joseph was born at Walthamstow on 26 December 1798. He was educated by private tutors and then at Trinity College, Cambridge where he graduated B.A. in 1819. He was ordained deacon by the Bishop of Ely in 1822 and priest in the following year by Dr. Howley, then Bishop of London. In 1827 he was appointed assistant preacher at St. James, Westminster and in the same year became Secretary of the National Society which had been formed in 1811 for the provision of Church schools. He held this post until 1839 when he first came to reside in Hampshire, becoming the Rector of East Tisted. In 1837 he married Susan Maria, daughter of Peter Arkwright of Willersley, Derbyshire, with whom he had six sons and three daughters.

In 1847 Wigram became Archdeacon of Winchester and in 1851 was installed as Rector of St. Mary's, Southampton. Both these nominations were in the hands of the Bishop, Charles Sumner. Southampton had been undergoing a remarkable expansion. With the opening of the railway to London in 1840, and the construction of the docks, the first of which was opened in 1843, the population of the town was booming. The employment of large numbers of men in the construction works, and in connection with the increasing trade of the port,

Sources

- Dictionary of National Biography
- A.T.Patterson, *History of Southampton,* Vol. II
- G.R.Sumner, *Life of Charles Richard Sumner*, p.397
- O.Chadwick, *The Victorian Church*, Vol.I
- White, *Hampshire Directory*, 1878
- A.I.Pearman, *Rochester* (in Diocesan History Series) 1897
- *The Gentleman's Magazine*,1867, Vol.I, pp.669-70
- *Hampshire Independent*, 1850, 1851
- Letters (D/Z 83/6, Southampton Record Office)
- *News and Views*, 1907, Southampton Record Office

brought many new residents. Development took place mainly in the area between the old town and the river Itchen, near the railway and docks and where there was still vacant land. The whole of this area was in the parish of St. Mary which was much the largest in Southampton and extended up the river Itchen where shipbuilding and related facilities were growing up. The population of St. Mary's grew from 4708 in 1821 to 21,250 in 1851.

Some advances had been made towards the foundation of new churches and the division of the large parish but there was a difficulty which affected the church as a whole in Southampton. The Rectory of St. Mary's was a wealthy living which had been held since 1797 by Francis North, Earl of Guilford, son of Bishop Brownlow North. It was not until his resignation in 1850 referred to in a local paper as the 'removal of the incubus' – that moves could go ahead to divide the parish and re-allocate the revenues. Within a short time the Rector was receiving about a third of the previous income, from which he paid several curates, and plans were in hand to use the endowments for the benefit of new and existing churches in the St. Mary's area and elsewhere in the town.

The speed with which plans were revealed make it clear that Bishop Sumner had already been working on the problems. Two weeks after the *Hampshire Independent* reported the resignation of the Earl of Guilford on 14 December 1850, the name of the new Rector was announced with the information that plans were in hand to divide the parish of St. Mary's. Wigram was inducted on 5 February 1851 and on 22 March particulars were given of the proposed changes. It seems likely that the Bishop had been working on these with his Archdeacon whom he planned to install in the parish as soon as possible. This was probably the most crucial problem in the southern part of the diocese at that time. Wigram soon showed himself to be active and concerned. By the middle of March he had arranged for prayers to be held every Wednesday and Friday, with a full service on Fridays; by July he had made available 20 acres of glebe land for use as allotments, revived the local Scripture Readers Association to help the clergy, and had set up a penny bank. Within the first year he 'won golden opinions from all sorts of people' by his 'dignified simplicity, suavity and kindness of manner'. The fact that his brother was a leading shipbuilder in the town, and his family were shipowners and merchants in London, no doubt aided confidence in his understanding of the needs of a growing port.

By March 1852 Wigram was persuading the directors of the leading steamship companies that chaplains were needed to minister to the seamen; an approach was also made to the Dock Company, another leading employer. In a letter to Brodie McGhie Willcox, MP for the town and one of the founders of the P&O Company, on 23 March the Rector stressed the urgent need; he explained that, while he understood the scruples of those of differing religious opinions (Nonconformity was strong in Southampton), he felt that action must be taken and that the established church should take the lead. This attitude was typical of Wigram; his work in St. Mary's was described as being of a 'most practical character'. 'Through his instrumentality the schools at Crabniton were built, and he started a printing office for boys and a laundry for girls so that in addition to the ordinary tuition the boys were afforded... practical knowledge of printing and girls taught useful work in the laundry'. His reputation, recalled many years later, was that he 'with Mrs Wigram and their daughters, were known as constant visitors to the homes of the poor, and their useful work and generous benevolence are still cherished memories in the parish.'

Wigram stayed in Southampton until 1860 when he became Bishop of Rochester. He was consecrated in the parish church of St. Mary, Lambeth, when Bishop Sumner was one of the consecrating bishops. In George Sumner's life of his father, he states that the Bishop and his Archdeacon had worked very closely together, and quotes a letter by the Bishop complaining that 'the Crown can make no high appointment in the Church at home or abroad without a foray into my diocese. In the present instance my right arm is cut off to furnish Rochester with its chief ruler'. However, he was confident that Wigram's capabilities would be more than adequate in his new role. 'He is a very stirring man – full of energy and devotion to his work – and himself the foremost in setting an example of labour and self denial in promoting it ... I cannot doubt that he will carry a blessing with him'.

The task facing Wigram in Rochester diocese was a daunting one. In 1846 the boundaries of the diocese had been changed to an extent which made it almost unrecognisable. There was need to provide for growing areas of population and the old diocesan structure, which was to give way later in the century to the creation of new dioceses, was subject to interim measures. Rochester was given responsibility for a large area north of the Thames which included most of Essex and the whole of Hertfordshire. South of the river, only the City and Deanery of Rochester were retained, the rest of the old diocese being divided between London and Canterbury. The episcopal residence was transferred from Bromley to Danbury Park near Chelmsford. Wigram's predecessor, Bishop George Murray who had been there since 1827, was a Tory aristocrat who seems to have been opposed to any kind of reform, so probably was not assiduous in coping with these changes.

It seems that Wigram attacked the task with his usual energy. An account in a diocesan history declares that he 'threw himself with great earnestness into the work of the diocese and went far to realize what in the popular phrase of the time was described as a 'gig-bishop' by visiting the remote villages of Essex in the most informal manner'. On the last day of his life, 6 April 1867, he had been at a confirmation and returned to London where he was to preach at St. James, Piccadilly, the following morning. On the next day he was to confirm at Braintree, on Tuesday at Gillingham and Chatham Barracks and on Wednesday at Gravesend. If this is an example of his normal schedule, it backs up the claim made for him especially as he had been told the previous year that the heart trouble he suffered from could prove fatal at any time. On the evening of 6 April, 1867, he was staying with relatives at 15A Grosvenor Square when he collapsed and died.

Wigram was buried at Latton church near Harlow with his wife who had died in 1864. Bishop Sumner wrote 'I have greatly felt the sudden death of the Bishop of Rochester. He was one of the most single-minded, straightforward men I have ever known, somewhat cold in manner, but full of energy and devotion to his work. The diocese will never have a more disinterested and unselfish head'. Another obituary adds a touch of humour. 'Dr Wigram was an evangelical in his religious views, and a year or two ago his somewhat injudicious denunciations *ex cathedra* of those of his clergy who played cricket with their parishioners on the village greens, or who wore moustaches or beards, caused no little indignation in Essex and ridicule in London'. However, the same writer went on to state that he was 'a very earnest, hard-working man, without any pretensions to oratorical powers or theological learning; but whatever faults his clergy might find with his discretion, no-one ever accused him of discourtesy, inaccessibility or indifference to the calls of duty'.

Philip Jacob

Archdeacon 1860 ~ 1884

1803 Born
1828 Graduated – Corpus Christi College Oxford
1831 Appointed Rector of St Mary's Crawley
1832 Married Anna Noel
1834 Installed as Canon Residentiary Winchester Cathedral
1860 Appointed Archdeacon of Winchester
1884 Died at Crawley

For over half a century Philip Jacob lived and worked in the diocese of Winchester. Indeed the links go deeper than this in that his father John Jacob had associations with the Channel Islands (attached to the Diocese of Winchester in 1499). John Jacob had been associated with 'Petite Marche' in Guernsey as well as 'Roath Court', County Glamorgan. Philip was the third son of John Jacob and Anna Maria Legrand, her father being George Legrand of Canterbury. Philip was educated at Corpus Christi College Oxford and graduated in 1828. He became Rector of the parish of St. Mary's, Crawley, under the patronage of the Lord Chancellor, in 1831. He married Anna, daughter of the Reverend and Honourable George Noel in 1832.

Philip Jacob's association with Winchester Cathedral began in 1834 when on the nineteenth of July, he was installed as a Canon of the Cathedral. And it was in 1860 on the presentation of Queen Victoria that he became Archdeacon of Winchester. For 53 years therefore, he was Rector of Crawley and from 1860 until his death on 21st December 1884 was also Archdeacon of Winchester. He was affectionately known by his parishioners as the 'old Archdeacon' and in his memory, above the altar at St. Mary's Church, there is a fine stained glass window, erected in 1887 with the inscription, 'for 53 years Father and Friend to all in the parish, given by those who love and mourn him'.[(1)]

Sources

1 *Crawley. Glimpses into the Past of a Hampshire Parish*, Privately published.
2 Hampshire Chronicle, January 1885.
3 ibid.
∻ *Crawley. Glimpses into the Past of a Hampshire Parish*, Privately published.
∻ *Winchester Cathedral Nine Hundred Years*, J Crook.
∻ Hampshire Chronicle, January 1885

Philip Jacob was a keen educationalist. He founded the Crawley Village School in 1835, and was well known for his promotion of the development of 'public instruction' in Winchester itself. He was renowned for his generosity and much loved. However, the Bishop of Winchester in paying tribute to the Archdeacon after his death said 'at one time there was a certain angularity of character about the Archdeacon which enabled him to manifest certain independence of character, but as that wore off one found underneath one of the kindest and warmest hearts that ever beat the human breast'.[(2)] He was also very knowledgeable in medical matters and put this knowledge to good use in his care of the sick in the parish. One parishioner commented that he was 'better than a doctor' and his epitaph notes 'he was a good man'. One of his sons Edgar became Vicar of Portsea and later Bishop of St. Albans.

From time to time Philip Jacob rode his horse over the open downland to the Church of St. James at Hunton where he would take divine service. However, on one occasion on his return he took a wrong turning and lost his way and as a result spent a cold and miserable night out in the open. In order not to get lost again, and indeed to assist other travellers in the future, he had a post erected at the highest point of his journey on which was fastened a lighted oil lamp. This was known for many years as the Archdeacon's lampost. The Victorian stained glass of the East window at Hunton Church was also added as a memorial to him.

The Hampshire Chronicle printed in full the text of a sermon given by the Reverend Canon Humbert and delivered to a large congregation of the parishioners at Crawley on a Sunday morning soon after his death. He took as his text the Acts of the Apostles chapter 13 verse 36 'after he had served his own generation by the will of God (he) fell on sleep.' It was a long sermon in which he paid tribute to the faithful service of their late Rector. He recalled a visit that he himself had made to the parish some 35 years earlier, remembering that the Reverend George Sumner was curate there at the time. Canon Humbert accompanied the Archdeacon on the Sunday and assisted in the church services as well as in the Sunday School, during the morning and the afternoon. As a young priest he remembered his gratitude for the hints and tips he had received, together with the kindly criticism and advice from Philip Jacob. He reminded the congregation of the Archdeacon's deep affection for the Cathedral and his annual autumn Residence in the Close, which he had completed as usual, as much as his final illness would permit, until a week before his death.

Archdeacon Jacob taking tea at rear of No. 8 the Close *(second right)*
(photograph: John Crook)

Interestingly, on the same Sunday evening at the Wesleyan Chapel in Winchester the Reverend R. W. G. Hunter preached a sermon to a large congregation in which he made special reference to the death of the late Archdeacon Jacob. He chose for his text the Acts the Apostles chapter 7 verse 60. He paid warm tribute to the Archdeacon but finished his sermon with a qualifying conclusion. He thought that some of his congregation may have felt it inappropriate to speak of a priest of the Established Church and to do so in such glowing terms but, for himself he saw no inconsistency. He explained that of course, he was a Methodist by ancestry, training and choice, principle and conviction but, 'he was an Englishman as well, and that was a larger term, and it was his aim to be a Christian, which was a larger term still. It might be said that there were evils and abuses in the National Church, but that was not the time to speak of them!' [3]

Early in 1885 on a Monday evening a meeting was called at the Guildhall to decide upon a fitting memorial to Archdeacon Philip Jacob. The Bishop of Winchester opened the meeting by reminding those present of the saintly qualities of the late Archdeacon. A number of different proposals for his memorial were discussed, but in the end the meeting voted by a large majority to restore the Great Screen in the Cathedral. Though it seems the decision caused some controversy, after much discussion and consultation the Great Screen was restored to the memory of Archdeacon Jacob. A memorial tablet to this effect is mounted on the back of the screen and includes those who subscribed to its repair and restoration and particular sponsorship of individual statues. The statue of Bishop Hedda, to the left of the high altar is made in the likeness of Philip Jacob.

George Sumner

Archdeacon 1885 ~ 1901

1824 Born the fourth child of Charles Sumner, later Bishop of Winchester
1845 BA
1848 MA and Ordained as priest, married Mary Heywood founder of the Mothers' Union
1850 Rector of Old Alresford
1857 Rural Dean
1885 Residentiary Canon Winchester Cathedral
1888 Bishop of Guildford until his death in 1909
1909 Died

When George Sumner died, at No. 1, the Close, on the 11th December 1909, work on the restoration of the Cathedral was still two years from completion. A vital part of the restoration was the placing of massive flying buttresses along the South wall. The two buttresses nearest to No. 1 bear memorials to George and Mary erected by the Mothers' Union perhaps, as Joyce Coombes in her biography of the Sumners speculates, as an intentional parable of the Sumners in stone. For the Diocese of Winchester had been George's home and the place of his Ministry for the whole of his life; he had lived at No. 1, The Close for twenty four years firstly as Archdeacon and later as Bishop of Guildford. His substantial achievements within the Church were overshadowed by the reputations of his illustrious father, as Bishop of Winchester and his uncle as Archbishop of Canterbury. George, a holy and humble man, intelligent and able but perhaps without the driving ambition or genius of his father, was apparently content quietly to serve the diocese throughout his lifetime and did so with much distinction.

Here was a man who loved life as a parish priest, and basked in the contentment of his home and the company of his friends. No doubt his comfortable background, free from financial cares, blunted the edge of his ambition; the Sumners were free to travel abroad at will, to indulge themselves in the arts and enjoy their friends and this they freely did. From the background of their happy

Sources

- Hampshire Record Office, 35M48/7/43 - 44, 47, 49 - 50.
- Joyce Coombs, *George and Mary Sumner: Their Life and Times* (London: The Sumner Press, 1965).
- Lady Horatia Erskine, *Mary Sumner Her Life and Work* (Winchester: Warren and Son, 1921).
- Mary Porter, *Mary Sumner Her life and Work* (Winchester: Warren and Son, 1921).
- *Memoir of G. H. Sumner, Bishop of Guildford*, (Winchester: Warren and Son, 1910).

domestic life and shared commitment to the Church emerged the Mothers' Union and George's part in this great achievement should not be underestimated. The contribution he made and the support he had given was clearly recognised when the Mothers' Union placed his memorial side by side with Mary on the Cathedral buttresses.

George was born in 1824, and was brought up at Farnham Castle, where the family moved when Charles became Bishop of Winchester and George continued to live there until his marriage to Mary Heywood, the daughter of a distinguished Herefordshire family. After Eton and Oxford, the newly-wed George spent a short time as curate at Crawley, Hampshire, to Philip Jacob, himself later to be Archdeacon of Winchester. Then in 1850 George was given the substantial living of Old Alresford. It is worth recalling that Charles Sumner had received in 1849, the resignation of Francis North, Earl of Guildford, from the long held benefices of Old Alresford, following the uncovering of his financial improbity as Master of St Cross, the gift of his father Bishop Brownlow North, and which was later satirized by Trollope in his book *The Warden.* The Sumners moved into the great house at Old Alresford Place no doubt with some trepidation bearing in mind the unsavoury reputation of their predecessor and with the reported words of the *Daily News* ringing in their ears; the new Rector was 'a young gentleman of very small pastoral experience, well fitted for a large house, a good income and little duty'. Given Old Alresford Place's size, sixteen bedrooms, grand reception rooms and extensive servants quarters, it is as well that the Sumners were blessed with private means. George immersed himself in the life of a country rector. From poor beginnings the church gradually filled as George and Mary worked together to involve the village, visiting regularly every home and starting, amongst a myriad of organisations, bible classes, a temperance society, a Sunday School, and a library and reading room.

In 1869, following Charles Sumner's resignation due to ill health, Samuel (Soapy) Wilberforce, Bishop of Oxford and second cousin to Charles Sumner, became Bishop of Winchester. The new Bishop was a frequent breakfast guest at Old Alresford, riding over from Winchester, having readily agreed that Charles Sumner should continue to live at Farnham. George's grasp of diocesan affairs was without equal and he often acted as Chaplain to Wilberforce as he had previously done for his father. In 1873, shortly before being killed in a riding accident, Wilberforce conferred an Honorary Canonry upon George. The new Bishop was Harold Browne, a man of delicate health, a conciliatory man of moderate view and moderate temper. George, although an Honorary and very junior member of the Cathedral Chapter quickly became, as he had for his father and Samuel Wilberforce, a steadfast supporter and right hand man.

George had been acquainted with Bishop Harold Browne since his school days and had got to know him well through Convocation. Since 1866 George had been a Proctor sitting in the Lower House whilst his father and Samuel Wilberforce were in the Upper House. In 1886, George was unanimously elected Prolocutor of Convocation. George proved to be a great success, scrupulously fair, with an astute grasp of procedure coupled with a dry wit. He assumed his office at a time when the House of Laymen was being established, promising, in fluent Latin, in his opening address, 'constantly and firmly to hold the Catholic and Apostolic Faith'. So where did George Sumner fit within the Church? The local Winchester Press categorised him as a moderate high churchman. He certainly was neither totally radical nor totally conservative. He had inherited the Erastian view, of the dominance of secular over ecclesiastical power, from his father. He was a passionate believer in the power of education as a means of liberating the minds of the poor, yet supported the system of tithing and was a strong proponent of the established Church at a time when dis-establishment was much discussed. It is fair to say that he was a man of progressive ideas, looking hopefully for reform whilst avoiding revolution. He held temperate but enlightened views on a raft of social issues.

Bishop Harold Browne made George Sumner Archdeacon of Winchester in 1885, with a permanent stall in the Cathedral and residence in No. 1, The Close. So after sixty years of living in large mansions, both Mary and George found themselves in a modest, for them anyway, seventeenth century house. The Sumners were faced with the stark problems of 'downsizing'; roomfuls of furniture had to be dispersed, books, records, letters destroyed, carriages and horses disposed of; on the positive side the new house nestled against the South side of the Cathedral, near to the east end with its garden stretching away to the grounds of the Bishop's Palace.

George was able to make an immediate physical impact upon the Cathedral for the environs of the Cathedral had become overgrown and sheep grazed right up to the walls themselves, washing was hung out to dry on its railings. With £100 from his own pocket and fifty men he set about cleaning the Cathedral grounds. Debris feet thick had accumulated against the walls of the North transept and the Nave. Its removal revealed a fine arch supported by Norman columns - what had once been an entrance to the church. Found, was the head and shoulders of a figure representing an aged God the Father, wearing a delicately carved papal tiara. It had been richly gilded and carefully coloured and dated from the fifteenth century.

Surprisingly little is recorded of George's time as Archdeacon, and Mary and the Mothers' Union dominate the bibliography of the Sumners. In any event, after only three years as Archdeacon, in 1888 at the age of 64, George was chosen to be the Suffragan Bishop of Guildford. It was a popular choice, for George had been a great success as Archdeacon. Bishop Harold Browne, aged and in ill health, was in sore need of support in managing his extensive Diocese and the re introduction of Suffragans was a timely measure. In practice George found himself carrying almost the full burden of the Diocese until Bishop Harold Browne retired in 1891. Much as he had liked and admired the Bishop the appointment of Anthony Thorold from Rochester to Winchester must have been a relief to George Sumner. Bishop Anthony Thorold had a reputation for energetic administration, but George's relief was to be short lived, as the new Bishop himself fell ill shortly after arriving at Winchester. Once more George, with his own health and vigour in decline found himself almost solely carrying the burden of the Diocese.

Bishop Anthony Thorold died in 1895 and was succeeded by Randall Davidson from Rochester. This proved to be a difficult time for George Sumner, at the age of 72, rheumatic and tired, had to cope with an ambitious Bishop in his mid forties; Davidson's first impression was 'I found Bishop Sumner of Guildford nominally a Suffragan but practically doing very little owing to failing health'. Although this comment does little justice to George for his past commitments to the Diocese it does show that he was running out of steam. In 1901, with evident relief, he resigned as Archdeacon after holding the office for 16 years. However, George was once more to be faced with shouldering the responsibility for the Diocese and this time for the Cathedral as well. On the death of Archbishop Frederick Temple, Randall Davidson became Archbishop of Canterbury, and in the same year the Dean of Winchester died, George nearly 80 years old, was once more in charge of Diocesan matters and, as Senior Canon, of the Cathedral administration.

Little has been said so far about George's involvement with the Mothers' Union. The idea for the Union had been Mary's in 1876, when she saw the need for a church fellowship for women. From its early beginnings the Mother's Union rapidly became a world wide organisation. George Sumner undoubtedly believed in the principles of the Mothers' Union and gave Mary his wholehearted support throughout, using his own ministry to advance its aims. In particular it is doubtful whether the movement would have achieved any momentum without his support and participation during the early days. From the first meeting, he was directly involved, replacing a nervous Mary in explaining the Union's aims and objectives. Thus the Mothers' Union was established but was to remain as a local movement until 1885, nine years later. By 1887 the society had spread throughout the Diocese and beyond. Given the closeness of their relationship one can imagine that George and Mary would have discussed and planned together every initiative taken for the development of the Mothers' Union. Mary was a strong intelligent woman but, given the nature of Victorian society, it would have been very difficult if not impossible for her to develop the movement without the participation and enthusiasm of George.

What has been written on the Sumners on occasion tends towards the hagiographic, but even so the towering goodness of George is a continuous and believable theme throughout. When in 1901, George relinquished the post of Archdeacon he was presented with an address signed by nearly a thousand clergy and churchwardens. Canon Lee used the following words in his presentation address: ' In all these varied offices you have been loved and valued, your rule has been just and fair and kind, you have never been a partisan, but the balance has been held with unswerving justice and unfailing kindness, so that all trusted you'. The rector of St Mary's Portsea, and Bishop of Stepney designate, Cosmo Gordon Lang, said – ' in some mysterious way George had combined the wisdom and guidance of the Father with the sympathy and large heartedness of the Brother ... they had never failed to be cheered, inspired and strengthened by his kindly presence and wise counsels'.

Randall Davidson's successor Bishop H. E. Ryle recognised the extent of George's standing in the Diocese and the enormous contribution he had made, George had held almost every office in the Diocese and had loyally served and supported five Bishops of Winchester. By 1904 George's ministry had to all practical purposes come to an end and in the year following he ceased to carry out the duties of Suffragan Bishop although keeping the title. The final four years of George's life were a period of steady physical decline. Ironically in 1905 as George declined so did the Cathedral building, enormous cracks appeared in the walls and the arches began to subside. The layer of peat under the raft of beech wood piles beneath the thirteenth century retrochoir had compressed and without extensive remedial work the Cathedral would have collapsed. The work of reparation required a major funding appeal and took six years to complete; the work of the diver William Walker was a major contribution. So long as he was able, George made the short journey from No. 1 to attend the Cathedral Services, sharing his daily prayers with the workmen. George would have been conscious of and probably welcomed the noise and bustle of the stonemasons and carpenters etc. working on the Cathedral throughout the last years of his life and drawn comfort from the progress made to save it.

The Hon. Arthur Temple Lyttelton

Archdeacon 1901 ~ 1903

1852 Born 7th January
1874 Graduated from Trinity College Cambridge BA, MA in 1877, DD in 1827
1876 Ordained Deacon
1877 Ordained Priest by the Bishop of Oxford and served first curacy at St Mary the Virgin, Reading
1879 Joined the staff at Keble College Oxford
1880 Married Mary Kathleen Clive
1882 Master of Selwyn College Cambridge
1891 Hulsean Lecturer at Cambridge
1893 Vicar of Eccles in Lancashire
1895 Chaplain to Queen Victoria
1898 Honorary Canon of Manchester Cathedral
1898 Bishop of Southampton
1901 Archdeacon of Winchester
1903 Died 19th February

Arthur Temple Lyttelton was born in London on 7 January 1852, the fifth son of George William Lyttelton, fourth Baron Lyttelton, by his first wife Mary, daughter of Sir Richard Glynne (eighth Baronet), the younger sister of Mrs Gladstone. His eldest brother became Viscount Cobham and among his other brothers were General Sir Neville Lyttelton, Canon Lyttelton, Headmaster of Haileybury and the Hon Alfred Lyttelton K.C., M.P.

Arthur was educated at Eton like his brothers and then went on to Trinity College Cambridge where he was placed in the first class of the Moral Science Tripos in 1873, he graduated B.A. in 1874 proceeding to M.A. in 1877 and D.D. in 1898. After a year at Cuddesdon Theological College he was ordained Deacon in 1876 and Priest in 1877, by the Bishop of Oxford. He served his first curacy at St. Mary the Virgin Reading.

In 1879 he moved to join the staff of Keble College Oxford which had been started nine years earlier by his brother-in-law Dr. Talbot. In 1880 he married Mary Kathleen, daughter of George Clive of Perrystone Court, Herefordshire and they had three children, two sons and a daughter. Three years later in 1882 at the age of 30 he was appointed Master of Selwyn College Cambridge, a college built as a memorial to a great bishop, first of New Zealand, then of Lichfield. Selwyn College was intended to be the Cambridge Keble and under Lyttelton's

Sources

- *The Winchester Diocesan Chronicle*
- *The Times* Obituary
- *The Hampshire Chronicle*
- *The Dictionary of National Biography*
- Miss Patricia Lancaster.

leadership its success was immediate and decisive for he inspired great confidence. As some of the rooms were small, but adequate and the hall and chapel were temporary buildings Lyttelton paved the way for the completion of the whole architectural scheme. Two years after his time at Selwyn ended Archbishop Benson dedicated the chapel. The church tone of the College was high and the chapel services were more frequent than in the older colleges, each day ended with Compline.

During his time at Cambridge he began a period when he was examining chaplain to the Bishop of Ripon, Dr Boyd Carpenter (1884-1888) and then to Bishop Creighton both at Peterborough (1891-1896) and London (1896-1898). He was liberal in his politics and in December 1885 he helped draw up a declaration on disestablishment signed by the liberal members of the Cambridge Senate. He was Hulsean Lecturer at Cambridge in 1891. He took as his subject 'The Place of Miracles in Religion'. These lectures were published in 1899 with some additions and corrections.

After eleven years at Selwyn College Arthur Temple Lyttelton felt he wanted to be involved in pastoral work so he became vicar of Eccles in Lancashire in 1893 on the nomination of the Lord Chancellor, Lord Herschall. In 1895 he was made Rural Dean and elected Proctor for the clergy in the York Convocation. He was made an Honorary Chaplain to Queen Victoria in 1895 and Chaplain in Ordinary in 1896. In his youth Lyttelton had been a page at the Court of Queen Victoria. In 1898 he was appointed to an Honorary Canonry of Manchester by Bishop Moorhouse.

He contributed the essay on the Atonement to *Lux Mundi*. This was an Oxonian publication and it is likely that he was invited to contribute because of his earlier connection with Keble College. His publications were few but he was a great reader and when his workload permitted he wrote criticisms on current literature.

In 1898 the Crown on the nomination of Dr Randall Davidson appointed Lyttelton to be Bishop of Southampton when Dr Fisher resigned. He was consecrated on 30 November 1898 (St Andrew's Day) in St Paul's Cathedral. In the same year he was made Provost of Lancing College which gave him authority over the southern group of Woodard Schools, a particularly appropriate appointment for a person so keenly interested in education on Church lines. He was installed in Lancing Chapel on 30 May 1899. A boarding house was named after him at St Michael's Petworth, the nearby girls' Woodard School; this school has now closed.

In 1901 Lyttelton became Archdeacon of Winchester, being installed by the Dean on Monday 4 February. He contributed valuable service to the Diocese in assisting the Bishop of Winchester in his Episcopal work and he was Warden of the Mission Staff. On the retirement of Canon Valpy, Bishop Littleton took over the control and management of Mission work in the Diocese. On Missionary Day in Bishop's Waltham on the 27 November 1899 he celebrated and preached. On 9 July the Bishop took the chair and gave the opening address at the Meeting of the Society for Promoting Higher Education in Religious Knowledge.

As Bishop of Southampton Lyttelton undertook a large number of engagements after his arrival, the following examples are typical of his work in the Diocese. In March 1899 there were only two days when he was not administering the sacrament of Confirmation and on some days there were two services. In May the Bishop addressed a meeting of the Cambridge Association, which supported Home and Foreign Mission Work. He commented that he thought it was a useful thing for graduates after they had started work in the world to be reminded of their Alma Mater and to realise how many there were up and down the Diocese who remembered their College with affection. In June he and his wife were among the speakers at the Mothers' Union Diocesan Conference. The Bishop gave an impressive address on the text 'For their sakes I will sanctify myself' John 8 v.19 and Mrs Lyttelton took as her subject 'The Principles of Character Training' on which she based some valuable remarks as to the best means of teaching children to know what is right, to find out what is right and to do what is right without murmur and misgiving.

Lyttelton seemed marked out for high office in the church, but sadly in 1902 he fell ill with cancer and he died at Castle House Petersfield on 19 February 1903, aged 51. His wife died on 13 January 1907 leaving their two sons and a daughter.

The following tribute appeared in the Winchester Diocesan Chronicle in March 1903-

> *For some time past it has been known to his friends that he was far from well, and early last autumn he was ordered to go abroad and take complete rest. In December when he returned home his illness was pronounced and malignant and he had a short time to live. Happily he did not suffer the severe bodily pain, which might have been anticipated, but physical weakness rapidly increased and he entered into rest on the morning of 21 February.*

His working day closed early, but in a short time he fulfilled a long time, and though his time of departure may seem to us, perhaps sadly inopportune, considering the bereft condition of the Diocese, yet we may say 'his soul pleased the Lord, therefore hasted He to take him away'.

Our loss is heavy; for us he was one who possessed in a marked degree the gift of right judgement, and he was a wise guide in all matters which concerned Church welfare.

He was described as a man whose 'wonderful recollectedness of spirit, gentleness of disposition, exact knowledge, and simple and strong holiness of life have left their mark in every home he visited', and we feel sure that in these words all who knew him will fully concur.

His published works include:

College and University Sermons (1894);
The Place of Miracles in Religion (1899);
After his death Modern Poets of Faith, Doubt and Unbelief and other Essays (1904)

The Thorold and Lyttelton Library is named after the two Bishops whose personal libraries formed the nucleus. This Library is situated in No. 11 The Close and is available for the use of students in the Diocese. It was opened in 1906. Since then the Library has expanded and new books are purchased regularly.

Dr W A Fearon

Archdeacon 1903 ~ 1920

1841 Born the third son of the Rev. Daniel Fearon, his forebears included Bishop Lancelot Andrewes and Christopher Wren

1864 Elected a Fellow of New College, Oxford after obtaining a double first in Moderations and Greats, ordained 1867

1868 Assistant Master and House Master, Winchester College

1884 Headmaster of Winchester College

1889 Honorary Canon of Winchester Cathedral

1903 Archdeacon of Winchester

1924 Died

Sources

- Hampshire Record Office, 44M68/G1/5.
- Hampshire Record Office, 44M68/B1/1 and 3.
- *Times Newspaper*, 30 April 1924.
- *Hampshire Chronicle*, 3 May 1924.
- A. K. Cook, *About Winchester College* (London: Macmillan, 1917).
- W. A. Fearon, *Sunday Mornings in Winchester* (1850).
- W. A. Fearon, *The Passing of Old Winchester* (Warder and Fellows, 1936).
- J. D'E Firth, *Winchester College* (Winchester: P. G. Wells, 1961).
- C. F. C. Hawkes, *St. Catherine's Hill, Winchester* (Winchester, 1930).
- James Sabben-Clare, *Winchester College* (Southampton: Paul Cave, 1981).
- Chrisopher Wilkes, *A Study of Winchester College* (London: Heineman, 1965).

Dr W. A. Fearon was Archdeacon of Winchester from 1903 to 1920 and was much loved and respected by the clergy. However, Fearon is best known as one of the great Headmasters of Winchester College. He could claim to have been almost born a Wykehamist. For his uncle had performed a financial service to the College about the time of his birth, and the Warden had, in return, promised to make his uncle's nominee a Scholar of the College and the place fell to the infant William. Fearon says that, 'at the first moment of consciousness I knew I was a Scholar of Winchester'. As we shall see the College was, together with his deep faith, to form the core of his life.

He was a brilliant and hard working schoolboy, becoming head of the school and in 1859 the first Winchester Scholar of New College, Oxford, to enter under a system based on merit. After a short time as a tutor he was appointed by Dr Ridding as an Assistant Master at Winchester. It is thanks to Fearon that we know so much about life at the college under Dr Moberly. In his little book of reminiscences of college life, *The Passing of Old Winchester*, he shows how his love of the place was formed from the very outset of his days there as a pupil. Viewed from today the regime was harsh and spartan, but Fearon revelled in it. He tells us that at age 13 he was already drifting into bad ways and that confirmation classes brought about his salvation and that for the rest of his life 'he manifested a degree of piety and earnestness which he tried, with no great success to transmit to the next generation'. He loved the Sunday service in the Cathedral. 'Dr Wesley, the organist, was in the habit before the sermon of extemporizing a voluntary on the organ to a greater length than the Canons sometimes approved'. He notes with pleasure that, on one occasion a chaplain delighted them by preaching for only five minutes commencing with the words: 'on these festival occasions it is desirable to avoid on the one hand a tedious prolixity, and on the other an unbecoming brevity'.

He was above all, at Winchester, a teacher, indeed he is rated as one of the greatest. A strict disciplinarian of great moral courage and with a certain fussiness tempered with a gleam of humour and understanding. His boundless enthusiasm brought history alive-pupils recalled gaining from him their first realization that the Greeks and Romans were men of actual blood and flesh. James Sabben Clare notes that Fearon was, 'besides being of prodigious energy, the master of all the tricks of dramatic utterance'. 'His voice would rise to a high tenor note, he would fling up his bearded chin, one or two warning fingers would be raised: and as he became fired by his subject, he would tilt his chair, coil one leg round the chair leg and slip his unemployed arm over the top of his head until he grasped the other ear'! He would tuck his gown under his arm and pace furiously up and down as he enlarged upon the unique significance of some episode in history.

Fearon in 1868 established the College's fourth house at 22 Kingsgate Street with just eight boys; meanwhile a permanent house was being built in Culver's Close. With the abolition of Commoners the new house soon filled up. A memorable feature of Fearon's House was his Sunday evening addresses later published, and every day at dinner in Hall he introduced discussions about current public affairs. In 1879 he married Mary, daughter of Archdeacon Freeman, of Exeter. In 1882 Fearon was appointed Headmaster of Durham Cathedral School, but he was to be separated from his beloved Winchester for only two years. In 1884 Dr Ridding accepted the Bishopric of Southwell. The election of Fearon as his successor was a foregone conclusion. He was Headmaster for 17 years, building on the high standards set by Ridding. His industry was extraordinary; he knew every side and aspect of the school and its life. In spite of a tendency to worry over trifles and a reluctance to delegate, he was an exceptional Headmaster who never lost his enthusiasm and energy. As a boy Dr Moberly had said to him: 'Fearon it's no good; you are like a cork, one puts you down and you are up again at once'. Fearon was as successful in making church questions come alive for the boys as he had been with history – as he himself puts it, 'how to make them other than repelling to the boy's mind'. First and foremost he ended the practice of weekly attendance at the Cathedral ordinary service, replacing it with a specially arranged service for the whole school on the 2nd Sunday of the month; achieving, as A. K. Cook tells us in his book on the college, 'the conversion of an institution which had its origin perhaps in mere slackness on the part of the Fellows and which to most had become irksome, into one which was at the time a valued privilege and later a happy memory'. The brief addresses he prepared for the short Sunday services were designed to 'capture the evasive minds of schoolboys', keeping a sense of proportion along with 'a certain vividness of impression'. These addresses were published on his retirement in '*Sunday Mornings at Winchester*' perhaps the most well known of his books.

Dr W A Fearon

During his time the College extended and developed its missionary activities in the deprived slums of Portsea, Portsmouth. He showed his ability to take a risk with the employment as College Missioner of Father Robert Dolling, a strange but brilliant high church priest, whose magnificent work amongst the poor led Fearon to say of him 'Dolling's religious methods and ritual were much out of harmony with the strict orthodoxy of the school religion, with him one has to accept perpetually the prospect of a crisis – but his unique work outweighed every other consideration'. Dolling after a time was able to claim that, besides much else, he had reformed 25 thieves, rescued 144 fallen women, started in life 100 young men living in the Parsonage and closed 50 brothels. Under Fearon's guidance the College entered wholeheartedly into the work of Dolling's Mission with regular weekend visits: Fearon tells us – 'Dolling's relationship to Winchester College was pure unbroken sunshine' It must have been very difficult for

Fearon when Dolling came into serious conflict with the new Bishop, Randall Davidson. After eleven years of dispute over ritual, matters came to a head when Dolling persisted, against the Bishop's advice, with the placing of an altar in the South aisle for Masses to be said for the dead. Fearon became an arbitrator between both parties, proving to be a loyal friend to both sides and easing the inevitable parting and repairing the damage as well as could have been done.

Although a forward-looking Headmaster, Fearon was a great lover of school tradition and did much to revive old customs where this could be done in a contemporary context. In 1894 at the start of each Summer and Winter term he revived, in modified form, the 300 year old tradition of 'Hills' with a pre-breakfast procession, at 8am, to St. Catherine's Hill. This also underlined Wykehamist's rights to disport themselves on 'Hills' at a time when threats had been made to fence it off. He also arranged for the much needed renewal of the clump of trees there, in 1897 adding some 50 firs and beeches. It had been Dr Fearon's dearest wish to build a new Chapel as a memorial on the occasion of the two quincentenary celebrations in 1887 and 1893, but Wykehamist sentiment was against this and he had to settle for a restoration of the Wykeham chantry in the cathedral and a museum building in the college grounds.

In 1901 Fearon retired as Headmaster. He was then sixty years of age, but more importantly, as J. D' E. Firth points out in his book on the college, 'he was a Victorian through and through and he had no message to give to the twentieth century'. For two years, after declining a deanery, Fearon retired into the country, the only time of leisure he had ever known. In 1903 Bishop Randall Davidson was elevated to the Archbishopric of Canterbury and Bishop H. E. Ryle became Bishop of Winchester. He was faced immediately with filling the vacancy of Archdeacon of Winchester and that of Suffragan Bishop of Southampton. It seems that William Fearon was offered the appointment of Bishop but preferred to be appointed Archdeacon. It is in character that he at once threw himself with his usual boundless energy into the work of the Diocese. What was outstanding about him was the encouragement and support he gave to all his clergy. Bishop Edward Talbot in his sermon for Fearon's funeral movingly said: 'he brought the energy of help and the living touch of sympathy to each of the clergy – encouraging lonely men, stimulating desponding ones and helping (more than was realised) needy ones'. There was a common saying that the Archdeacon was the youngest man in the Diocese.

From a letter to the Winchester Diocesan Chronicle of January 1905 we get an idea of his impact on the parishes: 'In the past few months an Archdeaconal Visitation has been translated from an oppressive phrase into a buoyant reality for numbers of the country clergy'. Fearon himself had a great sympathy for the work of the parishes and spoke at the Annual General meeting of the Bishop of Winchester's Fund in 1906 of – 'the clergy toiling under great difficulty underlining the debt that the nation owed them'.

In 1906 he was appointed a Canon Residentiary and he and Mary moved into No. 11, The Close, overlooking the cathedral he loved so much. He continued his interest in the Missionary work at Portsmouth and was instrumental in raising the £50,000 needed for the Portsmouth Church extension scheme. However, it is in two particular respects that his contribution to the Diocese is, perhaps, best remembered. Firstly, over a period of years and with the help of a number of the clergy, he put together a comprehensive collation and description of parish registers, published as – *The Parish Registers and Parochial Documents in the Archdeaconry of Winchester*, a social history still much used. He encouraged and supported the publication of related books such as *Hampshire Church Bells, The Church Plate of Hampshire* and an *Early Churchwarden's Account of Hampshire.* A country parson wrote to the Diocesan Chronicle – 'it is encouraging to be visited by an Archdeacon who has an archaeologist's appreciation of parochical antiquities, as well as a Churchman's interest in modern ecclesiastical efforts'. Secondly, it was due to his enthusiasm and personal generosity that the bequests of books made by Thorold and Lyttelton were transformed into a viable library for the clergy of the diocese. He was an energetic member of the Library's Trustees and, after his retirement, as Honorary Librarian. He made personal donations of over £2,000 to the library, a substantial gift, which provided the income needed to run the library. A cursory glance today over the library shelves, reveals the extent of his personal donation of books.

On retirement, in 1920, he moved to London and enjoyed nothing so much as keeping up with the many generations of Old Wykehamists. One of his greatest joys was Saturday meetings at the Athanaeum with Bishop Herbert Ryle, who had left Winchester for health reasons to become Dean of Westminster, where they would talk over affairs of church and state. At Winchester Ryle had found Fearon the most like minded with himself and theirs had been an enduring friendship.

Fearon died in 1924 aged 83, and his obituary describes him as 'A Wykehamist of Wykehamists', a phrase he would surely have approved. He had been associated with the College and the Diocese for 73 years of his life and during that time had never lost his enthusiasm for both of them. Bishop Edward Talbot started his sermon for Fearon with the words 'I put before you Dr Fearon as a great example of alertness in some of its noblest forms'. But as Talbot went on to say his alertness was tempered and controlled; indeed he had known few men so modest – he shrank from any reference to himself. Talbot concluded by attributing: 'the tempering of the fine metal of his quick energy to his deep religious faith'.

A E Daldy

Archdeacon 1920 ~ 1935

1865 Born
1888 Ordained as a deacon, and as a priest the following year
1904 Appointed Vicar of St. Peters, Bournemouth
1911 Appointed Honorary Canon of Winchester Cathedral
1920 Archdeacon of Winchester
1927 Master of St. Cross
1935 Died

Alfred Daldy was appointed to the Archdeaconry of Winchester in 1920 following the resignation of Dr W. A. Fearon. He was to remain in this post until his death in 1935 when the Bishop of Southampton, in his tribute, described him as a 'great Archdeacon, carrying in his heart the troubles of many parish priests'. He was born in 1865 and at the age of just sixteen, went up to Cambridge but never became a member of any college, reading quietly, living his own life. He took an ordinary degree in the same month as his nineteenth birthday and then left! In 1888 he obtained an M.A. and was ordained as a deacon in the London Diocese. In the next year he was ordained as a priest. For the next nine years he filled curacies in the diocese, firstly at Bromley and later at Barking.

A major change came to his ministry when he was invited by Arthur Lyttelton, then Bishop of Southampton, to become a missioner in the Diocese of Winchester and where he lived with his brother missioners at Wolvesey which had been adapted as the Mission Headquarters. His character and abilities developed under Lyttelton's inspiring leadership and in 1904, at the age of 39, he became Vicar of St. Peter's, Bournemouth. He was an ideal parish priest of the time; his deep faith and compassion were mixed with an unusual affinity for organization and administration. He spent sixteen years in the parish and under his guidance St. Peter's became the centre of a strong church life. His personal influence

Sources

- *Times Newspaper*, 5 May 1924.
- *Hampshire Chronicle*, 2 November 1935.
- *Hampshire Chronicle*, 9 November 1935.
- *Winchester Diocesan Chronicle*, December, 1935.
- Peter Hopewell, *Saint Cross, England's Oldest Almshouse* (Chichester: Phillimore & Co, 1995).

spread beyond parochial affairs into local civic and educational spheres. Debts were paid off, a church hall built, and his many diverse initiatives included the provision of a shelter for the cabbies at the local railway station. The railway company had refused to build one so Daldy set to to do so by public subscription. Whilst at St. Peter's, in 1908, Daldy married Constance Mary, the daughter of the Hon. Algernon West of Guildford and widow of the Revd Edgar Van der Noot, one time Rector of King's Worthy. Theirs was a happy marriage and under his wife's influence the vicarage became an important social centre.

Daldy's faith was unshakeable and his convictions impenetrable, he knew exactly where he stood and what he believed. He was a clear and forcible preacher, precise in manner. He held decided opinions on almost everything and liked to get his own way. At Bournemouth he usually got what he wanted as his parish had learned to trust his judgement. At all times outspoken, he once expressed his views on how a clergyman should behave in a holiday resort in the following words: 'he had always been astonished at the number of faddists and bores to be found amongst the residents of seaside resorts, but was glad that in those places the authorities often provided facilities for open air religious services - in carefully selected spots to which visitors never came. A parson at a seaside resort should always act like a parson. It was a mistake for him to lose respect with the visitors by dressing in flannels or a green suit with a red necktie'.

In spite of his forthright manner he was certainly not a self publicist and only those who lived and worked in Bournemouth and worked under him as Rural Dean would have been fully aware of how widespread and how great was his influence in every section of the community. A member of the Bournemouth Education Committee for some years, as well as Rural Dean at Christchurch, he was in 1911 appointed an Honorary Canon of Winchester. His influence at St. Peter's and the esteem in which he was held are illustrated by the gift bestowed upon him when he left the parish in 1920; an illuminated manuscript and a cheque for £600 for him to buy a motor car. A fellow missioner who lived at Wolvesey with him for four years recalled that he never once caught him off guard in word or deed. He noted that only two relationships are possible in the case of a leader as efficient as Daldy; he was either loved or not loved, but he could not be ignored.

It was the resignation of Dr W. A. Fearon in 1920 that led to Daldy's appointment by

Bishop Edward Talbot as Archdeacon of Winchester and his election as a Residentiary Canon. Daldy moved into No. 8 The Close with his wife. The beginning of Daldy's period as Archdeacon coincided with the debate within the Church of the necessity for a division of some of the larger dioceses into smaller more manageable entities. Daldy a strong proponent of division played a prominent part in the preparation for the division of the Winchester Diocese. He was asked by Bishop Talbot to introduce the Measure for division to the Church Assembly, and did so in a speech described as remarkable for its conciseness and lucidity. There was strong opposition, including that of Bishop Herbert Ryle and Dr Fearon his predecessor. The matter was referred to an appointed committee of supporters and opponents. Daldy, encouraged by the strong support for division from within the diocese, was unwilling to make concessions and so conciliate the opponents and by strength of will finally carried the day, the Measure being passed without substantial amendment. It was a great personal triumph for Daldy but the manner of the winning of it left considerable resentment in some quarters. Daldy's other great contribution was his part in framing the Clergy Pension measure and in developing the system for its administration.

Although he threw himself with great energy into the role of Archdeacon, he was never quite happy as a member of Chapter. He clearly missed not having a flock of his own to minister and care for and was deeply affected by the death of his wife suddenly in 1922, just two years after moving into the Close. However, there seems to have been a more serious clash of relationships, for Daldy was used to getting his own way and appears to have found the way Chapter worked, through consensus, rather frustrating. In addition there was the bad feeling left by the part he had played in getting through the Measure for division of the diocese. The Bishop, by then Theodore Woods, in 1924, wisely offered Daldy St. Mary's Southampton, a living that was within the gift of the Bishop. Daldy, in the West Indies in connection with a Mission of Help, cabled his acceptance from Trinidad. On his return in February 1925, Daldy resigned his appointment as Residentiary Canon but remained Archdeacon. He entered into the life of St. Mary's with the same extraordinary enthusiasm that had marked his time at St. Peter's.

However, by this time Daldy was aged sixty and St. Mary's was a busy important parish. Daldy was inevitably in much demand for his business skills and was unable to resist increasing his burden with such things as Chairmanship of the Management Committee for the Royal South Hants. and Southampton Hospital. All this, together with his continuing duties as Archdeacon were too much even for someone of Daldy's energies. The Bishop in 1927, three years after Daldy's appointment as rector to St. Mary's, therefore, offered him the Mastership of St. Cross, this proved to be a much better solution. Its beautiful church (or Chapel) was an ideal setting for a man so much a lover of worship; and happily for him, the Master was also responsible for the parish of St. Faith's, which not having its own church, had the privilege of worshipping in the St. Cross chapel. He was inducted as Master by the Bishop in February 1928 and for the next eight years proved to be a kindly, just and considerate Master. In 1929 he was re-appointed as an Honorary Canon of Winchester Cathedral.

Daldy died suddenly, aged seventy, at breakfast on the 29th of October 1935, found by his housekeeper still at the breakfast table as she took him the morning mail. He had been in apparent good health; he had attended two meetings the previous day and was about to catch the train to London, for a meeting of the Clergy Pensions Board, of which he was Vice-Chairman. The congregation for the first part of his funeral service in the Cathedral numbered some 1400 people from all walks of life. Daldy had attended a small party at a friend's house the night before his death and had left early with the words 'I have so much to do tomorrow'. A fitting epitaph for a man of such remarkable energy and dedication.

Edmund Robert Morgan

Archdeacon 1936 ~ 1943

1888 Born, 28th July
1912 Graduated from New College Oxford, B.A. Literae Humaniores
1913 Ordained Deacon
1914 Ordained Priest and served first curacy at St Andrew's Farnham
1915 Curacy at Eastleigh
1916 M.A.; Married Isabel Charlotte Jupp
1919 Domestic Chaplain to Bishop Talbot
1923 Warden of College of the Ascension Selly Oak Birmingham
1936 Rector of Old Alresford and Archdeacon of Winchester
1942 Residentiary Canon of Winchester Cathedral
1943 Bishop of Southampton
1951 Bishop of Truro
1955 Retired
1979 Died 21st September

Edmund Robert Morgan was born on 28 July 1888 He was educated at Winchester College, where he was top scholar of his year, and New College Oxford where he was also a scholar. He read Classics and was awarded 2nd class in Classical Moderations in 1909, B.A. 3rd Class in Literae Humaniores in 1912 and an M.A. in 1916 He also gained a diploma in Educational Method after six months training at Liverpool University. In 1912 he started his Theological training at The Farnham Hostel. He was ordained Deacon in Winchester Cathedral on Trinity Sunday 1913 to a title at St. Andrew's Farnham and he was priested a year later. It was at Farnham that he meet Isabel Charlotte Jupp to become his wife in 1916. She had been nicknamed Bluebell which was later shortened to Blue and she was known by that name.

In 1915 Edmund Morgan moved to a curacy at Eastleigh. The Parish Church dedicated in the name of the Resurrection had been enlarged considerably and a second church All Saints was built and dedicated, this was the one for which the curate had responsibility. The increasing population in Eastleigh was caused by the removal of the London and South West Railway works from Nine Elms to Eastleigh. His time at All Saints was fulfilling and he endeared himself to his parishioners. Two children were born during the Morgans' time at Eastleigh, Hugh in March 1917 and Robert in November 1918. Their third son, Geoffrey, was born in Farnham in 1920.

Source

∗ *Edmund Robert Morgan 1888-1979,* A. J. and E. M. Beach, published by the authors in 1981 *In the Preface Robert Runcie said "He made sanctity seem accessible to all."*

In 1919 Edmund Morgan returned to Farnham as Domestic Chaplain to Bishop Talbot, who, as bishop of the still undivided diocese lived in Farnham Castle. About the time that Bishop Talbot resigned the See of Winchester in 1923 Edmund Morgan was offered the Wardenship of a Church of England College in Selly Oak Birmingham to train women missionaries. So in 1923 he became Warden of the College of the Ascension at Selly Oak and was always known as 'Padre'. He remained there for twelve fruitful years and made a considerable impression on his students.

Mission was an important part of Edmund Morgan's thinking and after eight years at the College of the Ascension training women for work in the mission field he was invited to make a study of the relation of church history to work in the mission field. He had leave of absence from July 1931-January1932 to travel with a delegation headed by Professor Case of Chicago University and Professor Schermerhorn to Japan, Korea and China. On his way home he visited the Holy Land returning to Birmingham five months after he departed saying he had 'packed more experiences than most people have in a lifetime.'

Towards the end of this period Edmund Morgan began to feel he had done all he could for the College and so in 1936 when he was offered the post of Archdeacon of Winchester and Rector of Old Alresford he accepted. The idea of him being an Archdeacon struck him as rather comic. Anyone less like the popular notion of an Archdeacon at that time, gaiters and all, cannot be imagined.

Edmund Morgan moved to Hampshire and at the institution in March 1936 Cyril Garbett, the Bishop of Winchester, spoke of the value to the whole church of his work at Selly Oak and mentioned his previous connections with the Diocese. He went on 'I welcome him here. Early today I instituted him as Archdeacon of Winchester. I think it is an advantage that the two posts should be held together when the parish is a small one; also from the point of view of the Archdeacon, for he is in daily contact with the parochial problems amongst which he has to move. On the other hand, it is good for a parish that it should have, where possible, as its Rector one who is in direct touch with Church Movements in the Diocese.'

It seems that Edmund Morgan found some of the administrative duties of an Archdeacon uncongenial, he was much more interested in getting to know the clergy and their families and being involved in their joys and sorrows. He was popular with everyone in the Parish including the choirboys who found him good fun and they greatly respected him because they perceived he knew what he was talking about and expected the very best both in singing and deportment.

The Second World War caused changes in Alresford and tragedy to the Morgan family. In 1940, six months after War was declared Hugh, their eldest son, went off to India for three years on board the British India Steamship 'Domala' which was destroyed by enemy action. Hugh was serving as a junior engineer and this was his first voyage. The way Edmund and Blue Morgan faced their loss was an inspiration. In 1943 further tragedy struck. Robert their second son, was a Lieutenant in the Royal Navy and was serving on H.M.S.Hurworth operating in the Mediterranean. H.M.S. Hurworth was blown up going to rescue a Greek destroyer caught in a minefield in the Dodecanese. The news came through that Robert's name was not among the survivors of the ship. Many have spoken about the way Edmund Morgan helped the bereaved, he had been that way and found a way through.

There is not a great deal of information about Morgan's activities as Archdeacon. One amusing incident was a request from the Dilapidations Board to see an incumbent who had requested a 'loo' for each member of his family. He had five daughters! The shortage of petrol, masked headlights and lack of road signs made archidiaconal functions difficult.

At Easter 1942 Edmund Morgan was given a residentiary canonry by Bishop Haigh. This was to replace Canon Brabant who resigned his canonry to devote all his time to work on the staff of Winchester College. The Morgan family moved from Old Alresford to 15 Kingsgate Street as no house was available in the Close at that time. In 1943 they moved to No. 5 The Close where they remained till they moved to Truro. In 1943 Edmund Morgan was appointed Bishop of Southampton and was consecrated at St. Paul's on 3 June – Ascension Day. He relinquished the role of Archdeacon and was succeeded by Hedley Burrows. He cared for the clergy conscientiously and had special concern for those serving abroad, taking great trouble to see that they found the right niche on returning home. The younger clergy were also of special concern and he frequently ran courses for them.

Liturgy was a great interest; he would say 'Every occasional office should be a proclamation of the Gospel.' He composed two offices; one is An Office of Prayer for the Growth of the Younger Churches and An Office for a Missionary Gathering. There is also An Order of Service for a Missionary Festival for the Diocese of Winchester produced after 1949 which has all the marks of his influence.

Bishop Morgan became Bishop of Truro in 1951, succeeding Bishop Hunkin who died unexpectedly. He was enthroned on Thursday 14 June 1951 and given a very warm welcome with over 2,000 in the cathedral and the service was relayed to those outside. He was also installed as Dean because at that time the Bishop was automatically Dean of the Cathedral. In previous places he had been involved in Prayer Cells and found the experience strengthening. After only a few months in Truro he reported 'I have just brought off a cell of prayer on Religious Education, five priests and one sister of the Epiphany. Pretty Good' A senior priest said to the Rev Mother of the Community 'If only we had known this way years ago what a lot of mistakes would have been avoided". He wanted to nurture these prayer groups knowing what a difference they made to people's life and work. Gordon Cooke from the Diocese of Truro said 'The secret of this remarkable man lay in the fact that Edmund Morgan was a man under authority. He rose at six every morning and had an hour of prayer and meditation, which he regarded as absolutely vital and without which he could not have carried on his varied work.'

In 1955 Bishop Morgan was awarded a Lambeth D.D. In 1959 the office of Dean was made separate from that of Bishop and the first person to hold the post was Henry Lloyd. In the same year Bishop Morgan, aged 71, announced his retirement to much sadness in the Diocese. Many warm tributes were paid to the Bishop and his wife, who had been such a support, when they departed. The Rev. R. J. M. May paid a farewell tribute to the Bishop in the cathedral; he spoke of the way he had inspired the People and Parish movement and encouraged the formation of prayer cells. He also commented on the great joy experienced by those who attended the Bishop's retreats. Geoffrey Fisher, Archbishop of Canterbury said 'Morgan is the only one amongst us who hasn't got critics'.

The Morgans settled in a bungalow at Downton (near Salisbury) on Geoffrey's farm. In June 1960 Bishop Morgan was asked to take a Lectureship for the Easter Term Jan. – May 1961 at the Theological Seminary in New York, giving two courses of lectures in Ascetical Theology and the Interior Life. He accepted and it proved to be a very happy time. On returning to England they settled in Swanage. Blue died in February1964 having been a great support to her husband throughout his ministry. His final years were spent with Geoffrey and his family near Salisbury and there he had a constant stream of visitors. He died on 21 September 1979 aged 91.

Published Works include:

The Catholic Revival and Mission, 1932
The Mission of the Church, 1946
The Undiscovered Country, 1962

Editor of: *Essays Catholic and Missionary;* 1926, *East and West Review*, 1935-46; *The Mission of the Anglican Communion*, 1948. He also wrote two hymns one in Ancient and Modern Revised No. 20.

Hedley Robert Burrows

Archdeacon 1943 ~ 1947

1887 Born, Godalming Surrey
1909 Charterhouse New College Oxford (2nd class Modern History)
1911 Ordained Deacon (Winchester) Curate of Petersfield
1912 Ordained Priest (Winchester)
1913 Master of Arts Wells Theological College
1914 TCF
1917 Priest in Charge St Columba Kilmartin
1918 Res. Chaplain Archbishop of York
1919 Curate St Mary Southampton
1921 Rector of Stoke Abbott
1925 Vicar St. Stephen's Portsea
1927 Hon. Chaplain Bishop of Portsmouth
1928 Vicar Great Grimsby (also Rural Dean)
1933 Preb. Lincoln Cathedral
1940 Vicar St Peter with St Swithun Bournemouth
1943 Canon and Archdeacon of Winchester
1947 Dean of Hereford
1983 Died, Itchen Abbas

Source

∻ Information from interview with The Rt. Revd Simon Burrows (son).

Coming from a long-established clerical family Hedley Burrows served as Archdeacon of Winchester during the period which covered the end of the Second World War. He is still remembered in the diocese, not least for his marvellous sense of humour and is one of the last Archdeacons in this archdeaconry to have worn gaiters. On one occasion when it was suggested that perhaps he should give up this practice he is reported as saying, 'it's the only way to get a porter at Waterloo!'

Hedley Robert Burrows was born on 15th October 1887 and spent his early childhood in Godalming. He would talk about having seen Queen Victoria at Godalming station when he was a boy. His father, Leonard Hedley Burrows was so named in recognition of his family's admiration for a Captain Hedley Vickers, a Victorian evangelical soldier who died during the Boar War. In some ways therefore, in terms of Christian Ministry, Hedley Vickers became something of an icon to the Burrows family. Leonard, Hedley's father as Vicar of Hove became Bishop of Lewes and was later appointed as the first Bishop of Sheffield. Hedley was one of three children. His brother Righton was killed during the First World War and his sister Molly married another priest who later became Bishop of Selby. He was a pupil at Charterhouse and from there secured a place at New College Oxford. He graduated in modern history in 1909 and received his Master of Arts degree in 1913. Hedley became an ordinand at Wells Theological College and was then invited to serve his title in Diocese of Winchester as curate of Petersfield. He was made Deacon in 1911 and ordained priest the following year, staying in the parish until 1914 when at the beginning of the First World War he became an Army Chaplain. The experience of the war was harrowing, and in later life he talked endlessly about his experiences during those years, recognising that his service was quite short, in that he was invalided out in 1915. It is thought, that during his service as chaplain, and not knowing at the time, that he took the funeral service of his own brother.

The family feared for his life. Hedley was sent to Netley Abbey suffering from severe mental breakdown. However, after a long period of recuperation he re-emerged as a chaplain to a Laird in Scotland, a Colonel Campbell. He was made Priest in Charge of St. Columba, Kilmartin. An invitation followed to be residential chaplain to the Archbishop of York. This he accepted and lived and worked at Bishopsthorpe 1918-19. Hedley returned to the Diocese of Winchester as curate of St. Mary's, Southampton in 1919 being Curate in Charge of the Dock Street Mission. The incumbent of St. Mary's at the time was a Neville Lovett who later became Archdeacon of Portsmouth. As Archdeacon of Portsmouth he was charged with the task of creating the new diocese of Portsmouth, setting it up and acquiring a house for the new Bishop. To his surprise he was then invited to be Bishop of Portsmouth in 1927-28. Neville Lovett was translated to Salisbury in 1935. Hedley had married the Vicar's daughter Joan, and accompanied by his new wife he became incumbent of Stoke Abbot serving in the parish from 1921-1925. The population of the village was 165 at the time and Evensong was attended by 60 people! In 1925 Hedley was appointed incumbent of St. Stephen's Portsea, and also in 1927 became Honorary Chaplain to the Bishop of Portsmouth (his father-in-law). Once the new diocese of Portsmouth had been established the Burrows family moved to Grimsby, to the parish of Saint James Great, Grimsby living and serving there for eight years. Hedley returned to the diocese and to St. Peter's Church, Bournemouth in 1936. He was Vicar of Saint Peter with St. Swithun from 1936-43. Simon, (Hedley's son) remembers those days very clearly. The Church was 'packed' at the Sung Eucharist at 10 a.m. and again at Matins at 11.15 a.m. Sunday by Sunday long queues formed outside the Church in readiness for people to take up places once the Eucharist had finished. Hedley was a very good preacher and built on this reputation as Archdeacon. At the end of the Second World War he preached a course of sermons in the Cathedral, entitled 'Where do we go from here?' These sermons made a lasting and tremendous impression.

Hedley Robert Burrows was appointed Canon Residentiary of the Cathedral and Archdeacon of Winchester in 1943. His archdeaconry included the deanery of Winchester and the deaneries to the south. Hedley, his wife and family took up residence in number 11 The Close. Hedley and Joan had four children-Giles, (who died during the second world War) Gillian, Simon and Sarah. Simon was ordained priest in 1954 and appointed Suffragan Bishop of Buckingham in 1974.

In 1947 Hedley was asked to be Dean of Hereford Cathedral. This he accepted and served faithfully until his retirement in 1961. He retired to Itchen Abbas and Martyr Worthy, back in his 'home diocese', where he lived until his death in 1983.

Leslie Hamilton Lang

Archdeacon 1947 ~ 1962

1889 Born 27th May
1912 Graduated from Trinity College Cambridge, B.A. (2nd class History Tripos), M.A.1918.
1915 Ordained deacon at Winchester
1916 Ordained Priest , first curacy at St Mary's Portsea
Chaplain to the Forces during the First World War then to the Archbishop of York
1918 Married Janette Todd
1920 Vicar of All Saints Swanscombe
1922 Vicar of St George's Camberwell and Warden of Trinity Mission
1927 Vicar of Kingston on Thames and Rural Dean
1934 Residentary Canon at Winchester and Diocesan Missioner
1936 Bishop of Woolwich and Archdeacon of Lewisham
1947 Canon and Archdeacon of Winchester and Assistant Bishop
1962 Retired
1974 Died 12th March

Sources

- Crockford's Clerical Directory
- Times obituary, 13 March 1974
- Winchester Churchman
- *Edmund Robert Morgan 1888-1979,* A. J. and E. M. Beach, published by the authors in 1981
- *Cyril Forster Garbett, Archbishop of York,* Charles Smyth (1959)

Leslie Hamilton Lang, the son of Alexander Lang CMG from Scotland, was born on 27th May 1889. He went to Trinity College Cambridge where he graduated B.A.(2nd class History Tripos) in 1912 and M.A. in 1918. He started his Theological training at Bishop's Hostel Farnham in 1914. He was ordained Deacon in 1915, and Priest in 1916, in Winchester. He held his first curacy at St. Mary's Portsea (1915-1918). This parish had an unbroken succession of exceptional vicars over a period of 40 years, starting in 1878 with the Revd Edgar Jacob who was followed by Cosmo Gordon Lang in 1896. There were 14 or 15 curates and during Leslie Lang's time at St Mary's Cyril Garbett was the vicar. During the 1914-1918 war food was short and the curates found they were not getting enough to eat. Leslie Lang recalled that his fellow curates deputed him to see the vicar on the subject. He said 'It was the bravest thing that I ever did in my life!' Garbett was most reasonable and the situation improved. Nine of the Portsea curates went to serve as Army Chaplains, Lang being one. Garbett was greatly moved by a letter he received from these nine curates which said 'Dear Vicar, We, who are still curates of Portsea, have had it in our hearts for a long time that we would express in some simple way our opinion of the self sacrifice by which we were released for this special service. We speak with one voice when we say that in such a parish the real heroism is with those who have remained at their posts, bearing the burden and the heat with patience and courage, sustaining us all in prayer and pleading, moulding the younger generation to the mind of Christ, and ministering to those whose sorrows are deeper still when their men's sufferings are ended." They go on to say that they are proposing to send £200 a year for the Curates Fund. Lang was wounded when gallantly taking the place of a wounded stretcher bearer. For the rest of his life he had a permanently gloved hand. He always wore a black glove but exchanged it for a white one at Confirmations. By all accounts he was a handsome man. In 1918 he married Janette Todd and there were two sons.

After the war he was domestic chaplain to his cousin Cosmo Gordon Lang, the Archbishop of York. This was followed by Lang holding the living of Swanscombe where he was Vicar of All Saints 1920-1922. In 1922 he went to St. George's Camberwell and was also Warden of Trinity College Mission 1922-1927. From 1927-1934 Lang was of Kingston on Thames and Rural Dean from 1931-1934. He moved from there to become a Canon residentiary of Winchester in 1934. He was also Diocesan Missioner to the Diocese of Winchester. His stay was short, only two years, because Lang was consecrated Bishop of Woolwich in St. Paul's Cathedral on 30th November 1936. He also held the office of Archdeacon of Lewisham for the eleven years he was Bishop of Woolwich.

In 1947, after eleven years away from the Diocese of Winchester, Bishop Lang returned to succeed Canon Hedley Burrows (who was nominated to the Deanery of Hereford) as Canon and Archdeacon of Winchester and an Assistant Bishop. He was installed as Canon on 31st May. He remained in these posts until his retirement in 1962 when he and his wife went to live in Charmouth. His wife predeceased him. He died on 12 March 1974 in Fordingbridge aged 84 having spent a large part of his ministry in the Diocese of Winchester.

When Lang was in a nursing home at Fordingbridge, lame and feeling isolated and unhappy, Bishop Morgan visited him regularly. He gave the address at Lang's memorial service in Winchester Cathedral. He took as his text 'Then began I greatly to commend them that stood stiffly for the Lord' 2 Esdras 2 v 47. He spoke of Leslie Lang's service to the Church throughout his career and he ended with an affirmation of his faith in the continuing activity of those who have passed beyond the Veil.

The obituary notice in the Times on 13th March said 'He enjoyed life, could appreciate on occasion a good dinner or a good cigar and, like many such persons he was a good 'mixer'. He had the knack of putting all kinds of people at their ease in all sorts of situations and winning their confidence.'

The following tribute appeared in the Winchester Churchman contributed by R.M.R.

'The news of the passing of Bishop Leslie Lang on 12 March must have brought to many in this diocese-clergy and laity alike a sense of profound gratitude for his past ministry amongst us and of admiration for the quiet selfless way in which he triumphed over disability.

Leslie Lang was an intense lover of souls, and whether it was during a friendly chat at a social gathering or in a pastoral interview with a brother priest, he always made you feel that 'you' mattered. The general well being of clergy and their families was close to his heart, and as Chairman of the Dilapidations Board. When money was very scarce, he would groan in despair, and resort to a cigarette, as he strove to provide for their needs. I recall his expressed compassion concerning what he felt must at times be almost unbearable loneliness felt by a Diocesan Bishop faced with the many personal problems brought to him as Father in God.

His love for humanity was matched by – or did it spring from? – his love of God and the Anglican Church. 'This Church of England to which you and I have the honour to belong' – A sentence which occurred again and again in his sermons – will ever be remembered by those who were members of his congregation. It would come tumbling out, in a church packed with people, at a gathering of members of the Church of England Men's Society, of which he was Diocesan Chairman, or at a country Horseman's Service with a blacksmith's anvil as his pulpit.

God alone can measure the volume of counsel, guidance, and inspiration given by Leslie Lang to a multitude of persons corporately and individually. We salute him through our memories as with abiding affection we commit his soul to the Good God whom he served so well.'

J R Beynon

Archdeacon 1962 ~ 1973

1907 Born
1931 Ordained Deacon, curate of St. Barnabas, Homerton
1932 Ordained priest, after obtaining an L.Th (Durham) in 1931
1933 Served the church in India, becoming Archdeacon of Lahore in 1946
1948 Vicar of St. Mary's, Twyford
1952 Appointed Rural Dean, remaining Vicar of Twyford
1991 Died

James (Roy) Beynon, part of the Welsh clan of Ap Eynon as he was apt to remind one, was born on 16th September 1907 and educated in Llanelli. He attended St. Augustine College Canterbury in 1927, obtained a L.Th (Durham) in 1931 and was ordained priest in 1932. His first appointment was as curate at St. Barnabas in Homerton where he remained for just two years. As a young man of 26 he left England for India where he served until independence in 1947, some fifteen years later. His first appointment in India was as a chaplain at Sangor in the Punjab (now part of Pakistan). In 1937 he moved across the continent, to West Bengal, as Chaplain at the Eccles Establishment, Lebong, near Darjeeling. As a senior chaplain he moved the same year to Fort William close to Calcutta. The war years, after a short spell in the foothills of the Himalayas at Kasauli, were spent back in the Punjab, at firstly Peshawar, and then Quetta, where his parish extended to Eastern Persia. In the year preceding the partition between India and Pakistan, 1946, he became Archdeacon of Lahore, which encompassed the North West Frontier, Kashmir, the Sindh and Baluchistan as well as the Punjab. This was a period of turmoil and extreme violence, of civil war, as Moslems moved from India into the new state of Pakistan and Hindus fled the Punjab. Beynon would have been in the thick of it, a stressful and demanding time for him. In 1948 the Indian Ecclesiastical Establishment came to an end. Chaplains ceased to be

Sources

- Hampshire Record Office, 44M68/B2/5&6.
- Hampshire Record Office, 44M68/B3/3&4.
- Hampshire Record Office, 44M68/G2/20.
- *Hampshire Chronicle* (21 September,1973)
- Church of England Year Book 1965
- Doreen Pearce & Stanley Crooks, *Twyford, Ringing the Changes* (Winchester: George Mann Publications, 1999).
- *St. Mary's Twyford Parish Magazines* (1948 - 1973).
- *The Winchester Churchman No. 126* (September,1973).
- *Twyford 20th Century Chronicles,* ed. Stanley Crooks (Winchester: George Mann Publications, 2000).
- *Winchester Diocesan Leaflet* (February & June,1959).
- *Winchester Diocesan Leaflet* (September, 1962).

the responsibility of the Secretary of State for India, salaries no longer being paid from Indian revenues. Beynon returned to England as vicar of Twyford, a substantial living in the gift of Emmanuel College, Cambridge. He was installed as vicar at Wolvesey Palace on 17th July 1948, filling the vacancy caused by the death of the Rev Harold Morris .

After 15 years in India, at age 41, and after coping with the traumas of Partition, it must have been a difficult adjustment for him to make. In partial compensation he must have been delighted to have inherited a thriving parish together with a beautiful vicarage. The house, Mildmay House, had medieval beginnings, and with its classical seventeenth century Queen Anne facade, its Tudor bowling green and glorious river views it was indeed a delightful place to live. Roy Beynon proved to be a particularly conscientious and devoted parish priest. It must be borne in mind that Beynon's last experience of the Church of England had been in 1933. This showed in the way in which he ran the parish; an aloof formality, a rigid self certainty that today might be interpreted as pomposity, were the hallmarks of his ministry. This, at the time, suited the village which itself was still tuned to prewar values. The management of the parish rested in the hands of the better off village families, and Roy Beynon no doubt found this reassuring. He had recently served as Archdeacon in Lahore and was used to getting his views accepted. Music was one of Beynon's passions and he found, no doubt to his great pleasure, that it had strong roots at St. Mary's, with an able choir well led by Tom Tearell the organist. Soon after Beynon's arrival Twyford church was selected to provide the BBC Home Service broadcast on Christmas Day. Bellringing at St. Mary's was a thriving concern and Roy Beynon was happy to join the beginners class. Roy Beynon was very Welsh and, there was nothing he enjoyed more than singing Welsh hymns with the church choir. A member of the choir remembers him singing *Guide me, O thou great Redeemer, 'Bread of Heaven'*, with great verve, during which he remarked loudly to her – 'you're flat' she recalls lacking the courage to riposte 'so are you'.

In 1952, no doubt in recognition of his past contributions and knowledge of the Punjab he was made one of two Commissaries to the Diocese of Lahore, and remained so until 1968. Whilst no doubt content to settle into Twyford village life, given his administrative experience, it is not surprising that within ten years and still only 52, we find him as Rural Dean for Winchester. In early 1959 he had, for several months, stood in as Rural Dean during the illness of the incumbent, Canon Moloney. In the event, on medical advice, Canon Moloney stood down in June that year and Beynon took over officially as Rural Dean. In 1962 the much respected Bishop Leslie Lang, who had been Archdeacon of Winchester since 1947, retired and the new Bishop of Winchester appointed Beynon Archdeacon in his place. Not only was Beynon, with his administrative experience and his strong personality a natural and wise choice, but his selection fitted well into the Bishop's plan to offer a Residentiary Canonry to a scholar of international repute, namely, Emmanuel Amand de Mendieta. Mendieta, a Belgian, former Benedictine and former Roman Catholic, would fill the Residentiary Canon's stall previously occupied by the Bishop of Southampton and that vacated by Bishop Leslie Lang would, for the time being, be suspended. Roy Beynon, as Archdeacon would hold an Honorary Canonry, give up the appointment of Rural Dean but remain Vicar of St Mary's Twyford, at his own request and with the full support of the Churchwardens. Beynon would continue to live in Twyford's vicarage to his family's delight. Beynon saw no difficulty in managing to fill both appointments efficiently and the Twyford PCC, accustomed to his energy and dedication were confident that this was so.

Beynon, as Rural Dean was already Honorary Deputy Secretary and Treasurer of the Diocesan Board of Finance. He was heavily involved with the administrative work of the Diocese including the Church Building Committee, and Diocesan Information Committee. For the next ten years he immersed himself in his new appointment, at the same time fostering and shepherding Twyford Parish. Beynon brought the same dedication to his new role as he gave to Twyford Parish. He revelled in his new responsibilities, enthusiastically adopting formal dress, gaiters and frock coat, but advising his parishioners that they might still address him as Vicar. He was a man who provoked mixed emotions, on the one hand his devotion, kindness and unquestioning support were admired and loved but there is no doubting that he could be very difficult and off putting. At St. Mary's he rejected out of hand the PCC's proposal for a lavatory at the church, preferring still to rely on the vestry chamberpot. As Archdeacon, in the 1960s he vetoed proposals for bedroom central heating in the newly built Stanmore vicarage. His rigidity and formality were mitigated by his much loved wife Mildred who had found a special place in the affections of the village.

His four grown up daughters were living in Canada, and it is not surprising that in 1973, aged 66, he decided to retire and move there to be near them. He already had made his mark in Canada, during an 1968 visit he had appeared for half an hour on prime time

TV. In a lengthy interview with Chat Show host Edward Gloves on the CBC network he had given Canadians an insight into the History of Winchester Cathedral, enthralling them with the story of how William Walker, the diver, had saved the cathedral between 1906-11. However, his personality had not notably mellowed - when a Twyford resident met by chance the Canadian churchwarden from Beynon's Ontario church on a train through the Rockies, he remarked 'Oh yes, he can be a bit difficult'.

Twyford said goodbye to its vicar, and his wife Mildred, in style, with over 400 parishioners present. Beynon in his farewell speech paid tribute to his wife whom he described as the 'assistant vicar' and finished by quoting from the prayer 'O Lord I don't understand it all but I am glad I have had a part of it'. There were no marvellous peaks to Beynon's time at Winchester but the sum total of his service as Archdeacon and Vicar of Twyford were both substantial and valuable. An able administrator, a caring pastor, rather old fashioned in his attitudes, he fitted well into both roles within the church to which he had dedicated his life. Intelligent, with an austere countenance and sometimes forbidding manner, he was nevertheless a much loved and respected churchman. He also had a great affection for Twyford and the friends he had made over his long stewardship, returning for a visit most years, particularly after Mildred's death, to see old friends. Stricken with illness himself, in 1991 he wrote to express his love for Twyford and his friends there, something he would not have been able to do whilst still their Vicar.

David Cartwright

Archdeacon 1973 ~ 1984

1920 Born 15th July 1920
1941 Graduated from Selwyn College Cambridge, BA
1943 Ordained Deacon
1944 Ordained Priest served title at Boston Parish Church
1945 MA
1946 Married Elsie Rogers,
1948 Incumbent of St Leonard, Redfield Bristol
1952 Incumbent at Olveston with Aust
1956 Proctor in Convocation for Bristol Diocese
1960 Incumbent at Bishopston
1970 Honorary Canon of Bristol
1973 Archdeacon of Winchester and Vicar of Sparsholt and Honorary Canon
1984 Bishop of Southampton
1988 Retired
1997 Died 24th April

Sources

- *The Hampshire Chronicle.*
- *The Times.*
- Mr Graham Phillips

David Cartwright was born on 15th July 1920 in Lincolnshire, the son of a master butcher. He was educated at Grimsby Parish Church Choir School where he was encouraged by Hedley Burrows (later Archdeacon of Winchester and Dean of Hereford), then he went to Lincoln School. He went on to read Theology and History at Selwyn College Cambridge where he took a B.A. Degree in 1941 followed by M.A. in 1945. As an undergraduate he was influenced by the Student Christian Movement eventually becoming president of the Cambridge S.C.M. His theological training was undertaken at Westcott House, he was ordained Deacon in 1943 and priest in 1944. He served his title at Boston parish Church under the legendary Canon A. M. Cook. In 1946 he married Elsie Rogers and they had one son and two daughters.

After the war Cartwright spent 25 years in Bristol. He was the incumbent of St. Leonard Redfield 1948-1952, Olveston with Aust 1952-1960, and Bishopston 1960-1973. In 1970 Bishop Oliver Tomkins made him an Honorary Canon of Bristol Cathedral. He was highly regarded throughout Bristol and the Diocese for his lively and positive approach as Secretary of the Bristol Council of Churches, Chairman of Bristol Christian Aid Committee and for seven years as Secretary of the Bristol Diocesan Conference and Synod.

From 1956-1973 Cartwright served as a Proctor in

Convocation for the Bristol Diocese, his fellow clergy regularly re-electing him. His ecumenical and administrative skills were soon in demand nationally. He was involved both in Anglican- Presbyterian conversations and the Anglican-Methodist Unity Scheme. He was a Church Commissioner and a member of both the Central Board of Finance and the Church of England Pensions Board. Clergy housing and pensions were his special interests and he remained Chairman of Morley College until his death.

In 1973 he accepted Bishop Falkner Allison's invitation to become Archdeacon of Winchester and Vicar of Sparsholt (a nearby country parish) while continuing with his work in London. He was installed on 1st December 1973, succeeding the Venerable J. R. Benyon, former Vicar of Twyford. He was also made an Honorary Canon of Winchester Cathedral. His induction as Vicar of Sparsholt and Lainston was the previous day. Archdeacon Cartwright's hobbies included music and reading and now he hoped to grow roses as he had moved to a country area from Bristol.

He soon won the respect and affection of both clergy and laity in Hampshire where he was widely trusted, his wisdom and experience were greatly valued. He worked closely with the Diocesan Secretary and his staff and it was said he considered a day wasted if he had not attended at least one committee meeting. He was a great supporter of the Board of Finance and if ever there was a difficult motion to get through Synod David Cartwright was chosen to present it as he was very persuasive. During his Bristol days Cartwright was a notable trainer of curates and he continued to encourage younger clergy when he came to Hampshire.

In May 1984 it was announced that Archdeacon Cartwright was to be the next Suffragan Bishop of Southampton. He was consecrated on 2nd July by the Archbishop of Canterbury, Dr Robert Runcie. Bishop John Robinson gave David Cartwright his pectoral cross which was of a striking design. It was an unusual occasion since it was nearly a quarter of a century since the Archbishop of Canterbury had consecrated a bishop in Winchester Cathedral. The Archbishop also consecrated the Venerable Peter Coleman as Bishop of Crediton. It was a splendid event with a packed Cathedral and fine music under the direction of Martin Neary, Master of Music. Bishop Oliver Tomkins preached the sermon in which he said that bishops were called to lead 'But ours is not an autocratic and arbitrary leadership – the direction in which to lead is learned by listening'. At this stage Cartwright relinquished the post of Archdeacon but continued to live at Sparsholt in the Vicarage, which he named 'Jollers' after a name on an old map of the area.

At a Press Conference after the announcement of his appointment as Bishop of Southampton Archdeacon Cartwright described his job as one of 'management and maintenance' but as Bishop the emphasis would be more on pastoral care and mission, as a pastor to help and support people. He also took the opportunity during this Press Conference to say he thought unemployment was 'the supreme social problem facing the country at the moment' and suggested there should be a revolution in attitudes to deal with the problem. He would take a particular interest in the clergy and their families, people and community life as a whole, he was always the parish priest, he loved talking to people and was a great teller of stories. He also knew every clergy house in the Diocese. When any changes were requested his major concern was if it was going to work for the worship and pastoral needs of the parish. A Vicar asked via the Parsonages Board, if he could have a new wood store. This was refused as David Cartwright said from experience that it was quite unnecessary, he loved sawing, stacking and burning wood! .

The Bishop of Southampton was President of the Southampton Council of Churches and Chairman of the Hampshire and Isle of Wight and Channel Island Association for the deaf. In the 1983 and 1987 General Elections he chaired the meeting of all the Parliamentary candidates on one platform in the Winchester Constituency .He was a keen Liberal himself. He was also Patron of 'Freeze', the multi-lateralist group for nuclear disarmament. He was a Chaplain to Cunard, for whom he had great respect, and he went on many cruises. He blessed the QE2 after a refurbishment.

Bishop Cartwright retired in October 1988 after a varied ministry lasting 45 years. A large gathering in the Great Hall Winchester bore testimony to his great popularity and also showed the esteem in which he was held both in the Diocese of Winchester and the others where he had served. The Right Reverend Colin James, Bishop of Winchester, praised his colleague's ministry and paid particular tribute to the strength and companionship of his wife Elsie. The Bishop said 'They are a marvellous match and she has undoubtedly been a mainstay of support throughout Bishop David's ministry. He is a wise councillor to those in need, a great statesman in our Diocese and above all, a great friend. It is that most attractive side we see most. As a parish priest, he was always so good at solving problems and meeting difficulties; as a preacher, often thoughtful and refreshing. He and his wife have our unbounded admiration and affection'. Bishop James presented the Cartwrights with a framed painting of Winchester Cathedral and a cheque for £2000, raised by grateful parishioners and clergy. They retired to Wiltshire.

David Cartwright's Episcopal ministry was fruitful although he suffered ill health. He helped to make some enterprising appointments. Always a model of dignity and decorum, he nevertheless had a mischievous sense of humour, which enlivened many solemn ecclesiastical occasions with whispered asides.

He retired to Warminster where he spent his final years making new friends in the surrounding villages and studying the life of the Edwardian Archdeacon of Winchester W.A.Fearon whose fascinating parochial diaries he owned.

He died on 24th April 1997 aged 76. The funeral service was conducted by the Bishop of Salisbury, The Right Reverend David Stancliffe, and the sermon was preached by former Bishop of Winchester Colin James. The present Bishop, The Right Reverend Michael Scott- Joynt, read the Prayers of Commendation and the Rector of Littleton, the Reverend David Williams, read from the Gospels. There was a memorial service in Winchester Cathedral on June 6th and the Dean officiated assisted by the Reverend Tim Daykin, who lead the prayers, and by the cathedral clergy. Mr Roger Cartwright (son) and the Venerable Trevor Nash read the lessons. The address was given by The Right Reverend John Cavell.

Alan Geoffrey Clarkson

Archdeacon 1984 ~ 1999

1934 Born

1957 Christ's College Cambridge Bachelor of Arts

1961 Master of Arts

1957 Wycliffe Hall, Oxford

1959 Deacon

1960 Priest

1959 Curate Penn, Lichfield Diocese

1960 Curate St Oswald, Oswestry

1963 Curate Rington, Bath & Wells Diocese

1965 Vicar Chewton Mendip with Emborough

1965 Diocesan Ecumenical Officer

1974 Vicar St John Glastonbury with Godney

1980 Priest-in-Charge West Pennard

1981 Priest-in-Charge Meare

1982 Priest-in-Charge St Benedict, Glastonbury

1984 Vicar Glastonbury with Meare, West Pennard and Godney

1984 Archdeacon of Winchester and Honorary Canon of Winchester Cathedral

1984 Vicar Burley Ville

1999 Retired

Adrian Guy Harbidge

Archdeacon 1999 ~ 2000

1948 Born

1970 St John's College, Durham Bachelor of Arts

1970 Purser

1973 Cuddesdon Theological College

1975 Deacon

1976 Priest

1975 Curate Romsey Abbey, Winchester Diocese

1980 Vicar St Andrew's, Bennett Road, Bournemouth

1986 Vicar of Chandler's Ford

1993 Rural Dean of Eastleigh

1999 Archdeacon of Winchester

1999 Honorary Canon of Winchester Cathedral

2000 Archdeacon of Bournemouth

John Arthur Guille

Archdeacon 2000 ~ present

1949 Born

1967 Christ Church College, Canterbury
Certificate of Education

1970 Head of Religious Studies, Stockbridge County Secondary School

1972 Head of Religious Studies, St Sampson Secondary School, Guernsey

1973 Salisbury and Wells Theological College
Certificate in Theology

1976 Deacon

1977 Priest

1976 Curate, Chandler's Ford, Winchester Diocese

1979 Southampton University Bachelor of Theology

1980 Priest-in-Charge, St John's, Surrey Road, Bournemouth

1983 Priest-in-Charge, St Michael and All Angels, Bournemouth

1984 Vicar, St John with St Michael, Bournemouth

1989 Rector, St Andre de la Pomeraye, Guernsey

1996 Vice Dean of Guernsey

1999 Archdeacon of Basingstoke and
Residentiary Canon of Winchester Cathedral

2000 Archdeacon of Winchester

Archdeacons of Winchester 1100 ~ 2000

Year	Archdeacon	Bishop	Monarch
1100–1116	Henry	William Giffard (1100)	Henry I
Before 1128	Richard or Richer		
Before 1139–1142	Jocelin de Bohun	Henry of Blois (1129)	Stephen (1135)
1142 & 1147–1179/80	Ralph		
		Richard of Ilchester [*Toclyve*] (1173)	Henry II (1154)
1180–1207/08	Roger		
		Godfrey de Lucy (1189)	
			Richard I (1189)
			John (1199)
c1213 - 1230	M Bartholomew	Peter des Roches (1206)	
			Henry III (1216)
1231/32	Roger II		
1237 - 1253/4	Hugh des Roches		
		Will. de Raleigh (1244)	
c1254 - 1256	[unnamed Archdeacon]		
c1258 - 1260	[unnamed Archdeacon]		
1257 - 1261	Amaury Guiscard	Aymer de valance [*of Lusignan*] (1260)	
1263 - 1275	M. Henry de Helingeye	John Gervaise (1262)	
			Edward I (1272)
1276	[unnamed Archdeacon]	Nicholas of Ely (1268)	
1280 - 1285	M. Richard de la More	John of Pontoise (1282)	
1285 - 1304	M. Philip of St Austell *alias* Cornwaleys		
1304 -	M. Michael de Helleston		
1304 -	M. James Sinabaldi de Florentia or de Pulcis	Henry Merewell [*or Woodlock*] (1305)	
			Edward II (1307)
1325 - 1328	Philip Sapiti	Rigaud of Assier (1320)	Edward III (1327)
		John Stratford (1324)	
1328 - 1343	John de Podio Barzaco		
		Adam Orleton (1334)	
1343 - ?	M. Stephen de Malo Leone		
1343	Ayquelinus Guillelmi de Sparra		
1345 - 1361	Robert de Burton	William Edendon [*Edington*] (1346)	
1361	M. John de Wolveleye		
1361 - 1372	M. Robert de Wykford	William of Wykeham (1367)	

Year	Archdeacon	Bishop	Monarch
1372 – 1381	M. Nicholas de Wykeham	William of Wykeham (1367)	Richard II (1377)
1382 – 1387 (?)	M. John Bloxham		
1386 – 1389	William Forrester		
1387 – 1395	Roger de Walden		
1395 – (?)	Nicholas Daniel		
1395 – 1404	M. Robert Broun	Henry Beaufort (1405)	Henry IV (1399)
1428 – 1441	M. Nicholas Bildeston		Henry VI (1422)
? 1450	M. Stephen Wilton	William of Waynflete (1447)	
1450 – 1459	M. John Pakenham		
1459 – 1475	M. Vincent Clement		Edward IV (1470)
1475 – 1478	M. John Morton		
? – 1486	M. Robert Morton		Edward V (1483)
1487 – 1492	M. William Smith	Peter Courtenay (1487)	Richard III (1483)
			Henry VII (1485)
? – 1502	M. Robert Frost	Thomas Langton (1493)	
		Richard Fox (1501)	
1502 – 1511	M. John Frost		Henry VIII (1509)
1511 – 1520	M. Hugh Ashton		
1520 – 1527	M. John Fox		
1527 – 1529	M. Richard Pates	Thomas Wolsey (1529)	
1530 – 1552	M. William Boleyn	Stephen Gardiner [*deprived*] (1531)	
			Edward VI (1547)
1552 – 1554	John Philpot	John Ponet [*Poynet*] (1551)	
			Jane
			Mary (1553)
1554 – 1572	Stephen Cheston	Stephen Gardiner [*restored*] (1553)	
		John White [*deprived*] (1556)	Elizabeth I (1558)
1572 – 1575	John Ebden	Robert Horne (1561)	
1575 – 1609	Michael Reniger	John Watson (1580)	
		Thomas Cowper [*Cooper*] (1584)	
		William Wickham [*Wykeham*] (1595)	
		William Day (1596)	James I (1603)
		Thomas Bilson (1597)	

Year	Archdeacon	Bishop	Monarch
1609 - 1631	Ralph Barlow	James Montague (1616)	James I (1603)
		Lancelot Andrewes (1619)	
		Richard Neile (1628)	Charles I (1625)
1631 - 1653	Edward Burby	Walter Curll (1632)	
	Commonwealth period	Post vacant (1653–1660)	
1660 - 1661	George Roberts	Brian Duppa (1660)	Charles II (1660)
1661 - 1666	Thomas Gorges	George Morley (1662)	
1666 - 1684	Walter Dayrell		
1684	Robert Sharrock	Peter Mews (1684)	
1684 - 1700	Thomas Clutterbuck		James II (1685-1688)
			William III & Mary II (1689)
1700 - 1702	George Fulham		William III
1702 - 1743	Ralph Brideoke	Jonathan Trelawney (1707)	Anne (1702)
		Charles Trimnell (1721)	
		Richard Willis (1723)	George I (1714)
		Benjamin Hoadly (1734)	
			George II (1727)
1743 - 1749	Robert Eden		
1749 - 1750	Nicholas Lechmere		
1750 - 1756	Robert Lowth		
1756 - 1759	Robert Eden		
1759 - 1795	Thomas Balguy	John Thomas (1761)	George III (1760)
		Brownlow North (1781)	
1795 - 1807	Matthew Woodford		
1807 - 1814	Hon. Thomas de Grey		
1814 - 1819	Hon. Augustus George Legge		
1819 - 1829	Gilbert Heathcote	George Pretyman Tomline (1820)	George IV (1820)
		Charles Richard Sumner (1827)	
1829 - 1847	Charles James Hoare		William IV (1830)
			Victoria (1837)
1847 - 1860	Joseph Cotton Wigram		
1860 - 1884	Philip Jacob	Samuel Wilberforce (1869)	
		Edward Harold Browne (1873)	

Year	Archdeacon	Bishop	Monarch
1884 - 1901	George H Sumner	Anthony Wilson Thorold (1891)	Victoria (1837)
		Randall Thomas Davidson (1895)	
1901 - 1903	Arthur Temple Lyttelton	Herbert Edward Ryle (1903)	Edward VII (1901)
1903 - 1920	W. A. Fearon	Edward Stuart Talbot (1911)	
			George V (1910)
1920 - 1936	A. E. Daldy	Frank Theodore Woods (1923)	
		Cyril Forster Garbett (1932)	
1936 - 1943	Edmund R. Morgan	Mervyn George Haigh (1942)	Edward VIII (1936)
1943 - 1947	Hedley Burrows		George VI (1936)
1947 - 1962	L. H. Lang	Alwyn Terrell Petre Williams (1952)	
		Sherard Falkner Allison (1961)	Elizabeth II (1952)
1962 - 1973	J. Roy Beynon	Sherard Falkner Allison	
1973 - 1984	David Cartwright	John Vernon Taylor (1975)	
1984 - 1999	Alan Clarkson	Colin Clement Walter James (1985)	
		Michael Charles Scott-Joynt (1995)	
1999 - 2000	Adrian Guy Harbidge		
2000 -	John Arthur Guille		

Index